W9-AOP-999

New Jersey Reapportionment Politics

NEW JERSEY REAPPORTIONMENT POLITICS:

Strategies and Tactics in the Legislative Process

By

Alan Shank

Rutherford - Madison - Teaneck
Fairleigh Dickinson University Press

Library of Congress Catalogue Card Number: 69–18908

Associated University Presses, Inc.
Cranbury, New Jersey 08512

SBN
8386–6950–6
Printed in the United States of America

Acknowledgments

MY FIRST INTRODUCTION TO NEW JERSEY REAPPORTIONMENT politics was in 1962. As a graduate student in Professor Stanley H. Friedelbaum's constitutional law seminar at Rutgers University, I was fascinated by the implications of the unique state supreme court decision in the *Asbury Park* case. Here was an example of a state legislature refusing to reapportion. The state court threatened to impose a plan if the legislature refused to act. In a very lively description of the outcome of this case, Professor Friedelbaum showed how the legislature barely met the deadline for reapportionment in 1961.

My next contacts with New Jersey reapportionment took place in 1964–1965 as a result of a very rewarding research assignment with Dr. Ernest C. Reock, Jr., the Director of the Rutgers University Bureau of Government Research. Following the state supreme court adoption of the "one man, one vote" rule in 1964, Dr. Reock became very interested in examining the possibilities of district representation for the New Jersey Legislature. As his research assistant, I became involved with an historical-political analysis of New Jersey districting experiences in the nineteenth century. During this same time, Dr. Reock invited me to attend meetings of the New Jersey Committee for Fair Representation, where prominent attorneys and political scientists were trying to resolve the very complex problems of applying the "one man, one vote" rule to the New Jersey Legislature.

By this time, I was searching for a doctoral dissertation topic, and it appeared that New Jersey reapportionment experiences could be analyzed in depth. It was necessary to place New Jersey experiences into some kind of useful analytical framework. Professor Gerald Pomper of the Department of Political Science expressed interest in becoming my thesis advisor.

The success of this book, which is the product of nearly three years of extended study, is almost entirely due to the superior advice I have gotten from Professor Pomper. Without his assistance, this study could not have been completed. Professor Pomper has made me pay attention to detail, writing style, and theoretical analysis. He has been highly critical of my research, but his constructive criticism has resulted, I hope, in a book of which both of us can feel satisfaction.

In addition to his advice on substance, Professor Pomper was unusually prompt in returning drafts of the various chapters throughout the past two years. Our continual contacts by letter and long-distance telephone between New Brunswick and Boston might have complicated communications. But this problem did not occur, and I am most grateful that Professor Pomper recognized that distance was not a barrier to completion of my work.

Further useful assistance and advice has been provided by the other faculty members of Rutgers University, including Professors Stanley H. Friedelbaum and Judson L. James of the Department of Political Science; and Professor Richard P. McCormick of the Department of History. Many improvements in style and substance are due to their helpful comments.

Many political figures in New Jersey contributed their

time and advice on relating the complexities of reapportionment politics. I hope that none of these people will find my references to their interview comments injudicious. Most helpful to discovering "inside" views on New Jersey's past experiences were past Governors Alfred E. Driscoll and Robert B. Meyner. Incumbent Governor Richard J. Hughes and his special assistant, Joseph W. Katz, gave me their views on current reapportionment problems. Also I would like to express grateful appreciation for interviews extended by the following past and incumbent state legislators: Raymond H. Bateman, Dominic A. Cavicchia, J. Edward Crabiel, Marion West Higgins, Wesley L. Lance, John A. Lynch, William V. Musto, and William E. Ozzard. Also, useful information was provided by Attorney General Arthur J. Sills.

A book is more than the product of one individual and more than the compilation of substantive material required to complete the assignment. My typist, Mrs. Merle Byerlee, has in my opinion, produced a very fine manuscript. I have gotten much moral support in the last three years from members of my family, who have been very understanding. A special note of thanks is extended to my father-in-law, Samuel Spizer, for his constant encouragement. The most sincere appreciation is extended to my wife, Bernice and my children, Steven and Naomi. Without their constant kind consideration, this study would not have been completed.

Finally, I would like to dedicate my book to the memory of my father, Dr. Nathan M. Shank. His interest in my future was genuine, and I regret that he was not able to read the final product which is contained here.

Even with the academic and moral support provided by members of the Rutgers University faculty and my family, I alone must take responsibility for any of the shortcomings which may exist in this study. If there are criticisms and defects in my work, no other person is at fault. In the end, the author alone must bear the burden for producing his first book.

Brookline, Mass.
May, 1968.

Contents

List of Illustrations

List of Tables

New Jersey
Reapportionment Politics

1

Foundations of New Jersey Reapportionment Politics

A SPECTER IS HAUNTING THE UNITED STATES—THE SPECTER of reapportionment. The momentous decisions of the United States Supreme Court[1] are changing the nature of representation at the state level. The "one man, one vote" standard directly affects the balance of partisan power within state legislatures.

The reappotionment revolution needs to be examined from the inside. The New Jersey Legislature, which is the major focus of this study, has faced reapportionment problems throughout the twentieth century. Strategies and tactics have been used continually to resolve conflicts among competing legislative groups. The "one man, one vote" Court ruling thus represents only one part of a continuing struggle to resolve controversies over the representation system.

Relatively few studies deal with state reapportionment

[1] See *Baker v. Carr,* 369 U.S. 186 (1962) and *Reynolds v. Sims,* 377 U.S. 533 (1964).

in terms of internal legislative politics.[2] Traditionally, state legislative reapportionment activity has not included analysis of strategies and tactics employed by various groups. For example, numerous studies deal with such considerations as the criteria of fair apportionment,[3] the consequences of malapportionment,[4] the clash of urban and rural interests,[5] and the effects of apportionment on party competition in legislatures.[6]

When these aspects of apportionment are combined with particular responses of various legislative groups, a clear perspective of reapportionment politics emerges. The legislature is uniquely concerned with reapportionment for reasons of self-preservation. In resolving conflicts, the legislature has a direct impact on the representation system. Therefore, the strategies and tactics employed in the legislative process are significant in understanding the exercise of power and influence by various competing groups.

The New Jersey Legislature has been selected for a study of reapportionment politics. As a highly urbanized state and with a legislature tied to the past, New Jersey responses to reapportionment controversies indicate how political power is retained, altered, or redistributed in a legislature. This study attempts to establish a foundation for relating the criteria of fair and equitable representa-

---

[2] Perhaps the best study is found in Gilbert Y. Steiner and Samuel K. Gove, *Legislative Politics in Illinois* (Urbana; University of Illinois Press, 1960), pp. 84–117. See, also: Gordon E. Baker, *The Politics of Reapportionment in Washington State* (New York: Holt, Rinehart and Winston, 1960) and Malcolm E. Jewell, Ed., *The Politics of Reapportionment* (New York: Atherton Press, 1962).

[3] Alfred de Grazia, "General Theory of Apportionment," *Law and Contemporary Problems,* Vol. 17 (Spring, 1952), pp. 256–267.

[4] Paul T. David and Ralph Eisenberg, *Devaluation of the Urban and Suburban Vote* (Charlottesville: University of Virginia, Bureau of Public Administration, 1961).

[5] Gordon E. Baker, *Rural versus Urban Political Power* (New York: Random House, 1955).

[6] Malcolm E. Jewell, *The State Legislature* (New York: Random House, 1962).

tion to the various strategies and tactics employed by groups in conflict situations. The major goal will be to discover how competing claims were accommodated in the legislative process by analyzing legislative responses to all New Jersey apportionment problems in the twentieth century.

New Jersey reapportionment history prior to 1900

New Jersey reapportionment politics is conveniently divided into three general historical periods, under which various fundamental legal charters or constitutions were in effect. Examination of these past developments indicates the role of constitutional provisions, county representation, and political parties in shaping legislative responses to reapportionment: (1) New Jersey's experiences as a proprietary and royal colony, 1664–1776; (2) Major trends in the legislature under the first state constitution of 1776; and (3) Developments following adoption of the 1844 constitution, and until 1900. Important influences for twentieth century reapportionment politics are revealed in a brief examination of these three historical periods.

Experiences as a proprietary and royal colony, 1664–1776

New Jersey's first system of government emerged soon after the Duke of York granted the colony to Lord John Berkeley and Sir George Carteret in 1664. The first document that might be called a constitution, "The Concession and Agreement of the Lords Proprietors," established a governor, an appointed council, and elected deputies.[7] The

[7] Stanley H. Friedelbaum, "Apportionment Legislation in New Jersey," *Proceedings of the New Jersey Historical Society,* Vol. 70, No. 4 (October, 1952), p. 262.

twelve deputies were elected at-large. The legislature, designated as a general assembly, became a bicameral body when the councilors and deputies decided to meet separately at their first session.[8]

Territorial representation as a basis of apportionment was first established when the colony was divided into East and West Jersey in 1676. The "Fundamental Constitutions" of East Jersey provided for an assembly apportioned on the basis of towns.[9] The West Jersey "Concessions and Agreements" of 1677 constituted assembly representation on the basis of geographical divisions called tenths, with ten representatives elected from each tenth.[10] Between 1681 and 1692, the four West Jersey counties of Burlington, Salem, Gloucester, and Cape May were created.[11] By 1701 these counties had replaced the tenths system and each county elected ten members to the West Jersey assembly.

New Jersey was reunited in 1702 under the direct control of the British Crown. Lord Cornbury, the first royal governor, brought the Commission and Instruction, which fixed the assembly at 24 members equally divided between the eastern and western divisions.[12] The East Jersey counties of Bergen, Essex, Middlesex, Monmouth, and Somerset, created between 1675 and 1688, each had two assemblymen along with the city of Perth Amboy.[13] The four aforementioned West Jersey counties also had two assemblymen each supplemented by two representatives for the

---

8 *Proceedings of the New Jersey State Constitutional Convention of 1844,* Compiled and edited by the New Jersey Writers' Project of the Works Progress Administration with an Introduction by John Bebout, Sponsored by the New Jersey State House Commission, 1942, p. xiii.

9 Friedelbaum, *op. cit.,* p. 263.

10 *Ibid.*

11 Harris I. Effross, "Origins of Post-Colonial Counties in New Jersey," *Proceedings of the New Jersey Historical Society,* Vol. 81, No. 2 (April, 1963), p. 104.

12 Friedelbaum, *op. cit.,* p. 263.

13 Effross, *op. cit.,* p. 104.

towns of Burlington and Salem.[14] This system could not be changed unless an assembly act was approved by the board of trade in London. An effort to adopt a population-based apportionment system in 1704 was rejected by the Crown.[15]

The rejection of population-based apportionment and the practices of town and geographic representation reflected prevailing British practices. The House of Commons did not have population apportionment.[16] In New Jersey, developments after 1704 shifted to geographical fights over reapportionment. The admission of new counties was balanced so that the east and west were equally represented. The board of trade, moreover, did not act quickly in granting the new counties assembly representation.

The 24-member assembly remained intact until 1728, although Hunterdon County had been created in 1714. Hunterdon did not have representation until the royal governor requested that the board of trade approve a shift of the two seats from Salem Town, located in South Jersey, to Hunterdon, which was located in the northwestern section of the colony. The shift of seats was approved and made a part of an assembly act in 1728.[17]

Geographical compromises and balances characterized the efforts to retain equal county representation to the end of the colonial period. Morris County (created from Hunterdon in 1739) was balanced by Cumberland County (created from Salem in 1748). Then Sussex County was carved from Morris in 1753.[18] The three new counties had to wait for assembly representation until 1768. In that year the British authorized an increase in assembly mem-

[14] *Ibid.,* p. 105.

[15] Friedelbaum, *op. cit.,* p. 264.

[16] Malcolm E. Jewell and Samuel C. Patterson, *The Legislative Process in The United States* (New York: Random House, 1966), p. 49.

[17] Friedelbaum, *op. cit.,* p. 264.

[18] Effross, *op. cit.,* p. 105.

bership to 30.[19] Equality of representation between the east and west counties ended at this time. New Jersey now had seven western and six eastern counties, a pattern that was to continue until 1824.[20]

The constitutional developments of legislative representation during the colonial period took place amid a political conflict between royal governors and legislatures.[21] The assembly was broadening the bases of self-government in opposition to royal prerogative.[22] From 1703 to 1738, when the royal governor was simultaneously governor of New York, the assembly sought to extend suffrage, assure county representation, and conduct regular elections.[23] The assembly continued to assert control over representation during the time when a separate royal governor was sent to New Jersey, 1738–1776.[24] By 1776, on the eve of independence, royal governors had not been able to prevent the development of popular control in the assembly. The assembly controlled the governors' salaries and this perhaps was the major reason for hesitancy by the governors in alienating the assembly in matters of representation.[25]

By 1776 the following elements of legislative representation appeared established: (1) The assembly was the popularly-elected house of the legislature; (2) The county was the basic representative unit; (3) Counties had equal assembly representation; (4) Newly-created counties were established to achieve geographical balance and were sub-

---

19 *Ibid.*

20 The county lineup by 1768 was as follows: East Jersey—Bergen, Essex, Middlesex, Monmouth, Morris, and Somerset; West Jersey—Burlington, Cumberland, Cape May, Gloucester, Hunterdon, Salem, and Sussex.

21 Duane Lockard, *The New Jersey Governor* (Princeton, New Jersey: D. Van Nostrand Company, 1964), p. 12.

22 *Ibid.*, p. 27.

23 *Ibid.*

24 *Ibid.*, p. 34.

25 *Ibid.*, p. 22.

sequently given assembly representation; and (5) Assemblymen were elected at-large on county-wide tickets.

Developments under the constitution of 1776

The constitution of 1776 did not radically depart from the apportionment principles developed under colonial experiences. The upper house, newly-designated as the legislative council, was elected with one member from each county.[26] Upper chamber equal county representation remained unchanged through the constitutions of 1844 and 1947. Although the eight counties created between 1824 and 1857 were given upper chamber representation, no effective reapportionment took place until 1965. The upper chamber remained traditionally bounded by the one-member-per-county system for 189 years.[27]

The general assembly had a modified apportionment system following colonial experiences. The new constitution immediately increased the size of the assembly to 39 members. Article III gave the legislature considerable flexibility in reapportioning general assembly seats among the counties by authorizing that seats could be increased or diminished by majority vote "on the principles of more equal representation" within the 39 member proviso. Furthermore, the apportionment provision was followed by Section IV, dealing with qualifications of electors, which was interpreted to mean that all three members of the general assembly from each of the thirteen counties should be elected at-large on county-wide tickets.[28]

---

[26] *Constitution of 1776,* Article III.

[27] For the effects of equal county representation in the senate on constitutional revision and reapportionment, see Chapters III and V.

[28] *Constitution of 1776,* Article IV specified; That all inhabitants . . . shall be entitled to vote for representatives in council and assembly; and also for all *other* public officers that shall be elected by the people *of the county at large.* (Emphasis added.)

The legislature departed from the concept of equal county representation in the assembly following the census of 1790, which indicated that population was shifting throughout the state. With a new interpretation of "the principles of more equal representation," the legislature began moving in the direction of both a population basis for assembly apportionment and an increase in the total membership of the lower house. The 1797 reapportionment resulted in single seat gains for Burlington, Hunterdon, and Sussex counties offset by losses of two seats for Cumberland and one seat for Cape May County.

Population gains, accounting for seats given to Essex, Cumberland, Morris, and Monmouth counties between 1804 and 1818, raised the size of the assembly to 44 members. This figure remained unchanged through the admission of Warren County in 1824, at which time Warren was given two seats and Sussex County was reduced by two seats.

The most substantial increase in assembly membership took place after the 1830 census when seven counties (Burlington, Essex, Gloucester, Hunterdon, Middlesex, Sussex, and Warren) were given additional seats and no county was reduced in representation. The assembly increased to 54 with the admissions of Passaic (two seats) and Atlantic (one seat) counties in 1837. The 54-member assembly existed at the time of the 1844 constitutional convention, although Mercer, Hudson, and Camden counties were created between 1838 and 1844. The representation given to these three counties was taken from counties that had originally included their territories.[29]

Apportionment experiences under the 1776 constitution reveal three general trends. First, the principle of equal county representation was established for the upper

[29] Thus, Mercer gained two seats taken from Hunterdon County; Hudson gained one seat from Bergen County; and Camden gained two seats taken from Gloucester County.

chamber. By 1844, 19 counties were represented by one member in the legislative council. Second, the basis of assembly representation shifted from equal county to population apportionment, although no county had more than four members and all 19 counties had at least one member. Population apportionment did not present difficulties as long as roughly equal distribution existed among the counties. In fact, only Cape May County fell below the representative ratio throughout the period—that is, the total population of the State divided by the total number of assembly seats.[30] The third trend was in the direction of increasing the total size of the assembly. When new counties were created, seats were assigned on the basis of assemblymen who had originally represented existing counties.

Further changes under the constitution of 1844

The assembly apportionment provision of the 1844 constitution incorporated most of the principles previously developed. One change fixed the upper limit of members at 60, but this presented no problems with population apportionment at this time. Otherwise, Article IV, Section III continued the principles of county representation, population apportionment and periodic reapportionment:[31]

> The General Assembly shall be composed of members annually elected by the legal voters of the counties, respectively, who shall be apportioned among the said counties as nearly as may be according to the number of

---

[30] Ernest C. Reock, Jr., *Population Inequality Among Counties in the New Jersey Legislature, 1791–1962* (New Brunswick, New Jersey: Bureau of Government Research, Rutgers—The State University, 1963), p. 20.

[31] The constitutional provision is cited in full, because it was unchanged through the Constitution of 1947, thus placing a limiting condition on assembly apportionment in the twentieth century. See, also, Chapter III, below.

their inhabitants. The present apportionment shall continue until the next census of the United States shall have been taken, and an apportionment of members of the General Assembly shall be made by the Legislature at its first session after the next and every subsequent enumeration shall have been taken; *provided* that each county shall at all times be entitled to one member; and the whole number of members shall never exceed sixty.

The constitution also continued equal county representation in the senate, although prior convention debate indicated urban county dissatisfaction with this system. A delegate from Essex County argued that political power should be shared among citizens rather than counties.[32] The convention delegates defeated a proposal whereby 15 senators would be elected from five districts of nearly equal population, with the districts composed of whole counties electing three members each.[33] The only change made was to increase the terms of senators to three years.[34]

Closley related to the apportionment provisions were the increased powers of the governor. The governor became the one popularly-elected executive official and was given a three-year term. He was not permitted to succeed himself. His legislative responsibilities consisted of authority to convene the legislature, recommend measures to it, and veto bills. In turn, the legislature could override the governor's veto by simple majority vote.[35] These powers enhanced the governor's role in future issues related to apportionment.[36]

---

32 *Proceedings, op. cit.*, p. 283.

33 *Ibid.*

34 *Constitution of 1844,* Article IV, Section II.

35 *Constitution of 1844,* Article V, Paragraphs 1, 2, 3, 6, and 7.

36 See, especially, Chapters III, IV, and V, below. The New Jersey governor was an active participant in twentieth century reapportionment politics. As it will be shown later, the governor's formal-legal powers were part of his resources for developing strategies in reap-

An important omission from both the assembly apportionment provision and the suffrage section[37] concerned the method of electing members to the assembly. No reference was made in either section concerning at-large elections. The result was that in future years it could be argued by many persons that the state constitution placed no restriction on the legislature for alternative methods of electing members to the general assembly.[38]

In 1852 the legislature departed from the tradition of at-large county-wide elections for assemblymen and instituted a system of single member districts. Assembly districts continued until 1893, when the state supreme court ruled districts unconstitutional and ordered a return to at-large elections.[39] While the districting system has been analyzed in detail elsewhere,[40] it is important to review briefly the effects of districts on assembly reapportionment. First, the amount of vote distortion,[41] that is, the percentage of popular vote received in comparison with legislative representation, was decreased under districts. Second, the statewide degree of inequality of representation, measured by the average relative deviation from the statewide average of population per assemblyman,[42]

portionment controversies. In exercising leadership, for example, it will be shown that a veto was employed in one case, 1921–1922. Also, the *threat* of a veto by Governor Hughes was very important in the 1964–1965 senate reapportionment case.

[37] *Constitution of 1844,* Article II.

[38] See Alan Shank and Ernest C. Reock, Jr., *New Jersey's Experience with General Assembly Districts, 1852–1893* (New Brunswick, New Jersey: Bureau of Government Research, Rutgers–The State University, 1966), p. 7.

[39] In the case of *State v. Wrightson,* 56 N.J.L. 126 (1893) and affirmed by the Court of Errors and Appeals in *Smith v. Baker,* 74 N.J.L. 592 (1906).

[40] Shank and Reock, *op. cit.*

[41] *Ibid.,* p. 92.

[42] See Reock, *op. cit.,* p. 10. The entire population of the state is first divided by the number of legislators in order to obtain the average or ideal figure. The resulting figure, the "representative

reached a peak under assembly districts that was matched only by the legislative failure to reapportion in the 1950's.[43] Third, the districting experience inaugurated the practice of gerrymandering, whereby the drawing of district lines alternated among the controlling legislative parties in an effort to retain power.

By the end of the districting experience (1893), the legislature was so embroiled in the politics of gerrymandering that it was becoming increasingly difficult to design either fairly-drawn districts or provide for apportionments based on the principle of equal population. While the degree of population inequality was attributable to both districts and the 60-member constitutional restriction, the major reason for inequality was a direct result of the growing urbanization of the state. By 1890 the state ranked third in the nation in population density. More than 50 percent of the state's 1,445,000 population lived in places classified as urban areas. The three largest cities, Newark (Essex County), Jersey City (Hudson County), and Paterson (Passaic County), contained 30 percent of the state's population. The state ranked eighteenth in the nation in total population and fifth in manufacturing output.[44]

Thus, industrialization, large-scale immigration, and concentration of population in urban places had a direct impact on Assembly apportionment. New Jersey was experiencing an urban-rural dichotomy in the distribution of population that was to have an important influence on the politics of reapportionment within the legislature.[45]

---

ratio," is subtracted from the population actually represented by each legislator, and the result is expressed as a percentage of that ratio.

43 Shank and Reock, *op. cit.*, p. 96. See, also, Chapter IV, below.

44 These figures are taken from John E. Bebout and Ronald J. Grele, *Where Cities Meet: The Urbanization of New Jersey* (Princeton, New Jersey: D. Van Nostrand Co., 1964), pp. 33–34.

45 This development was also occurring in many other American states at this time. See Baker, *Rural versus Urban Political Power*, *op. cit.*, pp. 3–4.

Table 1.1 below[46] compares the degree of inequality resulting from assembly reapportionment with that caused by districts between the years 1852 to 1894. It is clearly evident that the counties were relatively equal in population at the beginning of the period. Inequality of representation increased as several counties fell below the representative ratio. By 1862, Cape May and Ocean counties were below the statewide average. By 1892, these two counties were joined by Hunterdon and Warren counties.[47] Thus, the counties experiencing rapid growth could not receive a proportionate share of increased representation due to the twin constitutional restriction of the 60-member limit and the guarantee of at least one assemblyman for each county.

TABLE 1.1. Degree of inequality of representation in the New Jersey General Assembly as caused by apportionment of seats and by districting, 1852–1894[48]

Legislative Year	Amount due to county apportionment of seats	Amount due to districting within the counties	Total
1852	8.8%	0	8.8%
1862	7.5%	7.2%	14.7%
1872	9.9%	5.7%	15.6%
1882	7.2%	5.4%	12.6%
1892	10.1%	14.3%	24.4%
1894	10.1%	0	10.1%

Constitutional restrictions and the developing urban-rural dichotomy in the state were two limiting conditions that forecast legislative struggles over reapportionment in the twentieth century. The inflexibility of the constitution served to entrench rural power in the legislature (and

46 Source: Shank and Reock, *op. cit.,* p. 97.

47 Reock, *op. cit.,* p. 20.

48 Using the measure of average relative deviation from the statewide average of population per assemblyman.

especially in the senate).[49] Rural power was enhanced by failure to reapportion at regular intervals and maintenance of the *status quo* despite evident population shifts.[50] The urban-rural conflict was particularly pronounced when the senate and assembly adopted conflicting strategies over the same issue.

The urban-rural clash was also evident in future efforts to revise the state constitution. A law of political survival dictated that rigid apportionment provisions would not be changed, particularly because those members who stood to lose the most power were the direct participants in any revisions of the constitution.[51]

Another important development under the 1844 constitution was the emergence of a strong two-party system in New Jersey. This pattern closely followed other northeastern states, where it has been observed that rural power is focused in Republican legislative parties, while the urban areas have most influence within Democratic party ranks.[52] The Republican party's rise to power in the state was marked by the election of the first Republican party governor in 1856. By 1900 the Republican party was clearly in control of the legislature, while the Democrats had more success in winning the governorship. The result was that future apportionment conflicts involved divided party control of the legislature *vis-a-vis* the governor. The Republican legislative party most often exercised the dominant influence in reapportionment policy-making. The gover-

---

[49] Charles R. Erdman, Jr., *The New Jersey Constitution—A Barrier to Governmental Efficiency and Economy* (Princeton, New Jersey: Princeton University Press, 1934), p. 13. See, also, Chapter III, below.

[50] See, particularly, Baker, *Rural versus Urban Political Power, op. cit.*, pp. 11–15. See, also, Chapter IV, below.

[51] Duane Lockard, *The Politics of State and Local Government* (New York: Macmillan Co., 1963), pp. 311–312. See, also, Chapter III, below.

[52] Jewell, *The State Legislature, op. cit.*, p. 9–33.

nor, in turn, either opposed Republican party plans or was the major force for innovation and mediation in legislative disputes.

Table 1.2 below indicates two major trends in the 109 years of two-party competition for legislative-executive control in New Jersey (1856–1965). First, the governor was a Democrat in every six out of ten years, while the legislature was controlled by Republicans in nearly seven of ten years. A Democratic governor was therefore most likely to face a Republican-controlled legislature when an apportionment dispute arose. Second, a Republican governor was more likely to have a Republican-controlled legislature during his term of office, although party similarity did not always ensure immediate success in all apportionment problems. A number of twentieth century apportionment disputes were bounded by conflicting and divided party interests of the governor and legislature. Bipartisan compromise and agreement were necessary to resolve disputes.

Thus, as the twentieth century began, New Jersey apportionment politics was bounded by fixed constitutional provisions, a return to at-large county-wide tickets for electing assemblymen, competition by two strong political parties, and a developing rural-urban clash for power among the state's twenty-one counties.[53]

Analysis of strategies and tactics in apportionment politics

The aforementioned boundary conditions of New Jersey apportionment politics do not provide explanations as to

[53] It should be noted that two counties were created after adoption of the 1844 constitution—Ocean (1850) and Union (1857). Ocean County was created as a response to population growth and the increasing economic development in southern Monmouth County. The incorporation of Union County resulted from the growth of the city of Elizabeth which became a rival to Newark in Essex County. See Effross, *op. cit.,* pp. 120–121.

TABLE 1.2. The legislature and the governor: party agreement and division, 1856–1965

	Under Democratic governors		Under Republican governors		Totals	
	Years	% of Years	Years	% of Years	Years	% of Years
Both houses Republican	39	59%	35	82%	74	68%
Both houses Democratic	11	17%	4	9%	15	14%
Split control	16	24%	4	9%	20	18%
Totals	66	100%	43	100%	109	100%
Republican assembly	39	59%	35	82%	74	68%
Democratic assembly	25	38%	7	16%	32	29%
Ties	2[a]	3%	1[b]	2%	3	3%
Totals	66	100%	43	100%	109	100%
Republican senate	53	80%	37	86%	90	83%
Democratic senate	13	20%	6	14%	19	17%
Totals	66	100%	43	100%	109	100%

	No.	Years	% of Years
Democratic governors	22	66	61%
Republican governors	14	43	39%
Totals	36	109	100%

[a] 1865, 1877 [b] 1919

how the legislature resolved conflicts over the representative system. An approach is required to analyze internal legislative politics. The research strategy is outlined below.

The legislative process can be analyzed in terms of

strategies and tactics employed in group conflict and accommodation.[54] *Strategies* consist of overall plans or courses of action to achieve a policy objective.[55] Reapportionment policy objectives might consist of preserving the *status quo,* assuring future legislative majorities, suppressing the minority party, or rewarding safe party members in particular counties.[56] *Tactics* are internal legislative maneuverings employed in specific cases.[57] Tactical maneuvering in reapportionment may include mobilizing a voting majority, establishing alliances and coalitions, etc. Several "rules" seem to be followed by legislators in the strategies and tactics of designing reapportionment plans:[58]

1. The legislative interest is clearly predominant in reapportionment policy-making. Each house should handle its own apportionment problem separately and the other house should accept the result. Each boundary problem should be handled by the dele-

---

[54] The most common approach to examining internal legislative politics in state legislatures is through analysis of party behavior. See, for examples, Thomas J. Anton, "The Legislature, Politics and Public Policy: 1959," *Rutgers Law Review,* Vol. 14, No. 3 (Winter, 1960), pp. 269–289 (on the New Jersey legislature); Thomas A. Flinn, "The Outline of Ohio Politics," *Western Political Quarterly,* Vol. 13, No. 3 (September, 1960), pp. 702–721; Malcolm E. Jewell, "Party Voting in American State Legislatures," *American Political Science Review,* Vol. 49, No. 3 (September, 1955), pp. 773–791; William J. Keefe, "Parties, Partisanship and Public Policy in the Pennsylvania Legislature," *American Politcial Science Review,* Vol. 48, No. 2 (June, 1954), pp. 450–464 and Duane Lockard, "Legislative Politics in Connecticut," *American Political Science Review,* Vol. 48, No. 1 (March, 1954) pp. 166–173.

[55] This definition has been adapted from Walter F. Murphy, *Elements of Judicial Strategy* (Chicago: University of Chicago Press, 1964), pp. 9–10.

[56] See Steiner and Gove, *op. cit.,* pp. 86–87; Royce Hanson, *The Political Thicket* (Englewood Cliffs, New Jersey: Prentice-Hall, Inc., 1966), pp. 35–36; and Jewell, *The State Legislature, op. cit.,* p. 18.

[57] Murphy, *op. cit.,* p. 9.

[58] This list represents a compilation of "rules" cited in Hanson, *op. cit.,* pp. 35–36; Jewell, *The State Legislature, op. cit.,* p. 18; and Steiner and Gove, *op. cit.,* pp. 116–117.

gation directly concerned. The legislature resents outside interference, whether by pressure groups, the governor, or the courts.

2. Reapportionment should focus upon maintaining the maximum number of incumbents. If incumbents must face each other after reapportionment, an attempt will be made to combine districts held by the minority party rather than by the majority party. The controlling political party will obtain maximum results by suppressing the minority party, especially when future legislative control is uncertain.
3. The maximum objective in reapportionment is to disturb the *status quo* as little as possible. This can be achieved either by refusing to reapportion; securing constitutional provisions that restrict change; or by passing bills that entrench prevailing political patterns.

Various analytical techniques are required to prove the employment of strategies and tactics in reapportionment politics. These fall into two general categories: (1) identification of legislative groups; and (2) analysis of group behavior.

New Jersey legislative groups have been identified according to affiliation by political party, urban and rural counties, and regions.

Political party alignments are necessary to show the extent and margin of legislative control, which in turn reveals which party exercised the dominant influence in policy-making. In the following chapters, the *margin of control* will refer to the number of seats held by a legislative party; the *extent of control* will indicate the relative percentage of years that a party has controlled one or both legislative chambers.[59]

---

[59] The classification scheme employed here is adapted from Richard E. Dawson and James A. Robinson, "Interparty Competition, Economic Variables, and Welfare Policies in the American States," *Journal of Politics,* Vol. 25, No. 2 (May, 1963), pp. 265–289.

Urban and rural classification of legislators by counties is based on the measure of population density. This is found by dividing the land area in square miles into the total population of the counties.[60] Using the census returns for the 100 years between 1860 and 1960, a distinct pattern of eight urban and 13 rural counties is found in New Jersey.[61] In all subsequent discussions, the urban and rural counties will be classified as shown in Table 1.3.

Regional groupings of counties may also account for differences in legislative responses to apportionment proposals. As shown in Figure 1.1, below, the regional groupings are nearly equal subdivisions of the urban-rural categories.[62] All of the Northeast and Central counties are urban; all of the Northwest and Seashore counties are rural; and, all but Camden County is rural in the Southern group. In subsequent discussions, these regional groupings will be correlated with urban-rural differences in reapportionment controversies. In summary, five county groupings form the basis of regional differences in the state:

Northeast Group	*Central Group*	*Northwest Group*
Bergen	Mercer	Hunterdon
Essex	Middlesex	Morris
Hudson		Somerset
Passaic		Sussex
Union		Warren

Seashore Group	*Southern Group*
Atlantic	Burlington
Cape May	Camden
Monmouth	Cumberland
Ocean	Gloucester
	Salem

---

[60] Using land area in square miles in the 1960 census. See: U.S. Bureau of the Census, *U.S. Census of Population: 1960*. Vol. I, Characteristics of the Population. Part A. Number of Inhabitants. Table 6, New Jersey: Area and Population of Counties, Urban and Rural, p. 32–13.

[61] Source: *New Jersey Legislative Manual* (1966), p. 224.

[62] Source: John E. Brush, *The Population of New Jersey* (New Brunswick, New Jersey: Rutgers University Press, 1956), p. 6.

TABLE 1.3, New Jersey counties: rank by population density, 1860–1960

Counties: Urban and Rural	Population density by census years										
	1960	1950	1940	1930	1920	1910	1900	1890	1880	1870	1860
Urban											
Hudson	13,752	14,388	14,490	15,350	13,981	11,938	8,579	5,714	4,178	2,873	1,394
Essex	7,215	7,078	6,542	6,512	5,094	4,007	2,805	2,005	1,484	1,124	772
Union	4,896	3,865	3,188	2,963	1,943	1,361	965	704	540	407	270
Bergen	3,349	2,320	1,758	1,566	904	592	336	203	158	133	93
Passaic	2,906	1,737	1,595	1,557	1,336	1,113	800	541	355	240	150
Camden	1,774	1,361	1,157	1,142	862	643	487	397	285	209	156
Middlesex	1,391	849	696	680	520	367	256	198	168	144	112
Mercer	1,168	1,008	865	821	701	551	418	351	255	204	164
Rural											
Monmouth	701	472	338	309	220	199	172	145	116	97	82
Morris	560	351	269	236	177	160	140	116	109	92	74
Somerset	469	323	242	212	156	126	107	92	88	77	72
Gloucester	410	279	220	215	147	114	97	87	79	66	56
Atlantic	280	230	216	217	146	125	81	50	32	25	21
Burlington	274	166	118	114	100	81	71	71	68	66	60
Cumberland	212	176	146	139	122	110	102	90	75	69	45
Cape May	182	139	108	110	73	74	49	42	37	32	27
Warren	176	151	139	137	125	120	105	101	101	95	80
Ocean	169	89	59	52	35	33	31	25	23	20	17
Salem	168	142	121	105	105	77	73	72	70	68	64
Hunterdon	124	98	84	80	76	77	79	81	89	85	77
Sussex	93	65	56	53	47	51	46	42	44	44	45

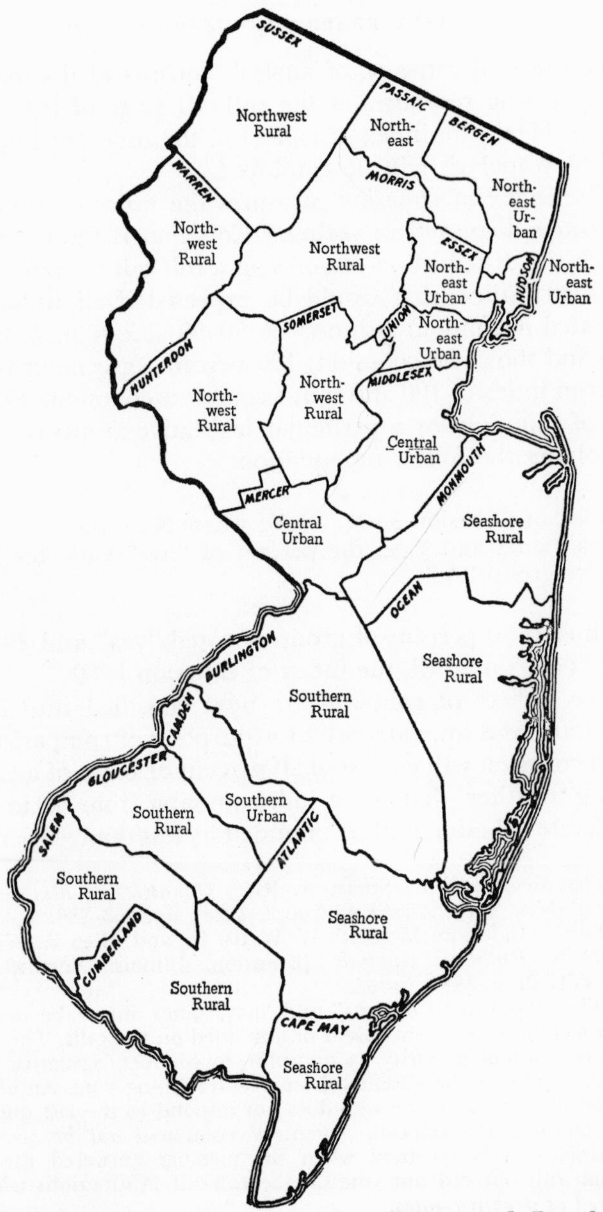

1.1 Map of New Jersey Counties, Urban and Rural and Regions.

The second category of analysis consists of discovering group voting responses at the roll-call stage of legislative action. Here, the index of cohesion, the index of likeness, and bloc analysis will be employed.

The *index of cohesion* measures the unity or cohesion of groups displayed in voting.[63] Cohesion is the extent to which the distribution of votes on a roll-call deviates from the distribution that would be expected if all influences operated in random fashion.[64] A 50–50 vote is an index of zero and shows no cohesion; 100 percent agreement represents an index of 100 and shows complete cohesion. The index of cohesion for a particular legislative group is found by solving the following equation:

> Index of Cohesion $= X_A - Y_A$ where $X =$ the percent of "yea" votes and $Y =$ the percent of "nay" votes for legislative group "A."

Thus, if 80 percent of group A voted "yea" and 20 percent "nay" on a bill, the index of cohesion is 60.

The indices of cohesion are next classified into high, moderate, and low categories for purposes of comparison.[65] High cohesion will consist of 90 percent or more of a group voting together, that is, an index ranging from 80 to 100. Moderate cohesion will be bounded by less than 90 percent

---

63 First developed by Stuart A. Rice, *Quantitative Methods in Politics* (New York: Alfred A. Knopf, 1928), pp. 208–209.

64 Lee F. Anderson, Meredith W. Watts, Jr., and Allen R. Wilcox, *Legislative Roll-Call Analysis* (Evanston, Illinois: Northwestern University Press, 1966), p. 32.

65 The employment of "yea" and "nay" votes must take into account members who were absent or abstained on roll-calls. The need for a constituent majority (a quorum) to conduct legislative business distinguishes the absentee from the abstaining vote. An absent member is defined as one who does not respond to the last quorum call preceding the roll-call. Absentees' votes *will not be counted.* An abstention is recorded when the member answered the last quorum call but did not vote on the roll-call. Abstentions *will be counted as negative votes.*

agreement but more than 75 percent agreement (an index ranging from 50 to 78). Low cohesion reflects less than 75 percent agreement (all indices below 50).[66]

The *index of likeness* measures inter-group differences.[67] This technique reflects the complement of the difference between the respective percentages voting "yea" in two groups.[68] For example, if both group A and group B divide 75–25 on a bill, the difference between them is zero and their likeness is 100. The index of likeness is found by solving the following equation:

Index of likeness $= 100-(X_A-X_B)$ where $X =$ the percent of "yea" votes for legislative group "a" and $X =$ the percent of "yea" votes for legislative group "B."

Thus, if group A voted 80 percent affirmatively and group B voted 75 percent affirmatively, the difference between them is 5 and their likeness is 95. High, moderate, and low "likeness" will be classified into categories similar to that for indices of cohesion.[69]

In order to find regularities in voting patterns, *bloc* analysis is employed.[70] A *bloc* is defined as a cluster of inter-

---

66 The classification of indices of cohesion into high, moderate, and low categories is, of necessity, arbitrary. The author inspected all roll-call votes and concluded that party or group unity was considerably weakened when less than 75 per cent (an index below 50) voted together. When 90 per cent or more voted together, there was either high party agreement or a strong blocking coalition. All other agreements between 75 per cent and 90 per cent thus formed the category of moderate cohesion.

67 This measure was also developed by Rice. See Rice, *op. cit.*, pp. 210–211.

68 Anderson, *et. al., op. cit.*, p. 44.

69 The same problem is evident in classifying categories of likeness as that of indices of cohesion. See footnote 66, *Supra.*

70 See Anderson, *et. al., op. cit.*, pp. 59–75; Herman C. Beyle, *Identification and Analysis of Attribute-Cluster-Blocs* (Chicago: University of Chicago Press, 1931); Stuart A. Rice, "The Identification of Blocs in Small Political Bodies," *American Political Science Review*, Vol. 21, No. 3 (August, 1927), pp. 619–627; and David B. Truman, *The Congressional Party* (New York: John Wiley & Sons, 1959), pp. 320–322.

related pairs of members voting together on a series of roll-calls.[71] The first step in identifying blocs is to find the number of times two legislators respond in the same way on a series of votes. Their agreements are then compared with other voting pairs and arranged in matrix form in the order of relative frequencies of agreement. Clusters of agreeing pairs appear in the matrix; the clusters form the *blocs* for analysis. The example below shows that legislators A, B, and C formed a strong bloc in contrast to outside member D. A, B, and C agreed on eight roll-calls, while D agreed with each of the other three members on only five roll-calls:

10 Roll-Call Voting Responses

	Yea	*Nay*
A	10	0
B	9	1
C	8	2
D	5	5

Matrix

	A	B	C	D
A		9	8	5
B	9		8	5
C	8	8		5
D	5	5	5	

Using the combined techniques of group affiliation and roll-call voting analysis, the following four chapters undertake a case-study approach to the study of legislative strategies and tactics in twentieth century New Jersey apportionment politics. The cases are treated chronologically, beginning with the five reapportionments of 1901, 1911, 1921, 1931, and 1941 considered together in Chapter II. The first forty years of apportionment activity were not as controversial or prominent issues within the legislative arena as later developments. Constitutional revision and the apportionment issue are examined in Chapter III, covering the years 1941 to 1947. The apportionment deadlock

[71] Truman, *op. cit.,* p. 320.

of the 1950's is presented in Chapter IV. Legislative response to court rulings on "one man, one vote" is the subject of Chapter V (1964–1965). New Jersey legislative strategies and tactics in reapportionment politics are reviewed in Chapter VI. Chapter VII is a theoretical exploration of strategies and tactics in the study of the legislative process.

2

The First Forty Years of Reapportionment Activity, 1901–1941

REAPPORTIONMENT HAS NOT ALWAYS BEEN A MAJOR LEGISLAtive concern in New Jersey. The first forty years of apportionment activity did not lead to the extensive legislative entanglements and disputes of later years. But even when the redistribution of assembly seats was accomplished, there were indications of controversy that would reappear later as full-blown political disputes. This chapter will first examine the necessary ingredients for adopting a non-controversial reapportionment plan. Attention will then shift to analysis of temporary disputes that required reconciliation among contending legislative forces.

Predictable majority party strategies in non-controversial reapportionments, 1901 and 1931

The reapportionment plans of 1901 and 1931 were summarily adopted by the legislature and appear to have been the only two genuinely non-controversial settlements in the twentieth century. Consensus characterized the legislative response in the two cases. Agreement was enhanced by two general preconditions: First, the reapportionment year was preceded by substantial one-party control of the legislature; second, the majority party was able to develop cohesion prior to the roll-call stage.

The Republican party was the undisputed legislative majority prior to both reapportionments. In 1901 the Republicans held 45 of the 60 assembly seats and 17 of the 21 senate seats; in 1931, the figures were 46 Republican assembly seats and 17 senate seats.[1] The 1901 session was preceded by seven consecutive years of two-chamber Republican party control, and the 1931 session by nine consecutive years of Republican dominance.

Republican party strength in 1901 was related to the return to at-large county-wide assembly tickets in 1895, although the last year under assembly single-member districts produced a Republican majority. Beginning with 1894, the Republicans controlled 74.2 percent of the assembly and 72.6 percent of the senate seats through 1901. (See Figure 2.1) In contrast, the Democrats held 65.3 percent of the assembly and 63.8 percent of the senate seats during the last five years of assembly districts (1889–1893).

Similarly, the Republican party enjoyed considerable success as the overwhelmingly superior legislative party between the years 1923 to 1931. Figure 2.2 shows Republican assembly strength ranging from low points of 42 seats in 1924 to highs of 48 seats in 1927 and 1929, following the great victory in 1921, when 59 Republicans were elected to the 60-member assembly. Republican control of the senate climbed to 18 of 21 seats in 1925, 1926, and 1928 after a "low" of 15 seats in 1921. Between 1923 and 1931,

---

[1] Unless otherwise noted, all figures concerning political party control of legislative seats are drawn from the *N.J. Legislative Manual.*

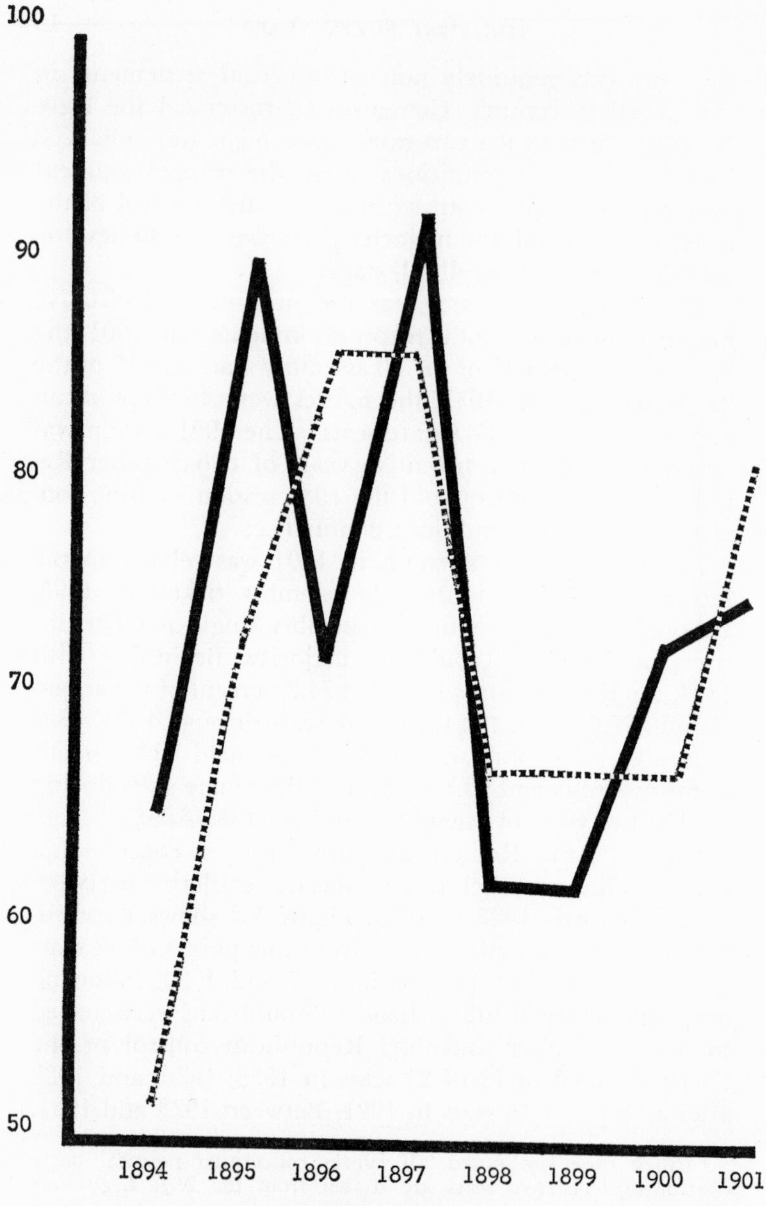

2.1 Republican Party Percentage of Seats in New Jersey Legislature, 1894–1901.

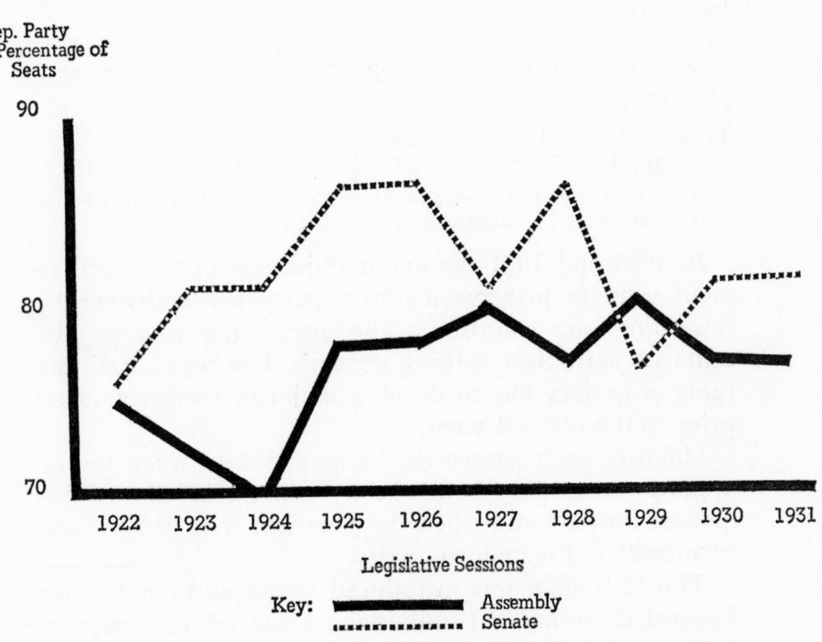

2.2 Republican Party Percentage of Seats in New Jersey Legislature, 1922–1931.

the Republicans controlled 76.8 percent of the assembly and 81.9 percent of the senate seats.

TABLE 2.1. Legislative sessions of 1901 and 1931 were preceded by Republican party control

	General Assembly		Senate	
	Republicans	Democrats	Republicans	Democrats
1894–1901				
Total seats	356	123	122	46
% of Total	74.2%	25.6%	72.6%	27.4%
1923–1931				
Total seats[a]	414	125	145	32
% of total	76.8%	23.2%	81.9%	18.1%

[a] One vacant assembly seat in Essex County in 1926; and two vacant senate seats in Camden and Middlesex counties in 1929.

In 1901 and 1931 the major objectives of reapportionment were to preserve majority party predominance by rewarding safe counties, while attempting to keep the minority party from gaining strength. The key to attaining these objectives was to develop majority party consensus prior to the roll-call votes.

Majority party agreement became evident when the reapportionment plan fulfilled the requirements of a mathematical formula and when the plan was endorsed by near unanimity of the majority party.

The 1901 plan was introduced by Republican Senator Edward C. Stokes of Cumberland County.[2] The reapportionment consisted of two seating shifts from the rural northwestern counties to the burgeoning urban northeastern counties.[3] Most of the population gains between 1890

[2] Source: *Journal of the Fifty-Seventh Senate of the State of New Jersey being the One Hundred and Twenty-Fifth Session of the Legislature,* January 14, 1901, p. 30. Hereinafter cited as *NJSJ.*

[3] New Jersey was rapidly meerging as an urban and industrial State through population shifts occurring during this time. See: John E. Bebout and Ronald J. Grele, *Where Cities Meet: The Urbanization of New Jersey* (Princeton, New Jersey: D. Van Nostrand Co., 1964), pp. 40–43.

and 1900 took place in the industrial northeast section of the state, while the rural northwest had gained little or no population during the decennial census interval. As shown in Table 2.2, below, the urban northeast ranked among the six leading counties in percentage of population gains between 1890 and 1900, while the rural northwest counties were clustered near the bottom of statewide population gains.[4]

The population considerations shown in Table 2.2 were closely correlated with the political party composition of counties in the 1901 legislature. The rural northwestern counties of Hunterdon and Warren were represented by Democrats and would yield seats to Republican-controlled Passaic and Democratic-controlled Hudson counties. Passage of the plan would result in a net gain of one additional Republican assembly seat and thereby strengthen the prevailing majority party.

The 1931 plan was proposed by Charles A. Otto, a Republican assemblyman from Union County and chairman of the judiciary committee.[5] Bergen (urban northeastern) and Morris (rural northwestern) counties were to gain seats from Hudson and Passaic counties, two urban northeastern counties. Table 2.3 reveals that while both Hudson and Passaic counties ranked lower than Bergen and Morris in decennial population gains between 1920 and 1930, Passaic County still had 2½ times more population than Morris and Hudson nearly twice the population of Bergen County. Thus, it appeared that the 1931 plan was intended to accommodate urban and rural county representation within the majority party.

Two additional considerations prompted the Morris

---

[4] Source: U.S. Bureau of the Census. *U.S. Census of Population: 1900*. Vol. I, Population. Part I. Table 5, Population of States and Territories by Minor Civil Divisions: New Jersey, pp. 267–271.

[5] Source: *Minutes and Proceedings of the One Hundred and Fifty-Fifth General Assembly of the State of New Jersey,* January 19, 1931, p. 74. Hereinafter cited as *NJAM*.

TABLE 2.2 Population gains in northeast and northwest counties between 1890 and 1900

Counties, 1901 Partisanship		Population Gain from 1890 Census	% of Population Increase from 1890	1900 County Rank in % of Population Increase
Urban Northeast:				
Bergen	Republican	31,215	66.1%	1
Passaic	Republican	50,156	47.7%	3
Hudson	Democratic	110,922	40.3%	4
Essex	Republican	102,955	40.2%	5
Union	Republican	26,886	37.1%	6
Rural Northwest:				
Morris	Republican	11,055	20.4%	11
Somerset	Republican	4,637	16.4%	14
Sussex	Republican	1,875	8.4%	17
Warren	Democratic	1,228	3.4%	18
Hunterdon	Democratic	– 848	–2.4%	20

gain. First, Morris was as safe a Republican stronghold as any other county within majority party ranks. From 1902 to 1931, Morris was solidly Republican in 27 of 30 legislative years, with the only exceptions occurring in 1911, 1912, and 1913. Second, Morris County had lost a seat under the 1922 reapportionment and was now designated to have that seat restored.

The second major objective of the 1931 plan was to continue to sap Democratic party representation in Hudson County. Hudson County had only a 9.8 percent population gain from 1920 to 1930, but even more important was the continuing Republican party attack on the Hudson-dominated Hague machine, which battled the Republicans in contests for the governorship.[6]

[6] Hudson County control over Democratic candidates for governor will be discussed subsequently in the 1921–1922 reapportionment case.

*TABLE 2.3. Both urban and rural counties ranked high in percentage of population increase between 1920 and 1930.**

Counties, 1931 Partisanship	Population Gain from 1920 Census	% of Population Increase from 1920	1930 County Rank in % of Population Increase
Urban Counties:			
Bergen Republican	154,274	73.2%	1
Union Republican	105,052	52.5%	2
Passaic Republican	42,955	16.6%	14
Hudson Democratic	61,576	9.8%	18
Rural Counties:			
Cape May Republican	10,026	51.5%	3
Ocean Republican	10,914	49.3%	4
Morris Republican	27,751	33.6%	9

* Source: U.S. Bureau of the Census. *U.S. Census of Population: 1930.* Vol. I, Population: Number and Distribution of Inhabitants. Table 3—New Jersey: Area and Population of Counties, p. 713.

Both the 1901 and 1931 reapportionment plans were consistent with a mathematical formula known as a variation of the Vinton Method.[7] Under this formula, the total population of the state is divided by the total number of

[7] See *New Jersey Legislative Reapportionment: A Summary of Legislative Proposals to Reapportion the General Assembly of New Jersey, 1951 to 1957* (Trenton: Law and Legislative Reference Bureau, Division of the State Library, Archives and History, New Jersey State Department of Education, November, 1957), p. 29.

assembly seats to obtain a preliminary ratio. Each county with a population smaller than this ratio is assigned one "guaranteed" constitutional seat.[8] The total population of the remaining counties is divided by the remaining number of seats to be allotted (the second ratio). The population of each of these remaining counties is then divided by the second ratio to obtain their exact quota of seats. After the whole number of seats is assigned, the remainder is distributed to those counties with the highest fractions in their exact quotas.

Under the variation of the Vinton Method, the 1901 plan produced the same seating gains and losses for the counties previously indicated. However, in 1931, Morris and Camden (urban-Southern) counties were tied according to the second ratio allotment. But the excess population over the second ratio whole number of seats was 39,409 for Morris as compared with 39,204 for Camden, so Morris County was assigned the surplus seat rather than Camden County. Thus, safe party affiliation, rural county status, and the politics of mathematics all worked in favor of Morris County in 1931 over the possible competing demands of the urban majority party counties.

Table 2.4 below summarizes the distribution of assembly seats to the counties most directly affected by the variation of the Vinton Method formula in 1901 and 1931.

Solid majority party agreement was evident when the 1901 plan was approved. Predictable strategy of maximizing gains and consolidating existing strength resulted in an optimum payoff for the Republicans as shown in Table 2.5 below.

Near majority party unanimity was similarly evident in the 1931 roll-call votes. Two roll-calls were necessary to pass the plan in the assembly, but the second vote was

[8] *Constitution of 1844,* Article IV, Section III.

TABLE 2.4. General assembly reapportionment by a variation of the Vinton Method, 1901 and 1931

Counties and Partisanship		Population	Second Ratio Allotment of Seats	Largest Fraction Surplus Seats	Total Seats
1901 Plan:					
Hudson	Democratic	386,048	12.00	0	12
Passaic	Republican	155,202	4.82	1	5
Warren	Democratic	37,781	1.17	0	1
Hunterdon	Democratic	34,507	1.07	0	1
1931 Plan:					
Bergen	Republican	364,977	5.13	0	5
Morris	Republican	110,445	1.55	1	2
Camden	Republican	252,312	3.55	0	3
Passaic	Republican	302,129	4.25	0	4
Hudson	Democratic	690,730	9.72	1	10

TABLE 2.5. Solid majority party voting cohesion was exhibited in 1901 reapportionment roll-call votes[9]

	General Assembly				Senate			
	Yes	No	Not Voting	Intra-party Cohesion	Yes	No	Not Voting	Intra-party Cohesion
Republicans	41	0	4	100+	13	0	4	100+
Democrats	0	13	2	100—	1[a]	2	1	33.4—
Totals	41	13	6		14	2	5	

[a] Affirmative vote by Hudson County senator

simply in response to a minor senate amendment.[10] Minor dissent was registered by the Passaic County senator and one Passaic assemblyman. These votes can be discounted as

[9] Source: *NJAM,* 125th, March 19, 1901, p. 418; and *NJSJ,* 57th, March 6, 1901, p. 216.

[10] Sources: *NJAM,* 155th, March 9, 1931, p. 279; *NJSJ,* 87th, April 8, 1931, p. 902; *NJAM,* April 21, 1931, pp. 809–810.

token resistance to the urban county seat loss with little impact on solid majority party cohesion.[11]

TABLE 2.6. Nearly unanimous majority party voting cohesion shown in 1931 reapportionment roll-call votes

	General Assembly[a]				Senate			
	Yes	No	Not Voting	Intra-party Cohesion	Yes	No	Not Voting	Intra-party Cohesion
Republicans	70	1	21	97.2+	11	1	4	83.4+
Democrats	1[b]	18	9	92.0—	0	3	1	100—
Totals	71	19	30		11	4	5	

[a] This is a composite of the two assembly roll-calls. The separate votes were 40–11 and 31–8. See *NJAM*, 155th, March 9, 1931, p. 279 and *Ibid.*, April 21, 1931, pp. 809–810.
[b] Hudson County affirmative vote.

The non-controversial reapportionments of 1901 and 1931 were enacted when the following requirements were met. First, close adherence to a mathematical formula, a variation of the Vinton Method, necessitated an increase in urban county representation at the expense of rural counties in 1901. When the rural counties were part of the legislative minority party, the majority party could proceed to increase urban county power. As it will be shown later, future legislative problems developed when rural counties within the majority party were designated for seat losses and refused to vote for them.[12] Second, the majority party chose to balance urban and rural county gains over an alternative shift focusing on a transfer of seats from urban minority party counties to urban majority party counties in 1931. This development indicated that

[11] Minor dissent really confirms the observation that the reapportionment bill would not pass without solid majority party support. See John C. Wahlke, *et. al. The Legislative System* (New York: John Wiley and Sons, Inc., 1962), pp. 345–346.

[12] See, particularly, the 1921–1922 case, below, and Chapter III, below.

the majority party can enact a plan when internal urban-rural accommodation is achieved. The assumption is that a possible rural county voting bloc could oppose a plan by joining forces with the minority party.[13] Then, no plan could pass because of the lack of a constitutional majority in the assembly. Third, both the 1901 and 1931 plans showed that the majority party exhibited internal strength and thereby handled the minority party without difficulty. Subsequent cases will describe the lack of majority party cohesion which, naturally, strengthens the blocking power of the minority party; or, magnifies the strategic position occupied by a key urban county delegation within the majority party.[14]

Having described the necessary ingredients for avoiding controversy, the next section identifies elements of conflict in the reapportionment process. The temporary disputes of 1911, 1921–1922, and 1941 were resolved only after reconciliation of competing demands within the legislature.

Roots of controversy in three reapportionments: 1911, 1921–1922, and 1941

Disjointed assembly majorities were the root-cause of reapportionment problems in 1911, 1921–1922, and 1941. Majority party division over proposed plans necessitated multiple roll-call votes. Each of the three cases contained political elements that reappeared in later prolonged controversies. The 1911 case represented an example of split party control of the legislature and Democratic party control of the governorship. In 1921, the Republicans had overwhelming legislative control, but the governor was a Democrat. Split party control of the legislature and the governor was similarly evident in 1922 and 1941.

Reapportionment disputes were caused by the 1911 as-

13 *Ibid.*

14 See, for examples, the 1941 case, below and Chapter IV, below.

sembly disagreement over a senate-sponsored plan; internal majority party disagreement along urban-rural lines in 1921; and powerfully located urban county delegations in 1921 and 1941, which temporarily blocked passage of plans.

Each of the three cases will be analyzed separately below to determine how effective assembly majorities were reestablished after initial disagreements. This will be followed by summary comparisons in which common points of conflict are identified for purposes of introducing the extended difficulties of the last quarter century of New Jersey reapportionment politics.

1911: The dispersed assembly majority of the Democrats

The 1911 assembly Democrats were not firmly united on a reapportionment plan that satisfied the expectations of competing county delegations. In contrast, the assembly Republicans remained relatively consistent in supporting a plan passed by the Republican-controlled senate. Minority voting cohesion in the assembly exploited majority party lack of agreement. The majority party eventually agreed to the senate plan in the absence of a suitable alternative.

The 1910 elections resulted in both a Democratic party victory in the assembly and the governorship. Woodrow Wilson became the first victorious Democratic party governor since 1895 by winning nearly 56 percent of the statewide vote.[15] Wilson's electoral margin was closely related to a turnover of 23 assembly seats, previously represented by Republicans. The Democrats made gains in eight previously solid Republican counties, [16] all of which voted for Wilson and Democratic candidates for assembly in 1910. When the 23 new Democratic assemblymen were added

[15] Source: *N.J. Legislative Manual* (1911), pp. 531–532.

[16] *Ibid.* The Democratic party assembly gains were in Bergen, Essex, Gloucester, Monmouth, Morris, Ocean, Somerset, and Union counties.

to 19 incumbent and returning Democrats, the party had its most substantial assembly majority since 1893.[17] The Democrats also made inroads on Republican control of the senate. Republican party control was reduced to a three-seat advantage with Democratic party gains in Bergen, Morris, and Ocean counties.[18]

With representation distributed along urban and rural county lines, the assembly Democrats were in a position to develop an apportionment plan to satisfy the various county delegations. The best strategy for the Democrats appeared to be a plan to consolidate new gains and enhance chances for retaining assembly control in the future.

The senate Republicans seized the initiative by passing the first reapportionment proposal. The senate plan focused attention on six counties: Atlantic, Bergen, Burlington, Cumberland, Essex, and Monmouth. As shown in Table 2.7, below, there were several calculations made by the senate Republicans in the plan. First, Bergen County (urban-northeastern), which would gain a seat, was expected to return to Republican party ranks in 1912.[19] Secondly, Atlantic County (rural-seashore), which had withstood the 1911 Democratic party sweep,[20] was designated for a seating gain to offset at least one of the seat losses for solidly Republican Burlington (rural-southern) and Cumberland (rural-southern) counties. Thirdly, a trade was proposed for Essex (urban-northeastern) and Monmouth (rural-seashore) counties. Essex County, which was somewhat "competitive" in previous assembly representa-

[17] In 1893, the Democrats held 39 of 60 seats. The last Democratic victory in the twentieth century was in 1907 when they controlled a bare majority of 31 seats.

[18] The 12–9 Republican advantage was the lowest since 1909, when a 13–8 alignment existed.

[19] Bergen County had solid Republican party delegations from 1902–1910.

[20] Atlantic County was solidly Republican from 1902–1910.

tion,[21] would gain a seat from Monmouth, which was more heavily weighted toward Democratic party representation.[22]

In summary, the senate plan calculated a net gain of one Republican seat in assuming that both Bergen and Atlantic counties would elect Republicans in 1912, while Essex County's future affiliation remained uncertain.

The senate minority Democrats challenged the Republican plan. Led by the Hudson County senator,[23] the Demo-

TABLE 2.7. Senate Republican calculations in 1911 plan

Counties 1911 Partisanship	Partisanship	Seating Gains and Losses	Partisan Advantage
Essex Urban Democratic	*Rep.* 1902–1906; *Rep.* 1908–1910 *Dem.* 1907	+1	"Competitive"
Bergen Urban Democratic	*Rep.* 1902–1910	+1	Republican Gain
Atlantic Rural Republican	*Rep.* 1902–1910	+1	Republican Gain
Monmouth Rural Split*	*Rep.* 1902, 1905–1907; 1909–1910 *Dem.* 1903–1904; 1908	—1	Democratic Loss
Burlington Rural Republican	*Rep.* 1902–1910	—1	Republican Loss
Cumberland Rural Republican	*Rep.* 1902–1910	—1	Republican Loss

* In 1911, Monmouth had 2 assembly Democrats and a Republican senator.

21 "Competitive" is used guardingly here, since Essex County had only one previous Democratic delegation between 1902 and 1910.

22 Democrats had previously controlled the Monmouth delegation in 1903, 1904, and 1908.

23 Proposed by Hudson Democratic Senator James F. Fielder. *NJSJ*, 67th, March 14, 1911, p. 347.

crats proposed a four-seat rearrangement with gains for Bergen and Essex counties offset by losses for Burlington and Cumberland counties. This alternative was immediately satisfactory to the Democrats. Bergen and Essex counties had Democratic representation in 1911 and if this continued in 1912 the Democrats would gain two seats. Atlantic County's gain was deleted as a partisan effort to offset the Republican rural county gain for two rural county losses. Also, Monmouth County was not included in the plan in order to protect Democratic party representation in a rural county.

The minority alternative was rejected when all twelve Republican senators lined up against eight of the nine Democrats. The senate Republicans then passed the original six-seat readjustment in a unanimous vote.[24] The Democrats were substantially cohesive in opposing the plan, as only the Morris County Democrat crossed party lines and voted with the Republicans.[25]

When the senate plan moved over to the assembly, two courses of action were available. First, the majority Democrats could mobilize party ranks on urban and rural lines and reject the senate plan. The Democrats could argue that the senate Republicans should not interfere with assembly reapportionment, because the chamber most affected should develop its own plan.[26] Secondly, the minority Republicans could attempt to exploit urban-rural divisions in the majority party by giving consistent

---

[24] *Ibid.*, March 15, 1911, p. 372.

[25] A possible explanation for the Morris County vote is that it represented an "independent" vote. The 1911 Legislative Manual describes the senator as not holding prior elective office, and that he was elected to the senate "solely on his own merits over a strong opponent." Furthermore, the Morris Democrat had broken a strong succession of Republican legislative victories in Morris County. The Morris Democrat was the first Democratic party senator in the twentieth century. Source: *N.J. Legislative Manual* (1911), p. 297.

[26] See: Gilbert Y. Steiner and Samuel K. Gove, *Legislative Politics in Illinois* (Urbana: University of Illinois Press, 1960), p. 117.

support to the senate plan. If the Democrats could not agree on an alternative, the minority Republicans might be able to attract enough majority party votes to pass the plan.

The assembly Democrats responded to the senate plan by dividing on urban-rural lines instead of mobilizing party ranks and passing an alternative. The urban Democrats decided to accept the senate plan because of an alternative set of calculations. The urban Democrats were willing to sacrifice a rural county seat loss in Monmouth for two possible seating gains in Bergen and Essex counties. If all county delegations retained the same party affiliation in 1912, the urban Democrats could expect gains in two counties while losing one rural seat. At the same time, the Republicans, while gaining a seat in Atlantic, would be losing two rural seats in Burlington and Cumberland counties. The overall result, as seen by the urban Democrats, would be a net gain of one urban Democratic seat in 1912, while the Republicans would suffer a net loss of one rural county seat.

Three roll-call votes were required in the assembly before the senate plan was finally adopted. The first vote fell short of a 31-member majority when only 13 Democrats joined 14 Republicans in a 27–22 division.[27] The lack of a majority was due to very weak Democratic party cohesion (31.6—negative) as 20 Democrats voted against the senate plan. In contrast, the Republicans had moderate cohesion (56) in an effort to remain relatively consistent on the Senate plan.

Democratic party division on the first vote was particularly evident in the urban county delegations with 8 members voting "yea" and 16 voting "nay." The 2–1 split was especially noticeable in the voting responses of Essex and Hudson counties, the two largest urban Democratic delegations. When these two counties could not agree on

[27] *NJAM,* 135th, April 20, 1911, p. 1304.

a plan, the assembly majority party was unable to act.[28]

Immediately following the initial failure to develop a majority for the senate plan, the assembly moved to a second roll-call vote to reconsider. The proponents of the senate plan assumed that at least four more votes could be attracted. The second vote reflected both the absence of a suitable alternative plan in majority party ranks and the necessity of a two-party coalition rather than a majority party bloc in passing a plan.[29] The vote to reconsider succeeded in a 38–5 victory for the senate plan proponents.[30] The minority Republicans were now firmly united over the first roll-call with 16 affirmative votes and two absences. The Democrats were still divided, but 22 Democrats joined the Republicans and agreed to reconsider the first vote. An urban-rural split continued to characterize the majority party voting pattern. Led by four vote changes in the Essex delegation (which split 8–1 on the second vote in contrast to the 4–6 division on the first vote), the urban Democrats divided 16–11 in favor of the reconsideration. The rural Democrats were considerably more divided with six in favor and five against.

The two-party coalition was now in a position to adopt the senate reapportionment plan. 29 Democrats joined 13 Republicans in a 42–7 vote with six abstentions and five absences.[31] Final opposition was confirmed to the Mon-

[28] Essex and Hudson counties controlled 23 of the 42 Democratic assembly votes. When these two counties were so badly divided, it was most difficult to form an effective majority party bloc vote for a plan. See also, David R. Derge, "Metropolitan and Outstate Alignments in the Illinois and Missouri Legislative Delegations," *American Political Science Review,* Vol. 52, No. 4 (December, 1958), pp. 1057–1058.

[29] The 1911 plan thus differed from both the 1901 and 1931 cases since both majority and minority party votes were needed to form a 31-vote legislative majority.

[30] *NJAM,* 135th, April 20, 1911, p. 1343. The vote was 38 yea, 5 nay, 11 abstain, and 6 absent.

[31] *Ibid.*

mouth County Democrats and a few regional allies.

Two reasons appear to explain why the assembly Democrats felt compelled to accept the senate plan. First, the senate Republicans seized the initiative by calculating gains and losses, mobilizing ranks, and passing a plan. The assembly Democrats could not develop a viable alternative plan due to the Essex-Hudson county division. Thus, the assembly Democrats were not "masters of their own house" when the senate plan finally prevailed.[32]

Second, the assembly Democrats were divided along urban-rural lines. The urban Democrats had fostered an intra-party split by focusing on expected urban county seating gains at the expense of rural county losses. Voting power was then dispersed among three definable blocs. The strongest affirmative-voting bloc on the three roll-calls consisted of Bergen County, which stood to gain a seat, and Hunterdon, Somerset, and Sussex counties. But this urban-rural bloc contained only five votes. The strong-negative-voting bloc consisted of Monmouth County, which was designated to lose a seat, and Ocean County. Again, however, the negative voting bloc held only four assembly votes. The remaining 33 majority party votes, consisting of both urban and rural counties, fell into a swing bloc. Within this crucial swing bloc, 70 percent of the Essex County votes were cast affirmatively and 30 percent negatively on the three roll-calls, while the Hudson County delegation was split 47 percent affirmative and 53 percent negative. Similarly the votes of the six other majority party county delegations changed during the three roll-calls. Obviously, then, majority party voting cohesion was very weak. A coalition was needed to cross party lines in view of majority party division.

---

[32] See Gilbert Y. Steiner and Samuel K. Gove, *Legislative Politicis in Illinois* (Urbana: University of Illinois Press, 1960), p. 117 for the following observation: "Redistricting decisions affecting each chamber are made within the particular house involved. . ."

TABLE 2.8. Majority and minority party voting cohesion on three 1911 votes

Counties	Yea	Nay	Index of Cohesion
Democrats-Urban	47	34	16
Democrats-Rural	17	16	3
Total	64	50	12
Republicans	43	8	68.6

In the final analysis the urban-rural majority split in 1911 represented a contrast to the usual dominance of party in passing reapportionment plans. When the two largest majority party delegations disagreed on a plan, several votes were required until a majority could be formed.[33]

1921–1922: Reward and punishment for Hudson County

Hudson County, a traditional Democratic party stronghold, was the focus of a series of legislative maneuvers in the reapportionment efforts of 1921 and 1922. The Republican assembly leadership developed a plan in 1921 that Hudson County opposed because of a "rule" that dictates county self-interest in preserving existing representation.[34] By establishing an alliance with a rural bloc, the Hudson opposition prevented adoption of the 1921 plan.

The party composition of Hudson County changed from Republican to Democratic in 1922. The 1921 plan was reintroduced and summarily passed as several rural counties broke with Hudson and displayed majority party loyalty.

[33] The reverse situation produces a deadlock in reapportionment. When the two largest county delegations form an alliance, no plan can be passed.

[34] See Malcolm E. Jewell, Ed., *The Politics of Reapportionment* (New York: Atherton Press, 1962), pp. 27–29; Jewell, *The State Legislature* (New York: Random House, 1962), pp. 18–20; and Steiner and Gove, *op. cit.*, p. 117.

Isolated in the legislative arena, the Hudson Democrats sought outside support to nullify the 1922 plan. The Hudson-controlled governor vetoed the plan, but Republican legislative majorities quickly responded and overruled the veto.[35] The last Hudson appeal was to the courts and this also failed when the state supreme court upheld the 1922 plan.[36]

Two major political events were at the base of the 1921–1922 reapportionment case. First, the overwhelming Presidential vote for Warren G. Harding in 1920 produced an extraordinary coattails effect[37] in normally Democratic counties.[38] The result was that 59 Republicans were elected to the 1921 assembly, leading to the most one-sided assembly majority in the twentieth century. Only Warren County withstood the Republican sweep and elected the lone Democrat. In the senate, six Democrats, who did not have to face election in 1920, were opposed by 15 Republicans. Thus, as the 1921 legislative session began, the Republican party had substantial control of both chambers.

Secondly, a Democrat, Edward I. Edwards, was the governor in 1921 and 1922. Edwards had been elected in 1919 and his victory was directly attributable to an overwhelming plurality produced by Hudson County.[39] Edwards was the handpicked candidate of Mayor Frank

---

[35] The Governor's action was unusual, since he seldom plays a forceful role in reapportionment controversies in fear of jeopardizing the rest of his legislative program. See: Jewell, Ed., *The Politics of Reapportionment, op. cit.*, p. 31.

[36] In the case of *Botti v. McGovern,* 97 N.J.L. 353 (1922).

[37] A one party sweep may sometimes result in disrupting the normal patterns of party control in a state. See Coleman B. Ransone, Jr., *The Office of Governor in the United States* (University Alabama: University of Alabama Press, 1956), p. 9.

[38] Harding got 70.4 per cent of the statewide vote and carried all 21 counties with a plurality of 256,887 votes. Source: *N.J. Legislative Manual* (1922), p. 534.

[39] Hudson County produced a 36,113 vote plurality for Edwards, which exceeded the plurality of 28,425 for the Republican candidate in 16 counties. Source: *N.J. Legislative Manual* (1922), p. 534.

Hague, the leader of the Jersey City and Hudson County machine.[40] The 1921 Republican sweep was a temporary setback for Boss Hague, but Governor Edwards stood as a bulwark of Hudson County interests.

The Republican assembly leadership united behind a plan designed to add seats to Bergen and Union counties and take seats from Hudson and Morris counties.[41] The plan was calculated to strengthen anti-Hague forces in the neighboring northeastern urban counties and reward the two fastest growing counties in the state.[42] Even though Hudson County had shifted to Republican in 1921, the future expectation was that the county would return to Democratic representation. The proposed seating trades would therefore result in a net gain of one Republican seat under more normal patterns of two-party competition.

The assembly plan had a predictably certain defect. Two conditions were necessary to pass the plan. Either the urban bloc, which had 32 assembly votes other than Hudson County, would have to demonstrate high voting cohesion, or an urban-rural coalition was needed to surmount Hudson and Morris opposition to seat losses. In contrast, Hudson and Morris counties together required 16 additional votes to block the plan. If a strong rural opposition bloc was established, it would be impossible to develop a 31-vote majority.

Within majority party ranks, a deliberate urban-rural blocking strategy was evident in the 1921 roll-call vote.

---

[40] See Dayton David McKean, *The Boss: The Hague Machine in Action* (Boston: Houghton Mifflin Co., 1940), pp. 46–50.

[41] The plan was introduced by Republican Assembly Majority Leader, T. Harry Rowland of Camden County. Source: *NJAM,* 145th, January 17, 1921, p. 55. Also see Newark *Evening News,* January 18, 1921. The bill was designed by Republican Assemblyman Arthur N. Pierson of Union County "on the basis of the 1920 census."

[42] Between the 1910 and 1920 censuses, Bergen and Union counties had increased in population by 52.7 per cent and 42.8 per cent, respectively.

Three rural and 21 urban Republicans voted in favor, while 11 rural and 18 urban assemblymen (including the lone Warren County Democrat) voted against. The plan failed to pass in a vote of 24–29 with two abstentions and four absences.[43] The two designated beneficiaries, Bergen and Union counties, were able to elicit support from only a portion of the other urban counties (15 votes out of a possible 26 non-Hudson urban votes) and weak rural county support (three votes from Atlantic and Ocean counties). In contrast, the Hudson-Morris opposing bloc got solid rural support from the northwestern counties,[44] and southern-seashore counties,[45] plus the urban county defections. The result of the 1921 vote was maintenance of the *status quo*. For the first time in the twentieth century, a reapportionment plan had not been passed in the first legislative session following release of the United States decennial census figures for New Jersey counties.[46]

The underlying cause for both the defeat of the 1921 plan and majority party refusal to press for additional roll-call votes was primarily due to the tenuous position of Hudson County. The 1922 Republican majority leader in the assembly explained that in 1921 there were no Democratic members from Hudson County and the Republicans preferred not to take advantage of that situation.[47]

The November, 1921 election victory of twelve Hudson assembly Democrats served as a prelude to Republican party reapportionment maneuvers in 1922. The Hague

---

[43] *NJAM,* 145th, April 4, 1921, p. 916.

[44] Consisting of Hunterdon, Somerset, Sussex, and Warren counties.

[45] Consisting of Burlington, Cumberland, Salem, Cape May and Monmouth counties.

[46] Refusal to reapportion is one of the major problems in state legislative reapportionment. See Jewell, *The State Legislature, op. cit.,* p. 20. See, also, Chapter IV, below.

[47] Newark *Evening News,* February 22, 1922.

machine produced an average vote of 81,323 for the 12 Democrats while the Republican incumbents received an average vote of 34,546.[48] The Democrats also retained the Warren County seat, and registered small gains in Essex (one seat) and Hunterdon (one seat) counties for a total of 15 Democrats in the 1922 assembly.

The assembly Republicans thereupon proceeded to re-introduce the 1921 plan, that is, seating gains for Bergen and Union counties and seating losses for Hudson and Morris counties.[49] To pass this plan, the Republicans needed an anti-Hudson voting alliance, which in effect was a relatively solid party vote on the roll-call. The only presumed obstacle was Morris County, which still opposed a seat loss.

The 1922 reapportionment plan passed the assembly by a vote of 34–18 with five abstentions and three absences.[50] The Democrats were solidly opposed, while the Morris County Republicans got scattered support from Burlington, Essex, Monmouth, Somerset, and Sussex counties. In contrast to the 1921 vote, the urban county Republicans were much more cohesive and contributed 29 of 30 available votes for the plan. Atlantic, Cumberland, Ocean, and Salem counties, from the southern seashore area, added five affirmative rural county votes. Thus, the significant reversal in the 1922 roll-call vote was within the majority party urban county delegations. When these counties combined their voting strength against a cohesive minority, the plan passed the assembly without difficulty.[51] The senate vote also demonstrated cohesive majority party support within the urban county delegations. The 12–3 senate

[48] *Ibid.,* November, 9, 1921.

[49] Re-introduced by the Assembly Majority Leader, John Y. Dater (Republican-Bergen). *NJAM,* 146th, January 30, 1922, p. 106.

[50] *NJAM,* 146th, February 21, 1922, p. 417.

[51] This confirms the hypothesis that urban county delegations will be on the winning side when they vote with high cohesion. See Derge, *op. cit.,* p. 1065.

approval revealed only rural county support for Morris County as Monmouth, Cape May, and Gloucester Republicans abstained or voted negatively.[52]

Majority party voting cohesion was maintained in the roll-call vote required to override Democratic governor Edwards' veto of the 1922 plan. The assembly Republicans nearly duplicated the urban county bloc vote displayed on the initial bill. Twenty-eight urban Republicans joined forces with nine rural Republicans and overrode the veto by a vote of 37–19 with four abstentions.[53] Morris County stood firm in opposition to a seat loss, and together with six negative and abstaining allies, crossed party lines and voted with all 15 minority Democrats. The senate vote followed a similar pattern. All but the Morris County senator voted to override the governor's veto on the Republican side, while the Democrats either abstained or were absent.[54]

Hudson County lost in the 1922 reapportionment plan, because there was no way that the powerful minority party delegation could prevent the outcome. There was no doubt that Hudson County would have lost the same seat in 1921

TABLE 2.9. Majority and minority party voting cohesion in 1921 and 1922 roll-call votes

	General Assembly			Senate	
	1st	2nd	3rd	2nd	3rd
Republicans					
1. Urban	5	93.3	80.6	100	100
2. Rural	60	23.1	28.6	20	77.8
	7.4	58.1	64.4	50	73.3
Democrats		100	100	100	100

52 *NJSJ,* 78th, February 28, 1922, p. 518.

53 *NJAM,* 146th, March 7, 1922, p. 713.

54 The Senate vote was 13–1 to override the veto. *NJSJ,* 78th, March 9, 1922, p. 712.

if it had been a Democratic party delegation. When the majority party controlled more than two-thirds of the legislative votes in both chambers in 1922, Hudson County was deprived of effective weapons to prevent the loss of an assembly seat.

The Hudson County position, however, does not fully explain the outcome of reapportionment in 1922. Also involved was the urban-rural split within the overwhelming majority party assembly advantage in 1921. A cohesive 31-vote majority did not form due to the strength of a blocking rural alliance which sided with Hudson County in opposing the plan. Urban county cohesion developed in 1922 as Hudson moved into minority party ranks. In 1922 the Hudson-rural alliance could not overcome strong majority party urban county voting strength.

A final consideration in the 1921–1922 case was the ability of the majority party to withstand outside pressures on legislative control over reapportionment. The governor's veto was overcome by a consistently strong majority party urban bloc. A final appeal to the courts similarly proved unsuccessful. Thus, in contrast to 1911, a cohesive majority party urban bloc paved the way for enactment of a plan.

1941: Strategic positions of urban county delegations

The strategic positions occupied by Essex and Camden counties precipitated the reapportionment conflict of 1941. Bargaining was necessary to negotiate an agreement when the assembly and senate passed conflicting plans. Essex County legislators exercised influence in a joint committee and gained support for a plan over the objections of Camden County. Essex assemblymen sought to retain all twelve of their seats, while Camden wanted a one seat gain.

The first reapportionment proposal was introduced in

the assembly by the Republican majority leader.[55] Bergen and Camden counties were to gain seats from Essex and Hudson counties. The plan reflected population and political considerations. In emerging from the economic crisis of the 1930's,[56] New Jersey had experienced the smallest population increase in forty years.[57] Most of the county population gains were in the rural areas. Salem, Somerset, Ocean, and Morris counties all ranked ahead of Bergen and Camden counties, but none of these rural counties had enough population to merit assembly seating gains. In addition, the Republican party leadership was continuing to employ the mathematical formula known as the variation of the Vinton Method.[58] Under this formula, Camden and Union counties were nearly tied in "second ratio" allotment, but Camden was designated a gain upon closer examination.[59]

Politically, the proposed plan had the unique element of exact balance between Republican and Democratic counties in 1941. Bergen Republican and Camden Democratic[60] gains would offset Essex Republican and Hudson Democratic losses. The proposal would also retain the balance of seats among the urban counties. A possible source of contention was the shift of one seat from the

---

[55] Introduced by John E. Boswell (Republican–Cape May). *NJAM,* 165th, January 27, 1941, p. 82.

[56] For a discussion of the effects of the Depression years on New Jersey, see Bebout and Grele, *op. cit.,* pp. 64–66.

[57] Statewide population increases over the first 40 years were as follows: 1900–30.4%; 1910–34.7%; 1920–24.4%; 1930–28.1%; 1940–2.9%.

[58] See *New Jersey Legislative Reapportionment, op. cit.,* pp. 28–29.

[59] See pp. 51–52 *Supra.,* for explanation of this method. The Camden allotment was 3.5096 seats, while the Union County allotment was 4.5062 seats.

[60] Camden County was in effect politically split in 1941 with three Democratic assemblymen and a Republican senator, but the Republican senator provoked the dispute by arguing for a Camden County seating gain in the assembly.

northeastern section of the state (Essex County) to the southern section (Camden County).

The initial assembly plan became controversial on closer examination. Essex and Hudson counties, the designated "losers", were the two most populous counties and had 22 assembly votes, while the "gaining" counties, Bergen and Camden, had a combined total of only eight assembly votes. If the Essex delegation crossed party lines in a 41–19 assembly lineup, the Republican majority would be reduced to 29 votes, or two under the 31-majority needed to pass the plan. Essex County had two alternatives in attempting to preserve its twelve seats: Either the Essex Republicans could join the minority Democrats and oppose the plan, or the Essex delegation could argue for an alternative within majority party ranks. Essex County representatives chose the second course of action.

The assembly judiciary committee heard the substitute plan offered by Essex County assemblyman Dominic A. Cavicchia.[61] The four-man committee then reported out the Essex alternate plan, which recommended only that Bergen and Hudson counties trade seats.[62] This plan not only preserved the 12 Essex seats, but also calculated an immediate advantage for the Republicans. Bergen County was a Republican stronghold, while Hudson County was solidly Democratic. The bill did not benefit the Camden Democrats, who were now excluded from consideration.

The substitute plan was adopted by the assembly in a nearly straight party line vote of 36–15 with nine absences.[63] Essex County provided eleven affirmative votes,

---

[61] The author wishes to thank Mr. Cavicchia for the useful information and assistance he provided in this section. Mr. Cavicchia was interviewed on May 11, 1965.

[62] The assembly committee was composed of Republicans from Cape May, Essex, Passaic, and Union counties. The bill was reported out on June 3, 1941. See *NJAM,* 165th, p. 827.

[63] *Ibid.,* June 9, 1941, p. 894.

indicating approval and bloc support for the Committee alternative. The threat of Essex resistance was the most notable element in the voting patterns. Essex County was in a strategic position to defeat a reapportionment by refusing to vote for it. Table 2.10 below, shows that if the 12 Essex votes had been added to the highly cohesive minority party opposition, a 31-vote majority would have been impossible to develop.

TABLE 2.10. First 1941 vote reflected the need for Essex County support in the assembly

	Yes	No	Not Voting	Bloc Cohesion	Intraparty Cohesion
Essex County Republicans	11	0	1	100	100
Other Republicans	25	1[a]	3		92.3
Total Republicans	36	1	4		94.6
Minority Democrats	0	14	5		100
Grand Total	36	15	9		

[a] The Burlington Republican assemblyman joined the minority Democrats in an independent vote, although he may have sympathized with Camden County interests. Also, see Footnote 11, *Supra,* p. 54.

In the senate the Camden Republican occupied a similarly placed strategic position as that of the Essex delegation in the assembly. As both senate majority leader and chairman of the judiciary committee, Camden County Senator Alfred E. Driscoll[64] objected to the Essex-prompted change in the reapportionment plan. Driscoll based his objections on two grounds. First, he argued that Camden County merited an additional seat on the basis of past

[64] Mr. Driscoll later became governor in 1947.

party affiliation. Camden County was Republican in seven of ten previous assembly sessions and ten of ten previous senates. The second objection was that the assembly substitute resulted in a break from the traditional employment of the variation of the Vinton Method in calculating assembly seating gains and losses. Camden County was excluded from a gain because Essex County was violating the "rules" of reapportioning according to a particular method.[65]

Senator Driscoll's influence was evident when the senate Republican caucus permitted a vote on an amended version of the assembly bill, which, in effect, was the original proposal for Bergen and Camden gains offset by Essex and Hudson losses. This proposal not only received the solid support of all Republicans (excluding Essex County) but all five minority Democrats as well. The 19–1[66] approval of Camden County's alternative plan presented the first time in forty years that the two chambers had passed conflicting plans.

The previously-noted Essex bloc vote was again shown when the senate alternative plan was sent to the assembly. Twenty-two urban and 13 rural county Republicans opposed the senate plan in a 16–37 rejection with seven absences.[67] The urban-rural county likeness was very high (95.4) among the assembly Republicans on this vote, while the minority Democrats voted substantially in favor (Democratic party cohesion was 75).

Negotiations were arranged between the senate and assembly to agree on a single plan when the senate president and assembly speaker, both Republicans, appointed legislators to a joint committee. The chambers agreed to

---

[65] It will be stressed in the summary of this Chapter that the mathematical formula for reapportionment was purely discretionary since it was not written into the constitution: See, also, *New Jersey Legislative Reapportionment, op. cit.*, p. 3.

[66] *NJSJ,* 97th, July 14, 1941, p. 855.

[67] *NJAM,* 165th, July 14, 1941, p. 1091.

weight the joint committee in favor of the assembly in view of the larger size of the assembly. A second decision reflected the partisan aims of reapportionment. Only Republicans were named to the committee. There were no intentions to develop a bipartisan plan. Appointed from the senate were the Bergen, Camden, and Essex senators; the assembly representatives were from Atlantic, Bergen, Cape May, Essex, and Monmouth counties.[68]

The joint committee, based on the previous roll-call vote position, had at least four and possibly five votes committed to the assembly plan. It was predictable that the four Bergen and Essex members would press for the assembly plan, while the Cape May assemblyman would also probably be a part of this group, since he had agreed to the judiciary committee substitute plan. The two neutral members from Atlantic and Monmouth counties had also followed the majority in the assembly. These two members would be affected only if the assembly majority leader (the Cape May representative) was sufficiently influenced by the Camden Senator to change his mind. The best that Senator Driscoll could hope for was a 4–4 tie vote, in which case a new alternative would have to be found. Driscoll's only hope was to change Boswell's (Cape May) vote and thereby establish a southern-seashore alliance against the urban northeastern bloc of Bergen and Essex counties.

When the joint committee reported out its recommendations in the form of a bill sponsored by Assembly Majority Leader Boswell of Cape May, it was evident that Essex County had gained support of at least three and possibly

[68] *NJSJ,* 97th, July 21, 1941, p. 884 and *NJAM,* 165th, July 14, 1941, p. 1091. Named by Senate President I. Grant Scott were Senators Lloyd L. Schroeder (Bergen), Alfred E. Driscoll (Camden), and Homer C. Zink (Essex). Speaker Roscoe P. McClave appointed John E. Boswell (Cape May), Herbert F. Myers (Bergen), Vincent S. Haneman (Atlantic), J. Stanley Herbert (Monmouth), and Dominic A. Cavicchia (Essex).

five other committee members. The agreement was to return to the bill originally passed by the assembly, that is, the Bergen-Hudson trade and to exclude the Camden-Essex shift. The Camden senator apparently lacked a convincing argument to sway the two neutral members and the assembly majority leader. In fact, the dispute really focused on only one question: Why should assembly and senate Republicans adopt a plan that was immediately beneficial to a Democratic county? Partisanship prevailed over retention of past reapportionment formulas and the committee agreed to employ a new formula to justify the Bergen-Hudson shift.[69]

Acting immediately on the committee's recommendation, the assembly initially rejected by voice vote a last-ditch effort by Camden Democrats to amend the bill with the addition of a Camden seat.[70] The assembly Republicans then united solidly behind the Bergen-Hudson plan and adopted it with a straight party line vote of 36–19 with five absences.[71] This vote was quite similar to the first assembly roll-call as 100 percent of the Republicans opposed 100 percent of the Democrats and no assemblyman crossed party lines. The senate agreed to the assembly plan in an 11–4 vote with the Camden senator getting token support only from three rural Republicans, who abstained, and the minority Democrats who added three negative votes.[72]

The 1941 reapportionment fight can be summarized in the success of Essex County legislators who remained consistent on a fixed theme—no county wants to lose seats in

---

[69] Assemblyman Cavicchia of Essex County takes credit for the use of the Vinton Method rather than the "traditional" variation of the Vinton Method to justify the Bergen-Hudson shift rather than the Bergen-Camden v. Essex-Hudson shift.

[70] Proposed by Assembly Democrat Joseph W. Cowgill, on July 21, 1941. *NJAM,* 165th, p. 1114.

[71] *Ibid.,* p. 1135.

[72] *NJSJ,* 97th, July 21, 1941, p. 906.

a reapportionment. Retention of existing seats is an expression of power in the New Jersey Legislature. Essex county assemblymen achieved their objectives by winning at all stages of the conflict. First, the originally proposed plan was amended at the insistence of Essex County; secondly, the joint committee agreed to the Essex viewpoint; and thirdly, both the assembly and senate adopted the Essex plan over the Camden County plan. The strategic position of Essex County in the assembly was evident in a powerful 12-vote resource, which could be employed to prevent the rest of the majority party from acting. In contrast, the one-vote resource of the Camden senator was insufficient to prevent a defeat, even though Senator Driscoll was the Republican party leader in the upper house. Essex County's legislators were so influential that even Democratic Governor Charles Edison did not veto the plan. Edison could have taken such action as expression of support for the Camden assembly Democrats. The governor did refuse to sign the bill, but he filed it with the secretary of state so that it became effective as a law.[73] As it will be shown in Chapter III, Governor Edison undoubtedly required the support of the 12-member Essex delegation in pursuing his objective of a revised state constitution. By not alienating Essex County on the reapportionment issue, Edison was able to attract important Essex votes for revision proposals in 1941.

Both strategic and tactical considerations were evident in the 1941 reapportionment dispute. The Essex strategy was to retain all seats in order to exercise the dominant influence within majority party ranks. There were advantages to the rest of the Republicans in accepting the Essex plan. No Democratic county would gain seats and the future prospect definitely favored the Republicans (in Bergen County) over the traditional opposition (centered in Hudson County). Tactically, Essex County was suc-

[73] See *New York Times*, July 29, 1941.

cessful by exhibiting a bloc vote in remaining consistent on one particular plan. When Essex County displayed its voting power as a lever for obtaining assembly approval, the weaker voting resource of Camden County in the senate became evident. The only alternative to the Essex position was stalemate. The reapportionment stakes of 1941 were not high enough to prolong a dispute beyond the point where Essex County would have certainly crossed party lines and caused an indeterminate deadlock.

Conclusions: foundations of conflict for the future

Examination of the first forty years of New Jersey reapportionment reveals that controversy was more prevalent than preliminary accommodation. The preconditions for non-controversial reapportionments, that is, prior trends of one-party dominance and majority party consensus before roll-call votes, were evident only in the legislative sessions of 1901 and 1931. In the sessions of 1911, 1921–1922, and 1941, several votes were required before adopting a plan.

Controversial reapportionments in all but one year (1911) were bounded by Republican party control of the legislature and Democratic party control of the governorship. New Jersey voters, as shown in Figure 2.3, were prone to elect Republican assemblymen and senators, while voting for Democratic party governors. This trend continued in the post-1941 period, and appears to change only in 1961. By 1961 the Democrats were getting a Statewide majority of the two-party vote in both the legislature and the governorship. Election returns are related to party control of the legislature. Here the trend is indisputable. Republican party control was continuous in the reapportionment years, with the lone exception of 1911 and the Democratic party upswing beginning in 1961 (See Figure 2.4).

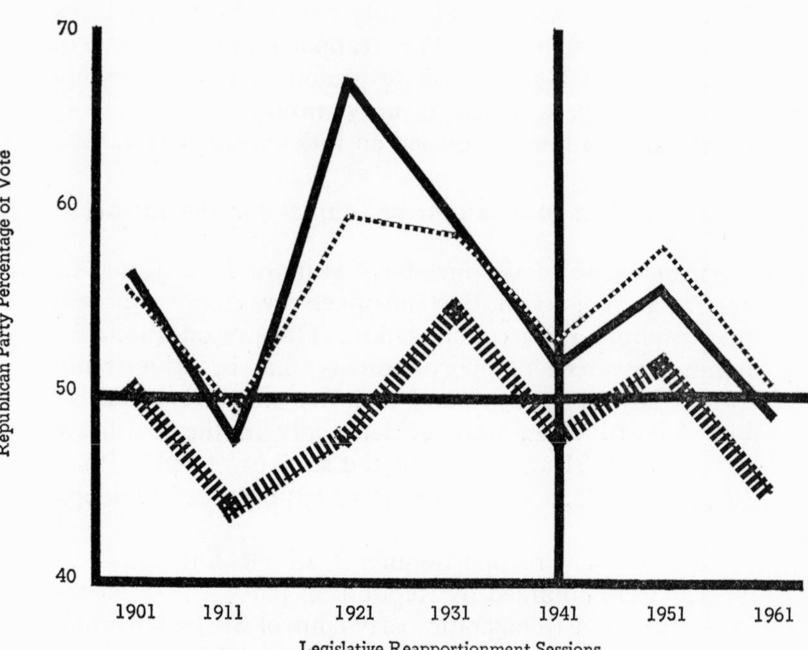

2.3 Republican Party Percentage of Popular Vote for New Jersey Governor, General Assembly, and Senate Preceding Reapportionment Years, 1901–1961.

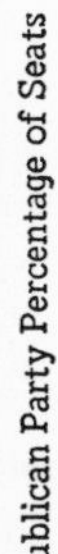

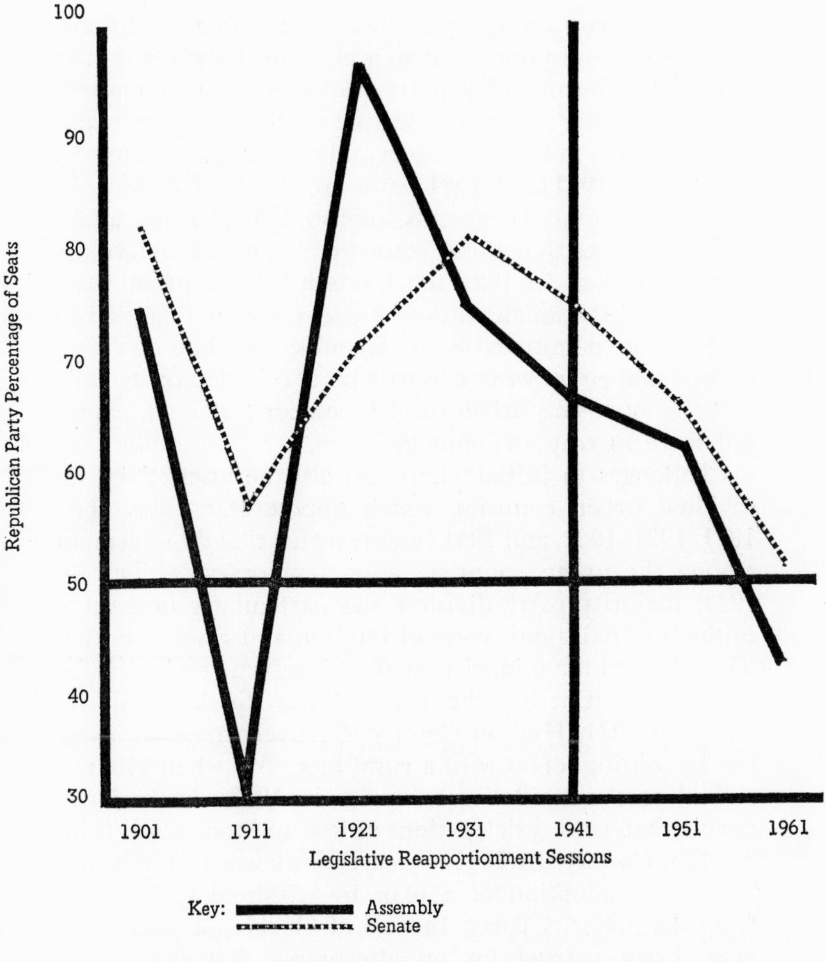

2.4 Republican Party Percentage of Seats in New Jersey Legislature in Reapportionment Years, 1901–1961.

Even with the established dominance of the Republicans as the legislative majority, reapportionment conflict took place. Problems arose when the various wings of the majority party could not agree on a plan. Initially, plans were offered by the majority party leadership. Upon reassessment, particular groups of counties challenged these plans, despite efforts to balance urban and rural county gains and losses. The 1911 and 1921 cases are illustrative here. In 1911 the assembly Democrats were so divided along urban and rural lines that three votes were required before approving a plan. In 1921 the Hudson-Morris, urban-rural bloc attracted enough votes to prevent passage of a plan in an assembly dominated by 59 Republicans. The two cases suggest that either weak majority party cohesion or strongly cohesive opposing urban-rural blocs can foster temporary stalemate in reapportionment issues.

Challenges to initial plans can also be asserted by individual urban counties, which oppose seat losses. The 1911, 1921–1922, and 1941 cases revealed that disagreement among the urban counties causes temporary conflict. In 1911, majority party division was particularly noticeable in the internally split votes of Hudson and Essex counties. This allowed the minority party to intervene and press for a plan by attracting the votes of the divided majority party. In 1921, Hudson County effectively opposed a seat loss by joining forces with a rural bloc. But when Hudson shifted to the legislative minority in 1922, the majority party urban county delegations united and took a seat from Hudson County. In 1941, Essex County was in a position to prevent adoption of a plan by withholding its votes from the majority party. Instead of blocking a plan, however, Essex pressed for an alternative that was finally adopted. The three cases all showed the importance of Essex and Hudson counties as keys to resolving reapportionment conflicts. Furthermore, the cases suggest that the legislative minority party is successful in promoting its interests when the majority is hopelessly divided. Conversely, strong urban county voting cohesion in majority party ranks is essential for developing effective assembly voting majorities.

A third observation relates to the lack of a specified reapportionment formula in redistributing assembly seats. While the legislature appeared committed to the variation of the Vinton Method, there were neither legal nor constitutional mandates requiring compliance to a particular formula. Neither the legislature nor the state courts defined the section of the constitution relating to apportionment "among the several counties *as nearly as may be* according to the number of their inhabitants."[74] (Emphasis added) In effect, the mathematical formula could be altered, as it was in 1941, to satisfy competing claims of particular urban county delegations. This suggests that future conflicts might focus on selecting among contrasting formulas, any one of which might satisfy one legislative group and antagonize another.

Finally, the early controversies illustrated the participation of both the senate and the governor in the reapportionment process. First, it appeared that the assembly, the chamber directly involved in seating changes, retained control as long as the majority party leadership agreed on a plan early in the legislative session. The 1911 case was exceptional. In that year divided party control of the legislature resulted in the senate seizing the initiative over a disjointed assembly majority. Assembly opposition to the senate proposal could not be translated into an effective alternative plan. But in 1941 the assembly did retain control even with a contrasting senate plan. In that case, a joint legislative committee was formed to resolve the two-house dispute. Both the 1911 and 1941 cases suggest that the legislative chamber most directly affected by reapportionment will try to prevent the other house from

[74] *Constitution of 1844,* Article IV, Section 3.

intervening. The affected chamber will lose control when the majority party is badly split.

Secondly, both chambers will resist outside interference from the governor, especially when the governor is a Democrat. In 1922 the governor's veto was overruled by the same urban county bloc that passed the reapportionment plan. The governor refused to intervene in 1941 even though the plan benefited the Republicans. The governor needs support for other legislative proposals and reforms and this suggests that a governor will be hesitant to alienate the legislature in reapportionment disputes. Direct executive leadership appears to be a last resort in reapportionment unless pressures are so great that a solution requires the governor's participation.

3

Constitutional Reform and the Senate Representation Issue, 1941–1947

CONSTITUTIONAL REFORM AND LEGISLATIVE APPORTIONMENT are closely related issues in state government.[1] The seven-year struggle to revise New Jersey's century-old constitution was directly related to the senate's insistence that no changes take place in the existing apportionment. The conflict between constitutional reformers and rural county senators was resolved after internal legislative agreement and accommodation between the legislature and the governor.

---

[1] See, for example, Gordon E. Baker, *Rural versus Urban Political Power* (New York: Random House, 1955), pp. 11–26; Malcolm E. Jewell, *The State Legislature* (New York: Random House, 1962), pp. 18–24; Malcolm E. Jewell and Samuel C. Patterson, *The Legislative Process in the United States* (New York: Random House, 1966), pp. 47–74; and William J. Keefe and Morris S. Ogul, *The American Legislative Process* (Englewood Cliffs, New Jersey: Prentice-Hall, Inc., 1964), pp. 32–38.

Several conditions affected the political environment of constitutional reform. These included the sources of voting strength in the legislature for each party; the extent of party competition for the governor; and the dominance of the Hague machine in the Democratic party.

By 1941 the Republican party controlled both houses of the legislature, but the pattern of control was sharply divergent. The rural counties were dominant in the senate, while the urban counties held a majority of the assembly seats. Over the first forty years of the twentieth century, statewide population gains occurred primarily in the urban counties, which subsequently gained increased representation in the assembly.[2] The senate did not reflect population changes because of the one-senator-per-county representation system.[3] Thus, the eight urban counties of the state held nearly 73 percent of the assembly seats over the decades following the reapportionments of 1901, 1911,

TABLE 3.1. Urban counties controlled assembly and rural counties controlled senate, 1902–1941

	General Assembly		Senate	
Decades	Total Urban Seats	% of Total	Total Rural Seats	% of Total
1902–1911	419	69.9%	130	61.9%
1912–1922	484	73.4%	141	61.6%
1923–1931	404	75.0%	107	60.5%
1932–1941	440	73.3%	127	61.7%
Totals	1747	72.9%	505	61.4%

---

[2] See John E. Bebout and Ronald J. Grele, *Where Cities Meet: The Urbanization of New Jersey* (Princeton, New Jersey: D. Van Nostrand Co., 1964), pp. 52–77.

[3] Ernest C. Reock, Jr., *Population Inequality Among Counties in the New Jersey Legislature,* 1791–1962 (New Brunswick, New Jersey: Bureau of Government Research, Rutgers—The State University, 1961), p. 21.

1922, and 1931, while 13 rural counties controlled 61.4 percent of the senate seats.[4]

Party control of the legislature from 1941 to 1947 can be shown by the sources of voting strength of the urban and rural counties. In the senate, the Republican party advantage was found in consistent representation in 10 rural and 4 urban counties.[5] The rural Republicans alone had an outright majority in six of the seven years. This meant that the rural Republican counties exercised effective control over constitutional revision bills within the majority party caucus. The assembly was controlled by the Republicans throughout the seven years, but the urban majority party counties had clear-cut voting majorities only in 1943 and 1947. The major findings of party control from 1941 to 1947 are summarized below in Table 3.2. The conclusion is that the urban-rural divergence established a pre-condition of possible conflict within majority party ranks.

TABLE 3.2. Summary of Republican party control of the legislature, 1941–1947

County and Party	General Assembly		Senate	
	Total No. of Seats	% of Total	Total No. of Seats	% of Total
Urban Republicans	202	48.1%	37	25.2%
Rural Republicans	104	24.8%	82	55.8%
Minority Democrats	114	27.1%	28	19.0%
Totals	420	100 %	147	100 %

Party control of the governor differed somewhat from the legislature. Prior to 1941 the Democrats were substantially more successful in competing for governors than

[4] Source: *N.J. Legislative Manuals.*

[5] The ten rural Republican counties were: Atlantic, Burlington, Cape May, Gloucester, Hunterdon, Monmouth, Morris, Ocean, Salem, and Sussex counties. The four urban Republican counties were: Bergen, Essex, Passaic, and Union.

in gaining control of the legislature. Over the first forty years of the twentieth century, the Democrats had two-house legislative control only in two years, while eight of fourteen governors were Democrats.[6]

Three governors, a Democrat and two Republicans, were elected to office during the seven-year period under consideration. Charles Edison, the Democrat, was elected by heavy pluralities provided by the urban counties in 1940. Edison tried to break away from the influence of Hudson County's Democratic party machine, dominated by Mayor Frank Hague, even though the Hudson County voting plurality for Edison nearly matched the rural county plurality for the Republican candidate. In fact, Edison carried only seven of 21 counties in 1940.

In contrast to Governor Edison's electoral strength, Republican party Governors Walter E. Edge and Alfred E. Driscoll won with overwhelming rural county support in 1943 and 1946. Not one rural county voted for the Democratic candidate in these two elections (two rural counties had voted for Edison in 1940). Both Edge and Driscoll got approximately the same high percentage of the vote from the rural counties, while Driscoll ran slightly ahead of Edge in splitting the urban counties. Even more important for the revision issue was the fact that both Edge and Driscoll were complemented by huge Republican legislative majorities in contrast to the split in party control while Democrat Edison was in office. Table 3.3 shows the sources of voting strength for the three governors according to the urban and rural county voting distribution.

A final boundary condition for the 1941–1947 period was the considerable legislative dominance of Hudson County within the minority Democratic party ranks. From 1900 to 1940, the Hudson County delegation was solidly Democratic in 37 of 40 legislative sessions. Hudson County's assembly delegations had been consistently reduced in

---

[6] Source: *N.J. Legislative Manual* (1966), pp. 712–714.

TABLE 3.3. Urban and rural county voting support in the gubernatorial elections of 1940, 1943, and 1946

	Urban Counties		Rural Counties	
Elections	Rep. Party % of Vote	Dem. Party % of Vote	Rep. Party % of Vote	Dem. Party % of Vote
1940	46.1%	53.9%	55.3%	44.7%
1943	51.7%	48.3%	67.2%	32.8%
1946	55.1%	44.9%	67.0%	33.0%

prior reapportionments,[7] but Hudson County still represented better than 50 percent of the Democratic party seats in the assembly. If Hudson County maintained solid voting cohesion in opposition to an urban-rural county Republican party conflict, the minority Democrats could wield important influence in the assembly.

Pressures for a new state constitution

Prior to 1941 all attempts to revise the state constitution had failed. The most concerted efforts at revision had taken place during the term of Governor Woodrow Wilson. In 1912 both Wilson and the proponents of constitutional reform in the assembly succeeded in passing a constitutional convention bill. The convention consisted of 60 delegates, apportioned among the counties in the same manner as the general assembly. The bill was supported by an outside reform group, the State Civic Federation. But the senate defeated the bill on the grounds that the rural counties feared "they would be deprived of their hold on the senate and be reduced to a shadowy minority of representation in both houses."[8] Wilson and the assembly

[7] Hudson had lost seats in the 1922, 1931, and 1941 reapportionments.

[8] John E. Bebout and Julius Kass, "How Can New Jersey Get a New Constitution?" *University of Newark Law Review,* Vol. 6 (March, 1941), p. 19.

Democrats then worked out a compromise whereby the proposed convention would consist of two delegates per county. Again the senate refused to pass the bill. In his last annual message, Wilson attacked senate recalcitrance and castigated the one-senator-per-county representation system on the grounds that the "powers of corrupt control have an enormous and abiding advantage under our constitutional arrangements as they stand."[9] The assembly thereupon passed another constitutional convention bill only to see the senate vote it down over the issue of preserving the existing senate representation system.[10]

The problems encountered by the governor, the assembly, and outside reformers in 1912–1913 were not unique in the efforts to achieve constitutional revision. Equal county representation for the senate had been endorsed in the 1844 constitutional convention over the objections of urban county delegates.[11] Four constitutional convention bills were passed by the assembly between 1881 and 1885, but each time the senate resisted change on the grounds of keeping intact the one-senator-per-county-system.[12]

When Charles Edison revived constitutional reform in his campaign for governor in 1940, the senate representation issue was still an outstanding problem. Using the 1940 United States census figures as a guide, the minimum population required to elect a majority in the senate was only 16 percent.[13] In contrast, 46.1 percent of the population was necessary to elect a majority in the assembly.[14] The 13 rural counties were 63.7 percent overrepresented in the senate, while the eight urban counties were 101 percent underrepresented.[15] In the assembly, by comparison, the

---

[9] Bebout and Kass, *op. cit.,* p. 19.
[10] *Ibid.,* p. 24.
[11] *Ibid.,* p. 13.
[12] *Ibid.,* pp. 16–18.
[13] Reock, *op. cit.,* p. 22.
[14] *Ibid.,* p. 15.
[15] *Ibid.,* pp. 28–29.

same 13 rural counties were 17 percent overrepresented and the eight urban counties 7 percent underrepresented.[16] Thus, any efforts to change the senate basis of representation would certainly result in diminishing the distorted influence of rural county power, because of the enormous statewide shifts in population that had taken place since establishment of the one-senator-per-county system in 1776.

The battle for constitutional revision begins

Charles Edison, the Democratic party nominee for governor in 1940, campaigned on two major themes. First, he asserted his independence from Mayor Frank Hague of Hudson County, even though Hague had previously interested Edison in running for United States Senator.[17] Edison, the son of the famous inventor Thomas A. Edison, had switched from Republican to Democratic party affiliation in the 1930's. President Roosevelt appointed him to serve on several New Deal agencies and, in 1937, he became Assistant Secretary of the Navy. By 1939, Edison was promoted to Secretary of the Navy. His national prominence resulted in a combination of labor leaders, liberal Democrats, and New Dealers attempting to convince Boss Hague that Edison should be drafted for governor in 1940.[18]

Edison's candidacy threatened Hudson County control in state politics. The formula for Hague's enormous power and influence consisted of hand-picked gubernatorial candidates, who won elections by huge Hudson County pluralities.[19] In return, the governor's patronage was at

---

16 *Ibid.*

17 Jack Alexander, "Ungovernable Governor," *Saturday Evening Post,* Vol. 215, No. 30 (January 23, 1943), p. 53.

18 Will Chasan, "The Decline of Boss Hague," *Nation,* Vol. 151, No. 24 (December 14, 1940), p. 606.

19 *Ibid.*

ments. The Republicans did not challenge Hague's control of the courts as long as they controlled appointments to the 80 administrative boards and commissions not directly under the governor's control.[20]

Edison demonstrated that he would not respond to Hague's control in a key campaign speech delivered before a huge rally at Sea Girt in August of 1940. Before an assemblage of 150,000 people, called by Hague, Edison declared, "If you elect me, you will have elected a governor who has made no promises of preferment to any man or group . . . I'll never be a 'yes man' except to my conscience."[21]

Edison's second campaign theme was to revive the issue of constitutional revision. He said that a constitutional convention would be proposed in his inaugural address. He conceded that the rural counties in the senate would be the major opponents of change and that the issue would generate statewide controversy. But he emphasized that "a democracy cannot permit itself to be frozen; it must change as times and conditions change. The Constitution must be made adaptable, more easily amended."[22]

The twin themes of independence from Hudson County control and support for constitutional change were to have a continuing impact on Governor Edison's relations with the legislature. As noted previously, the Hudson County vote was most important to Edison's electoral victory. But if Edison were going to challenge both the Hague machine and the rural county Republican senators, he would require support from other legislative groups in order to achieve constitutional revision.

Support for constitutional revision was also evident in Republican party ranks as Edison's gubernatorial op-
Hague's disposal, especially with regard to court appoint-

---

[20] Alexander, *op. cit.*, p. 53.

[21] Jack Alexander, "King Hanky-Panky of Jersey," *Saturday Evening Post*, Vol. 213, No. 17 (October 26, 1940), p. 11.

[22] *The New York Times*, December 28, 1940.

ponent, Robert C. Hendrickson of Gloucester County, promised to introduce a constitutional convention bill. Hendrickson, an incumbent senator from a southern rural county, sought reform that would be acceptable to the Republican-controlled legislature.

The 1940 elections resulted in a victory for Edison, who received 51.7 percent of the popular vote. Hedrickson was supported by 14 of 21 counties, including the southern-seashore and northwestern rural county blocs along with the urban northeastern counties of Bergen, Essex, and Union. The Republicans lost four assembly seats in Camden and Mercer counties, but still retained two-house legislative control with margins of 41–19 in the assembly and 16–5 in the senate. Hendrickson himself returned to the Gloucester County senate seat.

Before the inauguration of Governor Edison, Senator Hendrickson introduced a constitutional convention bill. Eighty-one delegates, apportioned among the counties the same as senators and assemblymen, would be elected by the voters.[23] The delegates would frame a new constitution and submit it for approval in a statewide referendum. Hendrickson's proposal represented an attempt to seize the initiative from Governor Edison. Presumably, other Republican legislative leaders would follow Hendrickson's leadership. Especially noteworthy was the 81-member plan, which would allow the rural counties to exercise a strong influence in the convention.

Governor Edison offered an alternative plan in his inaugural address. He called for a 100-member convention, which would consist of 81 delegates apportioned to the counties as senators and assemblymen, plus 19 members elected at-large.[24] Edison wanted to have the convention

---

[23] Source: *Journal of the Ninety-Seventh Senate of the State of New Jersey being the One Hundred and Sixty-Fifth Session of the Legislature,* January 27, 1941, p. 65. Hereinafter cited as *NJSJ.*

[24] *N.J. Legislative Manual* (1941), p. 664.

reflect urban interests, and he was assuming that the at-large delegates would be elected by the more populous counties. Furthermore, Edison supported the need for constitutional reform in terms of placing administrative agencies under the governor's control, reforming the court system, increasing the governor's term to four years, and eradicating "the existing representation inequality that permits a majority of the senate to be formed from the representatives of 15 percent of the people."[25]

Edison was particularly critical of Hendrickson's plan, and the governor launched an assault on overweighted rural county influence in a constitutional convention:

> Then there is the question about the wisdom of choosing delegates selected on the same basis as present legislative apportionment. A criticism that may be made about the upper house of our Legislature is that it constitutes a lawmaking body in which acres are represented rather than people. It might be that at the convention the acres would outvote the people. That has happened at times, I am told, in the Senate.[26]

Edison's "acres versus people" charge represented a direct challenge to the power and influence of rural county senators, who would have to agree to a convention bill before the constitution could be revised. The governor would have to seek support elsewhere or modify his criticism of rural county power in order to achieve his objectives. This was essential because the 1941 senate consisted of 11 rural and five urban county Republican senators. The rural Republicans formed an anti-revisionist voting bloc not only on roll-call votes, but also in the caucus. As long as the Republican caucus rule required a majority to approve bills before they were released for votes, the rural senators

---

[25] *Ibid.,* p. 665.

[26] Quoted from Newark *Evening News,* January 21, 1941.

could exercise a veto power and prevent roll-call votes from being taken.[27]

The governor's major support for a population-based convention was in the assembly, and especially in the Essex County delegation. Even though Essex County had elected 12 Republican assemblymen and provided a small plurality for Hendrickson in the 1940 elections, the party leader in Essex, Arthur T. Vanderbilt, was a devoted advocate of constitutional reform.[28] Vanderbilt agreed with Edison that the senate representation system must be changed. The Essex County leader argued that a bipartisan approach was necessary for a new constitution.[29]

In 1941, the urban counties represented 44 of the 60 assembly seats. If the urban counties, led by the 12 Essex County votes, formed a strong pro-revisionist bloc, they could withstand the opposition of anti-revisionist forces in Hudson County[30] and the rural counties. Twelve Essex votes added to 14 other urban Republicans and eight urban Democrats provided a possible 34–26 bipartisan alliance sought by Governor Edison. This alliance could allow for the defection of three votes and still retain the necessary 31-vote majority to pass a constitutional convention plan.

The first bill acted on by the legislature in 1941 dealt neither with the Hendrickson nor the Edison convention proposals. Assemblyman Wesley L. Lance, a Republican from Hunterdon County, offered a constitutional amend-

---

27 Until 1952 no bill or nomination could be reported to the senate floor unless released by a majority of 11 Republican senators in the caucus. See: Belle Zeller, Ed., *American State Legislatures* (New York: Thomas Y. Crowell Co., 1954), p. 207.

28 Duane Lockard, *The New Jersey Governor* (Princeton, New Jersey: D. Van Nostrand Co., 1964), p. 114.

29 Newark *Evening News,* September 18, 1941.

30 Hudson opposition was based primarily on Boss Hague's control over court appointments, which Edison proposed to reform in a new constitution.

ment under which future referenda on the constitution would be held at general rather than special elections.[31] On the surface, this proposal appeared to be a minor technicality and was supported by Lance in terms of reducing the cost of special elections.

Complex procedures governed the existing amending process.[32] A majority of both houses was required in two successive sessions to approve amendments. If approved, amendments were submitted for voter approval at special elections. Rejected amendments could not be considered again for five years.

Since any amendments would require at least three years before adoption, the rural counties endorsed this procedure as an alternative to constitutional convention bills. By supporting amendments, the rural counties would retain control over revision in opposition to the governor, and also exhibit "good faith" for revision while actually delaying comprehensive constitutional change. Opponents of the amending procedure concluded that the rural counties were engaging in diversionary tactics by preventing thorough reform at the earliest possible time.

The assembly voting pattern on the Lance amendment showed high voting cohesion among the rural Republicans and the minority Democrats, led by Hudson County. The Essex Republicans were badly split, while the other urban Republicans were cohesive. Two votes were taken. The first resulted in a 26–18 division with two abstentions and 14 absences.[33] The second vote saw a 43–4 majority, which was formed primarily by a switch in the Hudson County delegation from a negative to an affirmative vote.[34] The

[31] Source: *Minutes and Proceedings of the One Hundred and Sixty-Fifth General Assembly of the State of New Jersey,* March 10, 1941, p. 226. Hereinafter cited as *NJAM.*

[32] *Constitution of 1844,* Article IX.

[33] *NJAM,* 165th, April 29, 1941, pp. 642–643.

[34] *Ibid.,* April 30, 1941, p. 696. The Hudson County switch may be attributed to a dual blocking position by Hudson County. Hud-

vote illustrated two important requirements for further assembly action on revision proposals. First, a rural county-Hudson Democratic alliance could block efforts by the urban county proponents of full-scale constitutional change. Secondly, a divided Essex County vote weakened the position of the urban counties in promoting change. Table 3.4 summarizes the voting cohesion on the two-roll-calls.

TABLE 3.4. High voting cohesion by rural Republicans and minority Democrats exhibited in Lance constitutional amendment: two roll-calls

County Groups and Party	Party Cohesion	Inter-Group Likeness
Rural Republicans	85.6	96.6
Minority Democrats	92.6	
Urban Republicans (Minus Essex County)	90.0	33.9
Essex Republicans	22.0	

While the assembly shifted attention to constitutional amendments, the senate Republicans adopted stalling tactics by refusing to release Hendrickson's constitutional convention bill from the judiciary committee. This committee was composed of three rural Republicans from Monmouth, Hunterdon, and Gloucester counties; a rural Democrat from Somerset County; and an urban Republican from Camden County. Hendrickson could not get the support of either his Republican counterparts, or the rural Democrat. The other Republicans supported constitutional amendments for revision, while the rural Democrat favored Governor Edison's convention plan.[35] With

son could block any revision by opposing the Lance amendment; and could block revision under Governor Edison by supporting the amending procedure.

[35] Newark *Evening News,* February 19, 1941.

Governor Edison and Senator Hendrickson split over the method of apportioning delegates to a convention, the rural Republicans adopted a policy of inaction while the reformers disputed among themselves.

The Democratic party floor leaders, Senator James I. Bowers (Somerset) and Assemblyman Fred W. DeVoe (Middlesex), introduced Governor Edison's 100-delegate convention plan on May 26.[36] But neither the assembly judiciary committee nor the senate miscellaneous business committee would take action on the bill.[37]

With the 1941 legislative session nearing adjournment, Governor Edison sent a special message in June urging action on the 100-delegate proposal. Edison retreated somewhat from his "acres versus people" attack and stated that a new constitution would not threaten incumbent senators. He now emphasized the necessity for gaining control over administrative appointments in a new constitution:

> If the Legislature were confining itself to the lawmaking function, and administrative appointments were to be made by the Governor, I consider that the system of county representation might wisely be continued . . . Let us put across in bipartisan unity a revision of the Constitution to produce a simpler, more responsible, more efficient state Government.[38]

However, the governor's pleas fell on deaf ears. Each chamber blamed the other for refusing to vote on Edison's bill.[39] Finally, the governor called a special midnight session in July.[40] Both chambers still refused to act.[41]

---

36 *Ibid.*, May 27, 1941.
37 *Ibid.*
38 *NJAM,* 165th, July 28, 1941, pp. 1197–1198.
39 *The New York Times,* June 28, 1941.
40 *NJAM, Loc. Cit.*
41 Newark *Evening News,* July 29, 1941.

Governor Edison faced an obvious problem with the 1941 legislature. He lacked the necessary votes for a bipartisan alliance to pass a convention bill. By alienating the senate rural county Republicans, the governor had run into a roadblock, which could not be resolved without mutual compromise. The senate alternative of constitutional amendments blocked comprehensive revision. Edison thus faced a defeat unless the rural Republicans were convinced that revision would not threaten their existing power position.[42]

The 1941 deadlock was partially resolved when the senate Republicans agreed to a compromise plan in November.[43] The revision issue was delegated to a seven-member jointly appointed governor-legislative study commission.[44] The commission was charged with examining constitutional amendments and making recommendations to the 1942 legislature.

The study commission proposal represented a definite victory for the rural counties. Governor Edison had been prevented from getting approval for a convention. The legislature also retained the prerogative of rejecting the commission's recommendations. At the same time, Governor Edison had at least two spokesmen for full-scale reform on the commission. The governor could then use the group to dramatize the need for change, while retaining a maneuverable position to criticize rural county legislators if they refused to take action.

The senate approved the study commission by an 11–3 roll-call vote, with near Republican party unanimity and solid opposition by the minority Democrats.[45] Similarly,

---

[42] Rural counties want to retain control over constitutional revision which preserves rural conrol of at least one legislative chamber. See Jewell, *op. cit.*, p. 18.

[43] *The New York Times,* November 14, 1941.

[44] Introduced as Senate Joint Resolution 6 on November 13, 1941, by Senator George H. Stanger (Republican-Cumberland). Source: *NJSJ,* 97th, pp. 998–999.

the assembly endorsed the proposal by a non-unanimous vote of 49–0.[46] Four counties, Essex, Monmouth, Hudson, and Mercer, registered eight abstentions, but these votes did not represent any indication of bloc opposition. Rather, these votes appeared to represent cases of internal division within each of the four county delegations. Table 3.5 compares and contrasts the voting cohesion and likeness of the various groups in both chambers.

TABLE 3.5. Voting cohesion on study commission showed agreement among urban and rural Republicans and opposition by the minority Democrats

County Groups and Party	General Assembly		Senate	
	Party Cohesion	Inter-Group Likeness	Party Cohesion	Inter-Party Likeness
Rural Republicans	86.6		80	
		89.3		90
Urban Republicans	65.2		100	
Minority Democrats	68.4+		100—	

Anti-revisionists continue delaying tactics in 1942

The joint study commission departed from revision by separate amendments and offered instead a series of recommendations which threatened the blocking strategy of anti-revisionists. Led by its chairman, Senator Hendrickson, the commission proposed that a draft constitution be submitted for adoption in a statewide referendum.[47] This

[45] *NJSJ,* 97th, November 13, 1941, pp. 998–999.

[46] *NJAM,* 165th, November 13, 1941, pp. 1278–1279.

[47] The study commission consisted of Dr. John F. Sly, Director of the Princeton Survey; Arthur T. Vanderbilt, Republican leader of Essex County; Senator Crawford Jamieson (Democrat–Mercer); Common Pleas Judge Walter Van Riper; Freeholder-elect and for-

precluded both the need for a convention and limited legislative review of revision procedures. The "acres versus people" dispute was resolved by recommending continuation of the existing apportionment system.[48] The commission had apparently found a middle course to solve the governor-senate deadlock. First, no convention was required. Second, the one-senator-per-county representation system stayed intact. And third, neither the governor nor the legislature would clash, since the draft constitution was to be submitted directly to the voters for approval.

These recommendations were politically unacceptable to the legislative power structure. The Republican leadership did not want a Democratic party governor to receive credit for a new constitution during his tenure.[49] If Edison were successful, he would be in a position to assist Democrats in winning additional legislative seats, even though Edison himself was ineligible for a second term. Furthermore, if the new Constitution was quickly adopted, Edison might run for a new term with the demise of a non-succession restriction.

The anti-revisionists also had to avoid an indictment of obstructionism, which Edison could use as a political lever to focus criticism on the legislature. The new anti-revisionist strategy had three components. First, it was asserted that more time was needed to study the commission's proposals. Second, opponents argued that no action should be taken until after World War II so that all qualified New Jersey voters could endorse a new constitution. Third, the anti-revisionists hoped to continue their stalling tactics long enough to prevent action in time for the November,

---

mer Bergen County Assemblyman Walter J. Freund; James Kerney, Jr., Editor of the Trenton *Times* newspaper; and Senator Hendrickson. Source: *Report of the Commission on Revision of the New Jersey Constitution*. Submitted to the governor, the legislature and the people of New Jersey, May, 1942, p. 3.

48 *Ibid.*, p. 13.

49 Newark *Evening News,* May 19, 1942.

1942 elections. All three objectives were encompassed in a senate proposal establishing a new legislative commission "to determine the sentiment of the state" regarding proposed constitutional changes.[50] The eight-member commission was to conduct public hearings in the summer months of 1942 and present recommendations to both chambers.[51]

The senate quickly passed the anti-revisionist proposal by a non-unanimous vote of 16–0.[52] Essex County endorsed the plan as did three other urban Republican senators. Essex was guaranted representation on the commission. The rural Republicans voted with high cohesion, since the plan was designed within their ranks.[53] The Mercer and Middlesex urban senators broke with Hudson and Warren counties and opposed the new commission. The assembly followed suit by approving the commission in a voice vote.[54] Apparently, the reform forces decided to act within the framework of the rural county strategy. By doing this, the legislative commission might be prodded to recommend affirmative action in time for the 1942 elections. However, the commission made no recommendations. Despite Governor Edison's challenge to permit the voters to decide if they wanted a new constitution, the *status quo* remained intact throughout 1942.[55]

---

[50] Introduced as Senate Concurrent Resolution 19 on June 15, 1942. Source: *NJSJ,* 98th, p. 756.

[51] Subsequently appointed to he commission by Senate President I. Grant Scott (Rep.–Cape May) and Assembly Speaker John E. Boswell (Rep.–Cape May) were senators Schroeder (Rep.–Bergen), Summerill (Rep.–Salem), Pyne (Rep.–Somerset), and O'Mara (Dem.–Hudson); and assemblymen Amlicke (Rep.–Passaic), Cavicchia (Rep.–Essex), Haneman (Rep.–Atlantic), and Preen (Dem.—Hunterdon). Sources: *NJSJ,* 98th, June 15, 1942, p. 756; and *NJAM,* 166th, June 15, 1942, p. 829.

[52] *NJSJ,* 98th, June 15, 1942, p. 756.

[53] By Senator George H. Stanger, Republican–Cumberland.

[54] *NJAM,* 166th, June 15, 1942, p. 829.

[55] *New York Times,* September 18, 1942.

1943 compromise plan offered by assembly urban counties

Two Republican assemblymen from Essex and Union counties paved the way for adoption of a compromise plan in 1943.[56] Dominic A. Cavicchia (Republican–Essex) and Milton A. Feller (Republican–Union) employed a series of tactical maneuvers within the assembly majority party caucus to overcome the objections of anti-revisionists. The Cavicchia-Feller plan was to have a statewide referendum in 1943 by which the electorate would authorize the 1944 legislature to draft a new constitution. The two assemblymen had to answer three major anti-revisionists claims: (1) Even if the legislature controlled revision, the assembly might propose significant changes in the apportionment system which would arouse the opposition of rural county Republican senators; (2) No constitutional reform should begin while a Democrat was governor; and (3) All change should be postponed until the end of World War II.

In response, Cavicchia and Feller argued that (1) Legislative control over revision would protect the interests of the rural counties in the apportionment system; (2) Legislative control would preclude the necessity of a convention, and thus seize the initiative from Governor Edison; and (3) If the Legislature drafted a constitution in

---

56 The following account of caucus and legislative maneuvering was explained to the author in an interview with Mr. Cavicchia on May 11, 1965. Mr. Cavicchia's comments have been checked with newspaper reports during this period. Most of the commentary deals with the subsequent senate fight over protecting apportionment under a new constitution. Therefore, it is possible that the accuracy of Mr. Cavicchia's remarks may be questioned somewhat considering the lengthy time-lag that is involved. However, it may be said in Mr. Cavicchia's defense that he was very concerned that the story should be retold and that he tried to show the concern that the Essex County delegation had for revising the century-old state constitution.

1944, Governor Edison would no longer be in office.

To achieve their objectives, assemblymen Cavicchia and Feller used the weapons of caucus leadership and lobbying. Cavicchia introduced Feller's plan in the Republican caucus at a time when most other Republicans thought that no action would occur in 1943. As the Republican Majority Leader, Cavicchia called the caucus to order on the morning of April 2, 1943. He asked each Republican to speak on "pet" bills desired for home counties. Feller occupied the last chair on the right side of the room, and Cavicchia had begun with those sitting on the left side. When Feller requested that his referendum bill be given consideration, most others were inclined to withold support. But Cavicchia reminded all that he had the prerogative of calling for formal votes on controversial matters. A vote was taken and 27 Republicans expressed approval, but this fell four short of a 31-member majority for floor passage. Cavicchia adjourned the meeting until the afternoon. Feller then sought the additional four votes. He got assurances from the rural northwestern assemblymen, as well as scattered support from the South Jersey and seashore representatives.

Cavicchia's next move was to call for an immediate roll-call vote, rather than reconvene the caucus. This would prevent an urban-rural confrontation in party ranks and hopefully result in passing the Feller plan before the opposition could gather ranks. By splitting the rural counties, Cavicchia would preclude a possible counter-assault by the Hudson Democrats in getting rural county Republican support to oppose the Feller plan.

Speaker Manfield M.G. Amlicke (Republican–Passaic) told Cavicchia that he would not be present for the afternoon session and asked Cavicchia to be presiding officer. Here was the opportunity to bring the Feller bill to a vote. Cavicchia thereupon requested a roll-call while few assemblymen were present, thus precluding a heated debate. As the Republicans filed into the chambers, more and more votes were cast for the Feller plan until the bill passed by a 37–13 vote.[57]

Table 3.6 indicates that the urban Republicans voted with very high cohesion and provided 27 of 37 affirmative votes. The rural Republicans split, as a result of Feller's lobbying. The northwest counties supported the plan, while the South Jersey and seashore counties were divided. Burlington, Gloucester, and Salem counties broke with Cumberland and voted in favor, while Monmouth and Cape May supported and Atlantic and Ocean opposed. As expected, the minority Democrats, led by Hudson County, voted solidly against. Table 3.6 shows that high urban county voting cohesion (as well as outside rural county support) was essential for passing revision plans in the assembly.

TABLE 3.6. High urban county cohesion and outside rural county support produced a majority for the Feller plan in the assembly, 1943

County Groups and Party	Party Cohesion	Inter-Group Likeness
Urban Republicans	86.2	
		78.3
Rural Republicans	42.8	
Minority Democrats	100 (Negative)	

The same rural county Republican-minority Democratic opposition bloc was a formidable obstacle in the senate, and especially with the rural Republicans controlling a majority. The only hope for the Feller bill in the senate was accommodation with the rural counties. The rural Republicans refused to take action until Walter E. Edge,

[57] *NJAM*, 167th, April 2, 1943, p. 526.

a former governor and United States Senator, announced his candidacy for governor. Edge had enormous prestige as a Republican party leader.[58] He asserted that constitutional reform was an integral aspect of his candidacy and that he favored the Feller referendum plan.[59] His objective was to unite the Republican ranks for the Fall campaign.

Edge devised a compromise strategy with Republican senators. He presented three major arguments for the Feller plan.[60] First, he would not enter a primary fight for the Republican nomination. He wanted the full support of the party for his candidacy. His major purpose for running was to assist in the war effort and to unite the party. Second, Edge wanted endorsement from both county and senate leaders. In return, he demanded discipline from these leaders. Third, constitutional reform was a necessary element in a Republican victory. Edge promised to campaign for the referendum in the Fall elections.

Edge designed his strategy to overcome the "half-hearted"[61] support for constitutional revision among senate Republicans. He argued for quick passage of the Feller bill. Republican senators could then return home for their customary mid-session recess with the referendum issue resolved. This initial effort failed. Edge needed to give definite assurances to the rural senators that their interests were protected under the referendum plan.

The second effort succeeded. On May 6, 1943, Edge and the senate Republicans agreed to a compromise. In return

---

[58] Edge had been a state senator during Woodrow Wilson's governorship, and became governor in 1917. Professor Lockard describes Edge's leadership qualities in terms of "a driving will to succeed and the capacity to inspire loyalty and a high capacity for comprehension of complex issues." He was particularly interested in revision in order to improve state administrative efficiency. See Lockard, *op. cit.*, pp. 112–115.

[59] Newark *Evening News*, April 30, 1943.

[60] Walter E. Edge, *A Jerseyman's Journal* (Princeton, New Jersey: Princeton University Press, 1948), p. 253.

[61] *Ibid.*, p. 258.

for senate approval, Edge accepted a "non-apportionment"[62] amendment in the Feller bill. The compromise met the demands of rural county protection over the senate representation system. The opposition was reduced to senators who had participated on the legislative commission of 1942 and rejected revision until after the war;[63] a senator who still favored constitutional amendments;[64] and an unmoved rural county skeptic.[65] Otherwise, Edge got a party line vote for the amended Feller plan. On May 10, 1943, the senate approved the compromise by a 12–5 tally.[66] In effect, Edge had split the rural county opposition by his appeals to party loyalty.

The amended Feller plan immediately went to the assembly where the Republicans united on party lines and accepted the "no-apportionment" restriction attached by the Senate. In the 42–13 roll-call vote,[67] the Republicans voted with high cohesion (91) in contrast to the moderate party cohesion on the first referendum vote (72.1). The higher cohesion is explained by a net gain of three affirmative votes by the urban Republicans and an increase of two votes among the rural Republicans.

The minority Democrats, led by Hudson County in both chambers, were ineffective in preventing the passage of either the original or the amended Feller plan. Hudson County voting strength depended upon both a split urban Republican vote and a strong opposition bloc among the rural Republicans. When an outside leader, candidate Edge, appealed for party loyalty, the rural counties abandoned anti-revision tactics. Hudson Democrats were re-

62 That is, no changes in the existing apportionment system for either the senate or the assembly.

63 Senators Schroeder (Bergen), Summerill (Salem), and Pyne (Somerset).

64 Senator Lance (Hunterdon).

65 Senator Pierson (Morris).

66 *NJSJ*, 99th, p. 576.

67 *NJAM*, 167th, May 10, 1943, p. 667.

duced to impotence. Legislative reapportionment was dropped from revision; in return, the rural Republicans supported revision, especially knowing that they would still control the process hopefully under Republican Governor Edge, rather than Democratic Governor Edison. In this situation, Hudson County would have to concentrate on defeating the referendum outside the legislature in order to preserve control over the courts.

Table 3.7 below, summarizes the voting cohesion by groups on the amended Feller plan. The obvious conclusion is that Walter E. Edge broke the anti-revisionist bloc in the senate and weakened the minority Democrats.

TABLE 3.7. Party loyalty evident in senate and assembly votes on "No-Apportionment" compromise, 1943

County Groups and Party	General Assembly		Senate	
	Party Cohesion	Inter-Group Likeness	Party Cohesion	Inter-Party Likeness
Rural Republicans	71.4		27.3	
		85.7		80.3
Urban Republicans	100		66.7	
Totals	90.9		41.2	
Minority Democrats	100 (Negative)		100 (Negative)	

Passage of the Feller referendum plan represented an important step toward achieving constitutional reform. This was the first revision bill to pass both chambers.

From 1941 to 1943, the revision issue had promoted a series of responses which reflected the interest of three major legislative groups: the urban county Republicans, the rural county Republicans, and the minority Democrats.

The urban county Republicans, led by Essex County,

supported Democratic Governor Charles Edison in the objective of a new constitution. Realizing that the convention technique was difficult to enact, key urban Republican legislators developed a viable alternative. The referendum proposal offered the legislature an opportunity to control revision. These assurances were accepted by the rural assembly Republicans. Clever tactical moves to gain rural votes illustrated the need for rural Republican support of revision plans in the assembly.

The referendum plan had to meet the requirements of the second important legislative group, the rural county Republican senators. Historically opposed to revision, the rural Senators were most concerned with preserving county representation in the senate. When Governor Edison directly challenged the rural senators, the predictable response was refusal to support change. Constitutional amendments were supported, but this was a diversionary tactic to withstand comprehensive constitutional reform. The rural senators submitted to candidate Edge and his party loyalty appeal on the grounds that revision was essential to statewide party victory in the upcoming elections. But the "no-apportionment" amendment favorably preserved rural county control of the senate. The urban Republicans in the assembly accepted this restriction as the price for reform in the executive and judicial branches of state government.

The minority Democrats gave only weak support to Edison and lined up with the rural county opposition to block revision. The Hague machine opposed both an independent governor and threats to control over court appointments.

Comparisons of assembly voting patterns on delaying maneuvers[68] and the two Feller votes indicate the strength of the rural Republican-minority Democratic blocking

[68] Delaying maneuvers include the roll-calls on the Lance constitutional amendment (two votes) and the first study commission.

vote in the former three votes and the relative unity of the Republicans in the latter two votes. Lacking a clear-cut voting majority from 1941–1943, the urban Republicans had to vote with high cohesion to surmount the anti-revisionist bloc. But both the rural Republicans and the minority Democrats voted with higher cohesion than the urban Republicans on delaying maneuvers. This explains the failure of the assembly to pass a constitutional convention bill during Governor Edison's tenure. A compromise solution, the Feller plan, was necessary to draw the entire Republican party together. Thus, the higher urban Republican cohesion on the Feller plan promoted an urban-rural Republican likeness necessary to pass that plan. With the passage of the Feller plan, the minority Democrats were reduced to ineffectiveness since the opposition bloc was split.

TABLE 3.8. Summary comparison of group voting cohesion and likeness on delaying maneuvers and revision proposals in the assembly, 1941–1943

County Groups and Party	Delaying Maneuvers		Revision Proposals	
	Party Cohesion	Inter-Group Likeness	Party Cohesion	Inter-Party Likeness
Urban Republicans	60.6		93.2	
		87.3		82
Rural Republicans	86.0		57.1	
		98.3		21.4 (Neg.)
Minority Democrats	82.6		100	

Futher analysis of assembly voting responses on the five roll-calls revealed only one unanimously cohesive bloc of four rural Republican counties and one urban Republican county. Aside from rural Cape May, Gloucester, Sussex, and Somerset counties and urban Passaic County, there were so many split alignments within Republican and Democratic party ranks that no discernible pattern was evident. This finding appears to reflect competitive and shifting voting patterns in the assembly. Also, assembly voting blocs are complicated when various multimember delegations engaged in split voting.[69]

When the assembly Republicans are considered in terms of rural and urban voting blocs, the percentage of paired agreements is approximately the same (77 percent to 78 percent) for both groups, as well as among the minority Democrats.[70] When the paired agreements are considered by regional groupings of counties, the major finding is that the Northwestern rural, the Seashore rural, and the Southern urban-rural blocs were more cohesive than the Northeastern urban bloc on the five roll-calls. This finding emphasizes the weakness of the urban Northeastern counties on blocking maneuvers and the comparatively greater strength of the rural counties who joined forces with the minority Democrats.

Bloc analysis of the assembly reaffirms the necessity of high voting cohesion by the urban Republicans in developing a plan for constitutional revision. High urban cohesion and effective pressure tactics on the rural Republicans led to a situation where most rural Republicans voted on party lines rather than maintaining a separate bloc in opposition to the urban Republican counties. The rural Republicans and the minority Democrats were most effective when the urban Republicans voted with moderate to low cohesion.

---

69 Eight counties had split delegations on at least one of the five roll-calls and Essex County had three split delegations on five roll-calls.

70 Bloc analysis was attempted for the assembly during the 1941–1943 period to show responses to proposals by various groups. As shown in the text, the only clear pattern was a cohesive grouping of rural Republicans and minority Democrats opposing the urban Republicans. The urban Republican delegations were so divided that no consistent voting pattern was discernible.

TABLE 3.9. Bloc analysis of assembly Republican regional groupings on five roll-calls, 1941–1943

Northwest	Seashore	Southern	Northeastern
Sussex	Cape May	Gloucester	Passaic
Somerset	Atlantic	Burlington	Union
Warren	Monmouth	Cumberland	Bergen
Morris	Ocean	Salem	Mercer
Hunterdon		Camden	Essex
Number of Paired Agreements Among Bloc Members			
28 of 35	23½ of 30	22 of 29	34½ of 50
Percentage of Paired Agreements Among Bloc Members			
80%	78.3%	75.9%	68.5%

In the senate, the rural Republicans controlled a clear majority of the total votes (56 percent) from 1941 to 1943. The rural Republicans alone determined the fate of revision proposals and acted accordingly. Opposition to revision was shown in the maneuvers to delay change, where rural voting cohesion is highest.[71] Moderate voting cohesion by the rural Republicans on the two study commissions and the Lance amendment reveal that the rural Republicans did not need outside support. In contrast, the amended Feller plan did require an urban-rural alliance because of the residue of rural county opposition to change. The senate voting patterns show, therefore, that a strong bloc, the rural Republicans, alone can withstand efforts by a counterbloc as long as the dominant bloc retains a majority of the votes and exercises these votes effectively.

Bloc analysis of the senate reveals the similarity of the rural Republican county position of the revision issue. No less than seven rural county senators were in unanimous agreement on four of the five roll-call votes from 1941 to

[71] Delaying maneuvers consist of the two study commissions and the Lance constitutional amendment.

TABLE 3.10. Summary comparison of group voting cohesion and likeness on delaying maneuvers and revision proposals in the senate, 1941–1943

County Groups and Party	Delaying Maneuvers		Revision Proposals	
	Party Cohesion	Inter-Group Likeness	Party Cohesion	Inter-Group Likeness
Rural Republicans	81.8		27.3	
		93.7		80.3
Urban Republicans	69.2		66.7	
Minority Democrats	63.6		100 (Negative)	

1943. Only four urban county senators manifested unanimous agreement. A secondary bloc of three Northwestern counties (rural Republican) agreed on three of the four roll-calls. A third Republican bloc of Bergen (urban) and Salem (rural) voted for the study commission bills, but opposed the Lance amendment and the amended Feller plan. A fourth bloc consisting of Camden (urban) and Ocean (rural) county Republicans combined with Democrats from Middlesex (urban), Mercer (urban), and Somerset (rural) counties. Finally, Warren (rural) and Hudson (urban) county Democrats agreed on two roll-calls. The extent of paired agreement among twelve rural senate Republican counties was slightly higher (73.8 percent) than the agreement by six urban Republican counties (70.7 percent) on the five roll-calls. The minority Democrats had the highest percentage of paired agreements (75 percent).

Finally, the Northeast bloc of urban Republican counties had the lowest percentage of paired agreement (67.9 percent) in comparison with the predominantly rural Northwest (88.9 percent) and Seashore (71.4 percent), and the urban-rural Southern bloc (71.9 percent). Thus, regional bloc analysis of Republican voting patterns substantiates the previously described roll-call analysis. The rural Republicans controlled more votes and voted more often together than the urban Republicans in the Senate. As long as the rural Republicans opposed change, all revision efforts had to be directed at a compromise solution to satisfy the rural Republicans.

The 1944 legislature drafts a new constitution

Following the agreement between Mr. Edge and the senate Republicans in 1943 concerning legislative control of revision and the "no-apportionment" amendment, the next stage was ratification of the agreement in the November, 1943 elections. Edge was elected governor by a substantial plurality of 127,760 votes[72] and carried all but Camden, Hudson, and Middlesex counties. The senate remained controlled by 18 Republicans, while the 1944 assembly lineup was 44 Republicans and 16 Democrats. The Democrats gained three seats in Camden County, while the Republicans added the Warren County seat. Finally, the referendum was overwhelmingly approved by the electorate. The 154,424 plurality[73] represented a 62.1 percent affirmative response. The only resistance was from Hudson County which voted 73.4 percent against the referendum.[74] Thus, as the 1944 legislative session began, the Republican legislators and Governor Edge appeared firmly united in preparing a new constitution. United party control relaxed on the prior tension between Republican legislators and a Democratic governor. Bipartisanship did not appear necessary for revision.

Governor Edge was determined to implement the mandate for revision by recommending to the legislature that

[72] *N.J. Legislative Manual* (1945), p. 618.
[73] *Ibid.,* (1944), p. 552.
[74] *Ibid.*

changes be considered in the following areas. First, he suggested that the state's highest court, consisting of 16 members, be replaced with a seven-member body, serving with life tenure instead of seven-year terms.[75] Second, he recommended that the governor have a four-year term (in place of the three-year term) and a greater veto power (requiring more than a simple legislative majority of both houses to override). In addition, the governor should have greater control over appointment of department heads, instead of independent legislative appointments.[76] Finally, Edge proposed longer terms for legislators (two-year assembly terms and four-year senate terms in place of one-year assembly and three-year senate terms) and increased compensation.[77]

The legislature promptly responded to revision by establishing a joint committee on January 11, 1944.[78] The votes were unanimous in both chambers, with 43 Republicans joining 15 Democrats in the assembly, and 15 Republicans and two Democrats voting affirmatively in the senate.[79]

The joint committee was headed by Senator Howard Eastwood (Republican–Burlington), the 1944 senate president; and the two assembly proponents of the 1943 referendum, Dominic A. Cavicchia (Republican–Essex) and Milton A. Feller (Republican–Union). The committee was subdivided into three 14-member subcommittees on the judicial, legislative, and executive provisions of the new draft constitution. Each subcommittee had seven senators and seven assemblymen. Six Republicans and one Democrat were appointed to the respective subcommittees for each chamber.[80]

The subcommittee structure ensured Republican con-

[75] Edge, *op. cit.,* p. 261.
[76] *Ibid.*
[77] *Ibid.*
[78] Sources: *NJSJ,* 100th, p. 34; and *NJAM,* 168th, p. 43.
[79] *Ibid.*
[80] *Ibid.*

trol of revision, an objective originally proposed by assemblymen Feller and Cavicchia in 1943.[81] Also, equal geographic representation was ensured, as shown in Table 3.11.

TABLE 3.11. 1944 joint legislative committee reflected equal geographic representation among Republicans

Judicial Subcommittee		Legislative Subcommittee	
Senate	Assembly	Senate	Assembly
Bergen Mercer Passaic (North-east and Central)	Bergen Essex Middlesex (D) Union	Middlesex (D) Union	Essex Mercer Passaic
Somerset Warren (D) (North-west)	Morris	Morris Sussex	Hunterdon (D) Somerset Sussex
Burlington (South) Salem	Burlington Gloucester	Camden Cumberland	
		Ocean (Seashore)	Atlantic

Executive Subcommittee	
Senate	Assembly
Essex Hudson (D)	Bergen Essex Hudson (D) Union
Hunterdon	
Gloucester	Cumberland Salem
Atlantic Cape May Monmouth	Monmouth

[81] See page 102, *Supra*.

Further analysis of Table 3.11 reveals that all regions were represented on the subcommittees. Four counties (Camden, Cape May, Ocean, and Warren) had only senate membership. Fourteen counties[82] had dual membership, that is, at least one senator and one assemblyman on a subcommittee. Two counties, Bergen and Union, had three subcommittee members; and Essex County had four members.

The joint committee completed its work by April and endorsed all of Governor Edge's recommendations, including life tenure for the supreme court,[83] a four-year term[84] and increased veto power for the governor,[85] and lengthened terms for legislators.[86]

All but the Hudson Democrat voted for the draft constitution in the senate in a 20–0 roll-call.[87] The Hudson County delegation led minority Democratic opposition in the assembly, but the urban and rural Republicans united and voted unanimously for the draft proposal in a 42–15 roll-call.[88] Hudson County opposition to the draft was not only related to its previous anti-revision stands, but also to Boss Hague's anger at Governor Edge and his attorney general, who were conducting gambling raids in Hudson County.[89] Strengthened courts and more power for the governor under a new constitution threatened Boss Hague's control in Hudson County.

---

[82] These included Atlantic, Burlington, Cumberland, Gloucester, Hudson, Hunterdon, Mercer, Middlesex, Monmouth, Morris, Passaic, Salem, Somerset, and Sussex counties.

[83] See: *Proposed Revised Constitution* (1944), State Library, State House Annex, Trenton, New Jersey, Article V, Section II.

[84] *Ibid.*, Article IV, Section I.

[85] *Ibid.*

[86] *Ibid.*, Article III, Sections II and III.

[87] The Middlesex and Warren County senators voted with the Republicans, while the Hudson County senator abstained. See *NJSJ*, 100th, April 3, 1944, p. 529.

[88] *NJAM*, 168th, April 3, 1944, p. 609.

[89] Edge, *op. cit.*, pp. 264–266.

Hague saved his assault on the draft constitution until the last month prior to the November 8 elections. Hudson County tried to mobilize resentment among various groups with a propaganda campaign. The Hague machine told the labor unions that they would lose their rights; that school teachers' would lose their pensions; that police and firemen would lose tenure and security; that state civil service was to be ended; and that women would lose their civil rights.[90] The final charge was that Catholic priests would be required to testify in court on any criminal acts revealed in confessions.[91] The Hague machine never made an overall attack on the new document. As one charge was answered by the supporters of the draft, Hague and his machine levelled new attacks.[92]

The draft consitution was defeated by a 126,521 plurality with Hudson County providing nearly half of this total. Twelve counties voted against and nine in favor. The political causes of the defeat were attributable to the mistaken assumptions by Governor Edge and the Republican legislators. First, the Republicans followed a policy of one-party control over revision, when in reality, Hudson County was particularly influential in producing huge voting pluralities in general elections. Hudson County was strategically placed in the statewide electoral system and could generally determine the fate of statewide candidates (governors) or statewide referenda.[93] In this situation, Hudson opposition in the legislature should have been seen as a warning for the success of the draft document when it was presented to the voters. The Hudson County propaganda campaign was most effective in splitting the rural Republican counties, when 7 of 13 rural Republican

[90] Edge, *op. cit.*, pp. 281–282.

[91] *Ibid.*, p. 283.

[92] *Ibid.*, p. 282.

[93] Hudson County was as powerful in the electoral process in 1944 as Essex County was in the legislature in 1941.

counties voted against the new constitution. The second mistaken assumption by the Republicans was that the people of the state favored a new constitution in the absence of a strong promotional campaign. The referendum of 1943 had won a resounding victory at the polls; the draft document was pushed through the legislature on a single day. But, the reform groups that favored the 1944 document did not get their message across to the voters. In the absence of mobilizing support, the Hague machine put the reformers on the defensive, when in fact, the reformers should have been promoting the new constitution as effectively as possible.[94]

Rejection of the constitution represented a frustrating and embarrassing setback for the reformers. In the last two years of Governor Edge's term, the Republican-controlled legislature attempted to promote revision through a series of constitutional amendments. Separate amendments were introduced early in 1945 concerning the major reforms in the executive, legislative, and judicial branches included in the 1944 draft constitution.[95] However, neither separate amendments nor a jointly-appointed senate-assembly study committee achieved success. The Republicans still refused to take a bipartisan approach on revision,[96] and Governor Edge did not exercise leadership on the issue. Lacking a consensus, the Republicans failed to revise the constitution by the end of 1946.

A new constitution for New Jersey

Constitutional revision was finally achieved in 1947

[94] See Edge, *op. cit.*, pp. 280–281.

[95] See the amendments introduced by Senators Harold A. Pierson (Republican–Morris) and John G. Sholl (Republican–Gloucester), *NJSJ*, 101st, January 29, 1945, pp. 121–140.

[96] The senate Republicans defeated a proposal to make the study commission bipartisan as offered by Democratic Senator John E. Toolan (Middlesex). See *NJSJ*, 101st, March 16, 1945, p. 355.

under the leadership of Republican Governor Alfred E. Driscoll. Driscoll, a former state senator from Camden County, won an overwhelming victory in the November, 1946 elections with a 221,418 plurality from 19 of the 21 counties. Only Middlesex and Hudson counties voted for the Democratic candidate.[97]

Driscoll was successful because he overcame the legislative objections that had plagued both Governors Edison and Edge. Driscoll wanted a non-partisan approach to revision by means of an impartial constitutional convention.[98] To achieve revision, Driscoll hastily disposed of the apportionment issue by a direct reassurance to Republican rural county legislators in his inaugural address in January, 1947:

> It has long been assumed that a constitutional convention would mean the loss of the present basis of representation in the Legislature for such counties . . . I am convinced that political boundaries play a relatively minor part in a State Legislature; that group interests and party loyalties are in fact the principal factors through which legislation is evolved.[99]

Having made an appeal to the senate rural counties, Driscoll then dealt with the composition of the convention, a matter which had been a major stumbling block for Governor Edison. He proposed the following:[100]

1. A constitutional convention authorized by the people and restricted by them to protect our present system of representation;
2. The convention to be composed of 60 members elected from our counties, with each county to have

---

[97] Source: *N.J. Legislative Manual* (1946), p. 637.

[98] Governor Driscoll related the following events and considerations in an interview on May 18, 1965.

[99] *N.J. Legislative Manual* (1947), p. 705.

[100] *Ibid.*, pp. 706–707.

the same number of delegates as it has members in the House of Assembly;

3. The convention be directed to revise, alter and amend our present constitution and submit its final work for our approval or rejection by the people at the general election this November.

Aware of the previous objections to a convention among the rural legislators, Driscoll had purposely proposed a 60-member body in order to provide the rural legislators with a bargaining position. The governor wanted to forestall any attempts to delay revision and he wanted unanimous support for the convention to impress the electorate with the importance of adopting a new constitution at the earliest possible opportunity. Therefore, the governor "agreed" to a change in the composition of the convention from 60 to 81 delegates after meeting with senate and assembly Republican leaders. This guaranteed each of the rural counties at least two delegates in the convention. Delegates would then be chosen on the same basis as senators and assemblymen in the legislature. However, Driscoll held firm on his demand for nonpartisan slates of delegates to be elected from the 21 counties. Driscoll also met with Hudson County Democrats, who first opposed and later said they supported a convention. The governor could not account for the Hudson County change, except on the grounds that united Republican legislative support would pass the convention proposal over Hudson County's objections.

With the preliminary negotiations completed, the legislature unanimously passed a constitutional convention bill on February 10, 1947.[101] Subsequently, the electorate authorized the convention and selected delegates on June 3. The convention convened in the summer months of 1947,

[101] By votes of 20–0 in the senate and 59–0 in the assembly. See *NJSJ*, 103rd, p. 110; and *NJAM*, 171st, p. 186.

framed the new charter and submitted it to the voters in November, 1947, at which time the new constitution was adopted. The new constitution contained the same reforms proposed earlier by Governor Edge together with an unchanged apportionment provision for the senate and the assembly carried over from the 1844 Constitution.[102]

Conclusions

New Jersey got a new constitution after a protracted 7-year struggle between the legislature and three governors. The distribution of political strength in the legislature and the direct relationship between senate representation and revision precipitated the conflict. The Republicans clearly controlled both legislative chambers. Both Democratic and Republican party governors tried to develop effective legislative majorities, but (with the lone exception of Governor Edge) were continually stifled either by the rural Republicans or the Hudson Democrats.

New Jersey legislative politics from 1941 to 1947 can most accurately be described as bifactional rather than competition between two parties of approximately equal strength. The revision issue promoted one alliance between the governors (both Democratic and Republican) and the urban Republican legislators. But the urban Republicans were an effective voting bloc only when they voted with high cohesion and obtained outside support from the rural Republicans in the assembly. When the urban Republicans were divided, the governor could not get action from the legislature. The second alliance was between the rural Republicans and the Hudson Democrats, who both wanted to preserve the *status quo.* The rural Republicans listened

[102] For a summary of the events of the 1947 New Jersey Constitutional Convention, see: Richard N. Baisden, *Charter For New Jersey: The New Jersey Constitutional Convention* (Trenton, New Jersey: Division of State Library, Archives and History, 1952).

to a party loyalty appeal from Governor Edge, when an election victory appeared possible, but the Republican senators exacted a proviso that the senate representation system would remain intact. When strong leadership was not exerted by governors, either the rural Republican senators or the Hudson Democrats blocked action. Rural county power was most effective inside the senate caucus, while Hudson County power took place at the polls. The Republicans could pass a draft constitution inside the legislature, but Hudson County could roll up a huge plurality and assist to defeat the constitution in a statewide referendum.

The failures of both governors Edison and Edge can be traced to alienation of the anti-revisionist legislative bloc. Edison directly attacked the rural county senators and asserted independence from the Hudson County machine. As a result, the urban county revisionist bloc lacked enough votes to press for Edison's convention plan. The Feller referendum plan, passed at the end of Edison's tenure, was an urban Republican measure intended to bridge the gap between urban and rural differences which Edison alone could not resolve. Similarly, Governor Edge successfully reunited the Republicans in the legislature, but was ineffective in dealing with the Hudson Democrats. In contrast to Edison's approach, Edge delegated too much responsibility to the Republican legislators in drafting the new constitution. The Democrats were outnumbered on the legislative committees and could not properly present their point of view. Hudson County needed assurances from Governor Edge the same as the rural Republicans got under the Feller bill compromise. The Hudson propaganda campaign against the draft constitution of 1944 reflected the alienation of Hudson County in the legislature.

Governor Driscoll overcame the anti-revisionist opposition with skillful maneuvering. In avoiding the problems encountered by Edison and Edge, Driscoll immediately combined the 1943 "no-apportionment" compromise with a convention plan. But Driscoll also realized that a convention would not be acceptable to the legislature if it was weighted too heavily either in favor of the urban or rural counties, or if it was controlled by one party to the exclusion of the other. Therefore, Driscoll settled for an 81-member convention, which met the demands of both the urban and rural countries; and nonpartisan slates of delegates, which offset the possibility of political party disputes in the convention. With these elements, Driscoll achieved not only unanimous Republican party support (thus healing the urban-rural rift), but also the support of the Hudson Democrats, who would have a voice in the convention.

New Jersey got a new constitution in 1947, but at the cost of an agreement that no changes would take place in the reapportionment system. Governor Driscoll felt that it was important to achieve substantial executive and judicial reform. Reapportionment was not, in his opinion, absolutely essential to revision. More important, perhaps, is the fact that revision was impossible if the representation system was to be changed.

The failure to change the apportionment system in the 1947 constitution affected the apportionment deadlock of the 1950's, another protracted conflict which lasted for 11 years. This will be the subject of the next chapter.

4

The Apportionment Deadlock of the 1950's

PERSISTENT DEADLOCK WAS THE MAJOR THEME OF REAPPORTIONMENT efforts in the New Jersey Legislature from 1952 to 1961. The ten-year stalemate represented the most prolonged effort to find a reapportionment solution for the New Jersey General Assembly in the twentieth century.

Analysis of the legislative struggle reveals that particular legislative groups sought to maximize their power to the fullest possible extent. These groups came into conflict because of their contrasting objectives, and particularly those concerning retention of the *status quo* versus change; maintenance of an urban-rural balance; and maintenance of Republican and Democratic party interests.

Both Essex and Hudson counties defended the *status quo*. By opposing assembly seat losses, legislators from the state's two most populous urban Northeastern counties consistently defeated a number of proposed solutions. The two counties together held 21 of 60 assembly votes. By maintaining a cohesive voting position, attracting some outside county support, and crossing party lines in roll-call votes, they successfully blocked assembly reapportionment until 1961.

Opponents of the *status quo* consisted primarily of representatives from Burlington, Camden, Monmouth, and Union counties, each of which had gained population from 1940 to 1950 and felt it merited additional assembly seats. These four counties held only ten of the 60 assembly votes and had to attract outside support to achieve a favorable solution. These same four counties experienced the most frustration during the ten-year struggle, because they were not "rewarded" with additional seats until the very end of the reapportionment struggle. As the conflict remained unsolved, the four counties were gaining even more population, but could not achieve increased representation. Standing alone, the proponents of change could not force a solution to a problem that was essentially political rather than mathematical in nature.

Third, the two chambers conflicted. Atlantic County legislators, in asserting leadership for the rural counties in both the assembly and the senate, opposed proposals that reduced voting strength of the rural counties and increased the voting power of the urban counties in the assembly. Rural county voting cohesion in the senate effectively blocked these plans, while the same cohesion in the assembly represented a breakdown of Republican party discipline on key roll-call votes.

Finally, both Republicans and Democrats favored plans which resulted in retaining a party balance of power in the assembly. The parties did not try to protect opponents, but one-party solutions were generally viewed with suspicion by the minority party. As long as the Republicans and Democrats did not consult with each other, the minority party solidly opposed proposals. When the Republicans controlled both houses, Democratic party cohesion was remarkably high in opposing Republican plans. Republican party cohesion was similarly high in opposition when the Democrats gained control of the assembly.

The legislative political environment, 1952 to 1961

Further boundary conditions in the apportionment struggle may be found in any one or all of the following factors: (1) Party competition for governor; (2) Party control of the senate and general assembly; (3) Party composition of county delegations; and (4) Existing seating distributions among the counties affecting the formation of assembly voting blocs.

Republican Governor Alfred E. Driscoll, the architect of constitutional reform in 1947, was reelected for a four-year term in 1949. Driscoll proposed a plan in 1952 and 1953 during a time when the Republicans controlled both houses of the legislature. The plan was defeated by the narrow margin of one vote in 1952 and Driscoll was ineffective in achieving its enactment in 1953.

Throughout the remaining eight years of the apportionment struggle, 1954 to 1961, Democratic Governor Robert B. Meyner was in office. Meyner won elections in 1953 and 1957 through pluralities provided primarily by the urban counties.[1] Seven urban and five rural counties gave Meyner 54.3 percent of the two-party vote in 1953, and seven urban and seven rural counties combined to produce a 55.1 percent margin for his re-election in 1957.[2] But Figure 4.1 shows the dilemma faced by Meyner in exercising leadership to end the apportionment deadlock. From 1954 to 1957, Meyner was opposed by statewide voting pluralities favoring Republican legislators. The Democratic governor

[1] Only Bergen County, an urban Republican stronghold, did not vote for Meyner in either 1953 or 1957. See the voting returns for governor in the 1954 and 1958 *N.J. Legislative Manuals,* p. 638 (1954) and p. 695 (1958).

[2] *Ibid.*

could not force the apportionment issue in fear of alienating the Republican-controlled legislature on the rest of his program.[3] Meyner became effective at the very end of the struggle when his leadership was essential to spurring Democratic legislators in passing a reapportionment plan in the face of an ultimatum by the state supreme court.

Party control of the legislature was clearly demarcated by two distinct periods. From 1951 to 1957 the Republicans controlled both the senate and the general assembly. During this first period, as shown in Table 4.1, the Republicans held approximately 68 percent of the assembly and 74 percent of the senate seats. During this time, therefore, the Republicans were responsible for failing to enact an apportionment solution. Following the narrow defeat of a plan in 1952, the Republicans were so badly divided that nothing was done. Substantial one-party legislative control did not ensure enactment of a reapportionment plan.

In the second period of party control, 1958 to 1961, the Democrats controlled both the governor's office and the general assembly, while the Republicans continued to control the senate. Both divided legislative control and divided executive-legislative control characterized the second period. The Democrats were as badly split over the apportionment issue in this second period as the Republicans were from 1951 to 1957. The change in party control *per se* did not ensure resolution of the apportionment conflict.

Party discipline was weak during both periods of legislative control because of the independence asserted by county delegations that stood to lose seats. The senate, throughout the ten-year struggle, was characterized by one-party control of county delegations among both Democrats and Republicans. In fact a majority of the 21 one-member county delegations in the senate were represented by one

[3] See Malcolm E. Jewell, *The State Legislature* (New York: Random House, 1962), p. 30; and Jewell, Ed., *The Politics of Reapportionment* (New York: Atherton Press, 1962), p. 31.

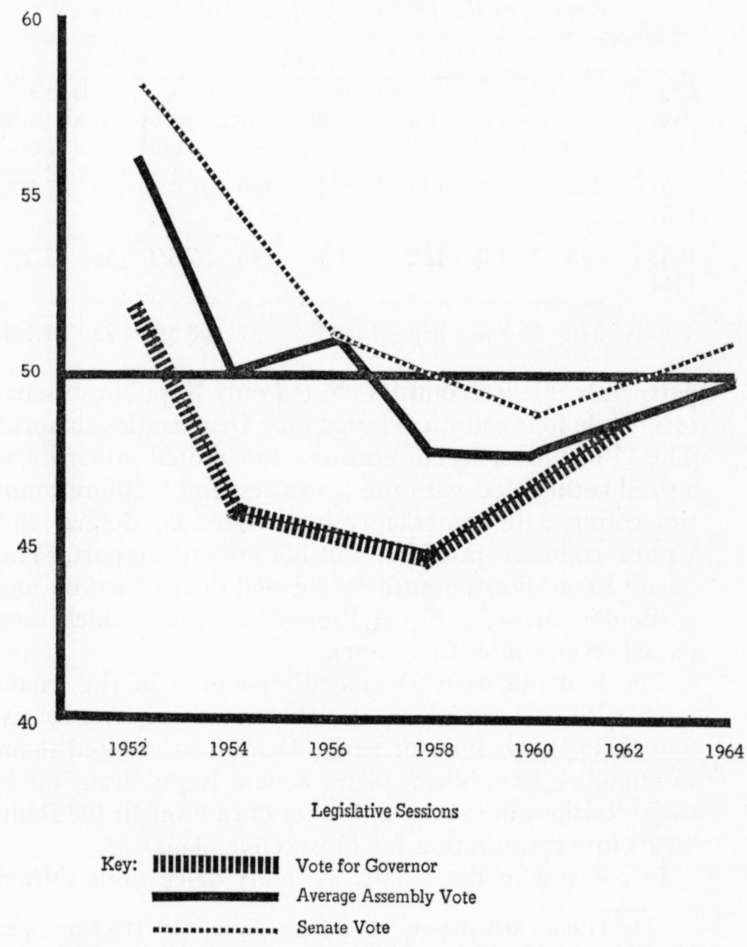

4.1 Republican Party Percentage of Popular Vote for New Jersey Governor, General Assembly, and Senate Preceding Legislative Sessions, 1952–1965.

TABLE 4.1. Two distinct periods of legislative control evident in the 1950's apportionment deadlock

	General Assembly				Senate			
	Reps.		Dems.		Reps.		Dems.	
Legislative Years	Total Seats	% of Total	Total Seats	% of Total	Total Seats	% of Total	Total Seats	% of Total
1951–1957	282	67.5%	136	32.5%	109	74.1%	38	25.9%
1958–1961	88	36.7%	152	63.3%	48	57.8%	35	42.2%
Totals	370	56.2%	288	43.8%	157	68.3%	73	31.7%

party only. Eleven counties elected only Republican senators, while four counties elected only Democratic senators.[4] The 11 one-party Republican senators united primarily as a rural voting bloc, with the Northwest and Seashore counties voting with remarkably high cohesion. Bergen and Union counties provided outside urban support. The senate Republicans eventually focused their efforts on one particular plan, the Equal Proportions Plan, which they passed seven consecutive times.

The four one-party Democratic counties in the senate were, with one exception, all urban counties. The consistent minority position of senate Democrats reduced them to opposing Republican plans. Senate Republicans made their decisions in caucus and never once brought the Democrats into consultation for prospective plans.[5]

In contrast to the senate, assembly delegations shifted

[4] The 11 one-party Republican counties were: (1) The Northwest rural bloc of Hunterdon, Morris, Somerset, Sussex, and Warren; (2) The Seashore rural bloc of Atlantic, Cape May, Monmouth, and Ocean; and (3) The urban Northeastern counties of Bergen and Union. The four one-party Democratic counties consisted of urban Hudson, Mercer, and Middlesex; and rural Cumberland.

[5] See Belle Zeller, Ed., *American State Legislatures* (New York: Thomas Y. Crowell Co., 1954), p. 207.

from Republican to Democratic party control throughout the apportionment struggle. Table 4.2 shows that 9 county delegations had at least one change of party affiliation, while 12 counties were either solidly Republican or Democratic. A coalition of county interests was the key to developing an effective apportionment solution in the assembly. The coalition was any combination of 31 assembly votes because of the lack of discipline in party ranks. The final solution had to be bipartisan, that is, a solution that mobilized competing county interests across party lines.

*TABLE 4.2. Classification of county delegations in the general assembly, 1951 to 1961**

Solidly Republican	Predominantly Republican	Competitive	Predominantly Democratic	Solidly Democratic
Atlantic	Burlington	Cumberland	Camden	Hudson
Bergen	Gloucester	Essex	Salem	Mercer
Cape May	Sussex	Passaic		Middlesex
Hunterdon		Union		Warren
Monmouth				
Morris				
Ocean				
Somerset				
(16)	(3)	(21)	(4)	(16)

* Classification shows that solid one-party counties had no changes; predominant one-party counties had one change; and competitive counties had more than one change in party affiliation over the 11 years. Figures in parentheses denote total assembly votes for each county grouping.

Republican or Democratic party control of one or both houses of the legislature was a major strategic consideration in the apportionment struggle. In general most counties not affected by the outcomes of various proposals voted the party line. The maintenance of party discipline was weakest, however, when the counties most affected by proposed changes refused to go along with the party position.[6] One of the most significant problems during the period was mobilizing an effective party majority when a party clearly controlled one or both houses of the legislature.

The importance of county delegation independence in the assembly can be shown further by the various blocs which formed throughout the period. In a 60-member assembly, 31 votes were required to pass a plan. Initially, it was most apparent that two key counties held the crucial votes for any apportionment proposal—Essex and Hudson counties. When the Republicans controlled the assembly, the 12 votes of Essex County were absolutely essential in passing a Republican plan. Only when Republican majorities exceeded 42 assembly seats was the Essex position somewhat weakened. Otherwise, the 12 Essex votes represented nearly 40 percent of the votes needed by the Republicans to attain a 31-vote majority. When assembly party control shifted to the Democrats, Hudson County played a key role. Democratic party majorities had to exceed 39 assembly seats to weaken the Hudson bloc vote. When Essex and Hudson County legislators joined forces in a 21-member voting bloc, neither party could pass a plan but required bipartisan support.

No other coalition of counties could form voting blocs to offset the existing power positions of either Essex or Hudson counties. The four counties that stood to gain increased representation, Burlington, Camden, Monmouth, and Union, together controlled only 10 assembly votes and could not form an effective counter-coalition to Essex and Hudson. Moreover, these four counties were split by party affiliation with Monmouth solidly Republican, Burlington predominantly Republican, Union competitive, and Camden predominantly Democratic. If Bergen County, solidly Republican, which gained a seat in the 1961 solution, is

[6] See V. O. Key, Jr., *American State Politics: An Introduction* (New York: Alfred A. Knopf, 1956), p. 277.

included among the "gainers," it can be seen that the five counties had 16 votes during the period of Republican control (1952–1957) and had to find 15 additional votes to pass a plan. However, Essex could cast its 12 votes with the minority Democrats, thereby making it absolutely essential for the Republicans to seek some Democratic party support to enact a plan. Democratic Camden County might have been a key to the solution, but, as it will be shown later, the Camden Democrats refused to go along with a plan that isolated them from the rest of the minority party.

Finally, there were two stationary blocs, consisting of Republican and Democratic counties that were not affected by the outcome. Included here were 14 counties, eight rural Republican, one rural and one urban competitive, and two urban and two rural Democratic counties. If the votes of the competitive counties are added to the party blocs during the two periods of party control, it is evident that the Republican stationary bloc had 15 votes and the Democratic stationary bloc had 13 votes. Thus, these two blocs alone could not decide the issue.

Table 4.3 provides the setting for analyzing voting blocs in the apportionment struggle. As long as Essex and Hudson counties were designated for seat losses and exercised a veto power within party ranks or formed an interparty coalition, no solution was possible. Other groups of counties could form veto blocs, but none could develop an effective and affirmative 31-vote majority to overcome Essex-Hudson resistance to change. Only when Essex County itself was split in 1960 and 1961 among both Democratic and Republican party assemblymen was the effectiveness of the Essex-Hudson alliance reduced. By adopting a bipartisan approach, the veto power of Essex and Hudson counties was surmounted and a final solution achieved. Until 1961, however, Essex County was in a position to block all Republican plans, while Hudson County could block all Democratic-proposed apportionment solutions.

TABLE 4.3. Classification of voting blocs in general assembly, 1952–1961

Gaining Counties		Stationary Counties	
Rep.	Dem.	Rep.	Dem.
Bergen (6)	Camden (3)	Atlantic (2)	Mercer (3)
Burlington (1)		Cape May (1)	Middlesex (3)
Monmouth (2)		Gloucester (1)	Salem (1)
		Hunterdon (1)	Warren (1)
Competitive		Morris (2)	
Union (4)		Ocean (1)	
Total Votes = 16		Somerset (1)	
		Sussex (1)	
		Competitive	
		Cumberland (1)	
		Passaic (4)	
		Total Votes = 23	

Losing Counties	
Rep.	Dem.
Essex (12)	Hudson (9)
Total Votes = 21	

The legislature took action on four basic reapportionment proposals from 1952 to 1961. These included: (1) the Cavicchia Plan, which employed the Vinton Method; (2) Equal Proportions Plans based either on the 1950 or the 1960 census; (3) the Arithmetical Eliminations Plan; and (4) Increasing the total membership of the assembly from 60 to 67 members. The first three proposals required the use of mathematical formulas, which will be explained below.

The Vinton Method, which was used in the 1941 reapportionment, consists of the following steps: The total population of the state is divided by the total number of assembly seats (60) to obtain a fixed ratio, which represents the ideal population per assemblyman. This fixed ratio is divided into the population of each county to obtain the exact quota of seats for each county. One seat is assigned to each county whose exact quota is less than one seat (as required by the constitution). Each county is assigned a number of seats equal to the whole number of its exact quota. The remaining number of seats to be allotted are assigned to those counties having the largest fractions in their exact quotas.[7]

The Equal Proportions method first assigns one "constitutional" seat to each of the 21 counties. Next, a priority list is established to distribute the remaining 39 seats. This is done by dividing the population of each county successively by the geometric mean (the square root of the product) of each pair of successive integers in the order of increasing magnitude until the number of quotients calculated for each county exceeds by at least one the number of additional seats allotted to that county. These quotients are arranged in the order of magnitude, beginning with the largest, to form the priority list. Finally, the 39 seats are allocated to the counties having the 39 highest positions on the priority list.[8]

The Arithmetical Eliminations Plan requires that a fixed ratio be obtained by dividing 60 seats into the total

---

[7] Source: *New Jersey Legislative Reapportionment* (Trenton, New Jersey: Law and Legislative Reference Bureau, Division of the State Library, Archives and History, New Jersey State Department of Education, November, 1957), pp. 7–8. The Vinton Method has generally been discarded because like all methods of reapportionment based on a fixed ratio, it is susceptible to a mathematically illogical and contradictory phenomenon. In certain situations, a county which has grown in population at a greater rate than any other county may lose a seat and the other slower-growing counties may gain seats despite an increase in the size of the assembly.

[8] *New Jersey Legislative Reapportionment, op. cit.*, p. 11. The Equal Proportions method is one of the formulas used to apportion legislative seats where the residents of each subdivision are entitled to at least one member of the legislative body. This method is presently used for the reapportionment of seats in the United States House of Representatives. The Equal Proportions method may dilute strict population apportionment depending on the size of the

state population. Each of the 21 counties is assigned one "constitutional" seat. The fixed ratio is then subtracted from the population of each county whose population exceeds this fixed ratio as payment for the "constitutional" seat. The remainder is labelled a "plus balance" and is used in the assignment of the remaining 39 seats. The population of each county smaller than the fixed ratio is subtracted from this fixed ratio to obtain a "minus balance." The total of these "minus balances" is prorated among the counties having "plus balances" in proportion to the size of their "plus balances" as "constitutional equalizers." The "constitutional equalizer" of each county is subtracted from its "plus balance" to obtain the "population remaining for allocation." One additional seat is awarded to each county for each whole fixed ratio contained in its "population remaining for allocation." The remaining number of seats are awarded, in order, to those counties with the highest remainders.[9]

Since the 1947 state constitution did not specify the method of reapportionment,[10] the "fairness" of any of the three mathematical formulas can best be determined by examining the criteria of population per assemblyman and the individual share in an assemblyman (based on the 1950 census figures for New Jersey counties).[11] The goal of the

---

legislative body and the number of subdivisions guaranteed the right to elect at least one member to that body. For examples, see: Advisory Commission on Intergovernmental Relations, *Apportionment of State Legislatures* (Washington, D.C., December, 1962), pp. A-26 to A-27.

[9] *New Jersey Legislative Reapportionment, op. cit.*, pp. 9–10. As with the fixed ratio used in the Vinton Method, the Arithmetical Eliminations method tends to cause some over-representation of underpopulated areas and does not fully maximize seating gains for heavily populated areas. See: William J. Keefe and Morris S. Ogul, *The American Legislative Process* (Englewood Cliffs, New Jersey: Prentice-Hall, Inc., 1964), p. 74.

[10] *Constitution of 1947*, Article IV, Section 3.

[11] See *Legislative Apportionment in New Jersey* (New Bruns-

first criterion is to ensure that the assembly represents, as nearly as possible, the same number of persons. If the population per assemblyman (80,588) [12] is made equal in each county, the apportionment is perfect.[13] The second criterion, the individual share in an assemblyman, is found by dividing the number of representatives assigned to a county by its population.[14] The concept is based on the assumption that each person in a county is entitled to a share of an assembly seat. If the figure is the same for each county, the apportionment is perfect.[15] Since it is nearly impossible to have either of these figures the same for all counties, the degree to which an apportionment approaches perfection must be measured by the difference from county to county in population per assemblyman and the individual share of an assemblyman.[16]

Table 4.4 below compares and contrasts the criterion of population per assemblyman for the seven counties involved in the three mathematical formula plans. The figures differ for particular counties because the three plans varied in the redistribution of assembly seats as follows:

County	*Present Seats*	*Vinton Method*	*Arith. Elims.*	*Equal Props.*
Atlantic	2	1	2	2
Burlington	1	1	2	2
Camden	3	4	3	4
Essex	12	11	11	10
Hudson	9	8	7	7
Monmouth	2	3	3	3
Union	4	5	5	5

wick, New Jersey: Bureau of Government Research, Rutgers–The State University, January, 1952), p. 2.

12 The result of dividing the 1950 State total, 4,835,329 by 60 assembly seats.

13 *Legislative Apportionment in New Jersey, op. cit.*, p. 2.

14 *Ibid.*

15 *Ibid.*

16 *Ibid.*

The major findings in Table 4.4 are that the Vinton Method produces both the two smallest and two largest deviations from the ideal population per assemblyman. The Equal Proportions formula results in the smallest range of deviations from the ideal, expressed either as absolute or relative differences, while the Vinton Method produces the largest range of deviations from the ideal. The Arithmetical Eliminations plan falls between the Vinton Method and Equal Proportions.[17] Similarly, when the individual share of an assemblyman is compared under the three plans, the Equal Proportions method emerges as the "fairest" plan.[18]

TABLE 4.4. Comparison of three reapportionment plans involving a mathematical formula: absolute and relative differences in population as compared with the ideal population per seat based on the 1950 census.[19]

Counties	Vinton Method		Arith. Elims.		Equal Props.	
Atlantic	51,881	64.3%	–14,388	–21.7%	–14,388	–21.7%
Burlington	55,322	68.6%	–12,633	–18.6%	–12,633	–18.6%
Camden	– 5,402	– 7.2%	19,660	24.4%	– 5,402	– 7.2%
Essex	1,771	2.2%	1,771	2.2%	10,007	12.4%
Hudson	342	.4%	11,903	14.8%	11,903	14.8%
Monmouth	– 5,479	– 6.7%	– 5,479	– 6.7%	– 5,479	– 6.7%
Union	– 960	– 1.2%	960	– 1.2%	– 960	– 1.2%

The Cavicchia Plan is proposed and defeated, 1952, 1953

Republican Governor Alfred E. Driscoll took the initiative in proposing the first reapportionment plan in 1952. Delay of the final census figures for all New Jersey counties had forestalled reapportionment in 1951.[20] Upon receiving the necessary information from the United States

[17] *New Jersey Legislative Reapportionment, op. cit.*, pp. 14–15.
[18] *Ibid.*, p. 16.
[19] *New Jersey Legislative Reapportionment, op. cit.*, p. 14.
[20] Newark *Evening News*, January 22, 1951.

Census Bureau, Governor Driscoll delegated responsibility to his Deputy Attorney General, Dominic A. Cavicchia, to design a plan.[21]

Cavicchia worked on a plan throughout 1951. In his effort to design a "fair" and "objective" assembly reapportionment, Cavicchia sought to apply the Vinton Method, with which he had been successful in the 1941 reapportionment. Cavicchia concluded that population gains and losses among the counties should result in the following realignment: Atlantic, Essex, and Hudson counties would each lose one Assembly seat, while Camden, Monmouth, and Union counties would each gain one seat.[22]

There were three political implications resulting from the Cavicchia Plan for the Republican-controlled assembly, which stood at a 43–17 advantage in 1952. First, owing to the existing party control of the various county delegations and assuming that Camden and Union counties were safe Republican counties, the plan resulted in a net gain of one Republican seat. Democratic Hudson County would lose one seat, while no other Democratic county would gain any new seats. Secondly, with regard to balancing urban county representation, the Cavicchia Plan called for a shift of one seat from the urban northeastern section to the southern section of the state. Union County, urban northeastern, would gain only one of the two seats lost by urban northeastern Essex and Hudson counties. The other urban county benefactor was Camden County, located in the southern section. Thirdly, the plan called for a balance in rural county representation by shifting seats in the sea-

---

21 Interview with Mr. Cavicchia, May 11, 1965.

22 The 1950 census figures showed that the three "losing" counties ranked at the bottom of the state in terms of percentage of population gains from 1940; while, the three "gaining" counties ranked as follows: Monmouth, 3rd; Union, 10th; and Camden, 12th. Source: U.S. Bureau of the Census. *U.S. Census of Population*: 1950. Vol. I, *Number of Inhabitants.* Table 5—New Jersey: Area and Population of Counties, Urban and Rural, p. 30–10.

shore area. Monmouth was to gain the seat lost by Atlantic County. Monmouth would then have three assembly seats, while Atlantic County was reduced to one seat.

The three political implications of the Cavicchia Plan had an important bearing on three major strategic considerations. First, Essex County, with 12 assembly votes (representing 20 percent of all potential assembly votes), would have to agree to a single seat loss and cast its votes with the Republican majority to facilitate passage of the plan. Secondly, Atlantic County, with two votes, would have to agree to a 50 percent reduction in representation or seek outside support to block the plan. Thirdly, the Democrats, led by Hudson County, would either have to go along with a Republican-sponsored plan, or oppose a plan that envisaged the loss of a Democratic seat in an assembly where the Democrats were already in a minority. The outcome, to be shown below, was (1) Essex County agreed temporarily to the loss of one seat on the grounds that this was the least possible loss that it could accept; (2) Atlantic County sought to block the plan from consideration in the senate, while mobilizing rural county opposition in the assembly; and (3) the Democrats solidly opposed any plans that reduced Democratic seats and did not give additional representation to Democratic counties.

The Cavicchia Plan was introduced in the assembly by the republican majority leader during the regular 1952 legislative session.[23] Since no action was taken by adjournment, Governor Driscoll considered that it was his constitutional duty to recall the assembly into special session after the November elections and request that a plan be passed.[24] Reapportionment had by this time been delayed for nearly two years since the 1950 census and Driscoll

[23] Source: *Minutes and Proceedings of the One Hundred and Seventy-Sixth General Assembly of the State of New Jersey,* March 21, 1952, p. 438. Hereinafter cited as *NJAM.*

[24] *Ibid.,* December 1, 1952, p. 1196.

thought it necessary to have a plan in effect for the 1954 legislature.[25]

During the three-day special session, Essex and Atlantic County assemblymen were at polar extremes concerning the merits of the Cavicchia Plan. The Essex County delegation gave support to the plan because it produced the least possible loss for Essex. The Essex delegation stated in a joint declaration that it only wanted to retain "that which is justly, lawfully and in good conscience Essex County's rightful representation in the assembly."[26] The two Atlantic County assemblymen firmly opposed the plan because it "emasculated"[27] that county by depriving it of one of its two existing seats.[28] Bolstering the Essex position were arguments made by the "gainers," Camden, Monmouth, and Union counties, all of which urged immediate action. Further delay, they asserted, would result in postponing new representation until 1956.[29] Finally, Hudson County Democrats, speaking for the Democratic minority, stated that they opposed the plan, because the Democrats were not brought into the preliminary discussions in developing the plan.[30]

When the Cavicchia Plan was voted upon, the strategies of the Essex and Atlantic County delegations significantly affected the outcome. Essex, with 12 votes, needed 19 additional votes to pass the plan, which were available if the other urban Republican counties voted as a solid bloc.[31] Atlantic County, with its two votes and the prob-

---

[25] *Ibid.*

[26] Newark *Evening News*, November 30, 1952.

[27] *Ibid.*, December 4, 1952.

[28] Atlantic County had maintained two assembly seats since the 1911 reapportionment. See Chapter II, *Supra*, pp. 56–58.

[29] Newark *Evening News*, December 4, 1952.

[30] *Ibid.*

[31] In effect, the urban Republican bloc had 29 votes and was hoping to attract the support of rural Monmouth (2 votes) which gained a seat under the Cavicchia Plan.

able solid minority party opposition (17 votes), needed 12 outside Republican votes to defeat the plan. These 12 votes were available from the other rural Republican counties. If the rural Republicans combined with the minority Democrats, the urban Republicans would fail to enact the plan.

Cavicchia Plan proponents were unable to form a 31-vote majority. The plan failed to pass the assembly by a single vote in a 30–24 roll-call.[32] What accounted for the failure of this plan when the opportunities for success were certainly available? The major reason for the failure was that the likeness of the rural Republicans and minority Democrats was higher than the likeness of the urban Republicans and the rural Republicans. The urban Republicans alone were unable to present a solidly unified front when one Bergen County assemblyman cast a negative vote and two members, one each from Essex and Union counties, did not appear and register their assent. Both of these absentees supported the same plan when it was reintroduced in 1953. In addition, only the rural Republican votes of Monmouth and Morris counties were cast in favor of the plan, while the remaining six rural Republican counties[33] followed Atlantic County's opposition. Monmouth County assented because it stood to gain a seat, while Morris County was probably moved by a party loyalty appeal. Otherwise, as shown in Table 4.5, the rural Republicans and minority Democrats combined to produce 23 opposition votes. Thus, the urban Republicans, who stood to gain most from the Cavicchia Plan and possessed superior voting power in the assembly, could not unify sufficiently to form a strong enough bloc when the opportunity existed to act.[34]

[32] *NJAM*, 176th, December 3, 1952, pp. 1251–1252.

[33] Burlington, Cape May, Cumberland, Hunterdon, Ocean, and Salem counties.

[34] This finding agrees with urban county voting at the roll-call stage in a study of the Illinois and Missouri State Legislatures. See:

TABLE 4.5. Cavicchia Plan failed to pass assembly by one vote, 1952

County Groups and Party	Yes	No	Not Voting	Party Cohesion	Inter-Group Likeness
Urban Republicans	26	1	2	92.6	
					69.8 (Affirmative)
Rural Republicans	4	8	2	33.3	
					66.7 (Negative)
Minority Democrats	0	15	2	100 (Negative)	
Totals	30	24	6		

Renewed efforts to reapportion in 1953 again revealed significant cleavages in the Republican assembly majority. In contrast to 1952, both the assembly and the senate passed plans. The senate backed the first Equal Proportions plan, while the assembly reintroduced the Cavicchia Plan.

Senator Albert McCay (Republican–Burlington) was the sponsor of the first Equal Proportions Plan.[35] While the plan was allegedly based on "mathematical fairness," it also had distinctive political implications. McCay backed the plan because it resulted in a one seat gain for his home county (Burlington) as well as one seat gains for Camden, Monmouth, and Union counties (which had been included in the Cavicchia Plan). Two seat losses were projected for Essex and Hudson counties, instead of the one seat losses in the Cavicchia Plan. Finally, Atlantic County retained its two seats by not being included in McCay's proposal.

David R. Derge, "Metropolitan and Outstate Alignments in Illinois and Missouri Legislative Delegations," *American Political Science Review,* Vol. 52, No. 4 (December, 1958), p. 1065.

[35] Source: *Journal of the One Hundred and Ninth Senate of the State of New Jersey being the One Hundred and Seventy-Seventh Session of the Legislature,* January 16, 1953, p. 242. Hereinafter cited as *NJSJ.*

The plan was notable for enhancing Republican control of the assembly, which stood at a 43–17 advantage (the same as in 1952) . The two Hudson Democratic seats would go to Republican counties. Also, in contrast to the Cavicchia Plan, three seats were shifted from the urban northeastern to the southern and seashore sections of the state (Burlington, Camden and Monmouth counties). Finally, the two rural counties, Burlington and Monmouth, gained new seats, while no other rural Republican county lost seats.

Both the Essex County senator and the minority Democrats argued against the plan, but their efforts were nullified by the overwhelming voting superiority and solid cohesion of the rural Republicans. The Equal Proportions Plan passed by a 14–6 roll-call vote.[36] The rural Republicans stifled objections raised by Essex County and the minority Democrats. Essex got the support only of Passaic County, while the other urban Republicans from Bergen, Camden, and Union voted in favor. The minority Democrats from Cumberland, Hudson, Mercer, and Middlesex counties were solidly opposed.

Agreement was necessary in the assembly to pass a plan, since the lower house wanted to exercise the decisive voice in settling its own reapportionment problem.[37] Before voting on the senate-passed Equal Proportions Plan, the assembly reconsidered the Cavicchia Plan. When the Cavicchia Plan was reintroduced, it was fully expected that the Essex and Union delegations would now cast all of their 16 votes for the plan. Thus, 15 additional Republican votes were needed to pass the plan. The strategy was simply to maintain the voting cohesion developed in 1952. Fifteen votes were available from the combination of Bergen (6) , Camden (3) , Monmouth (2) , Morris (2) , and

[36] *NJSJ,* 109th, February 16, 1953, p. 242.

[37] See Gilbert Y. Steiner and Samuel K. Gove, *Legislative Politics in Illinois* (Urbana: University of Illinois Press, 1960) , p. 117.

Passaic (4) counties. These calculations allowed for a two-vote defection in the coalition in forming a 31-vote majority.

Cavicchia Plan opponents, again led by Atlantic County, had to split the urban-rural Republican coalition to prevent passage of the plan. This could be done by arguing that the senate had passed an alternative plan that was even more favorable to Republican party interests than the Cavicchia Plan, since it resulted in a two-seat gain for all Republicans. Assuming that Essex County opposed the senate plan, assembly Republicans could form a favorable coalition to pass the senate plan over Essex objections by uniting on rural-urban party lines. The same coalition could isolate Essex County on the Cavicchia Plan.

TABLE 4.6. Projected bloc analysis for Cavicchia Plan and Equal Proportions Plan in general assembly, 1953

Cavicchia Plan Bloc				Equal Proportions Plan Bloc			
Republicans				Republicans			
Urban		Rural		Urban		Rural	
Bergen	(6)	Monmouth	(2)	Bergen	(6)	Atlantic	(2)
Camden	(3)	Morris	(2)	Camden	(3)	Burlington	(1)
Essex	(12)			Passaic	(4)	Cape May	(1)
Passaic	(4)			Union	(4)	Gloucester	(1)
Union	(4)					Hunterdon	(1)
						Monmouth	(2)
Total Votes = 33						Morris	(2)
						Ocean	(1)
						Somerset	(1)
						Salem	(1)
						Cumberland	(1)
				Total Votes = 31			

The Cavicchia Plan was defeated on two separate roll-call votes.[38] The Atlantic County strategy worked: The

[38] Sources: *NJAM,* 177th, February 2, 1953, p. 105; and *Ibid.,* February 16, 1953, pp. 283–284.

urban Republicans, while possessing sufficient votes to pass the plan, divided. Bergen and Union counties split their votes on both roll-calls, while Passaic County changed from support on the first to abstention on the second roll-call.

Table 4.7 indicates the nature of the split among the urban Republican counties. When the urban Republicans did not form a solid voting bloc, they could not pass a reapportionment plan.[39] Solid rural county cohesion was not required in view of the urban county split. The rural Republicans lost the support of Monmouth, Morris, and Somerset counties, but were still an effective anti-bloc by combining with the solidly unified minority Democratic opposition.

TABLE 4.7. Weak urban Republican cohesion leads to double defeat for Cavicchia Plan, 1953

County Groups and Party	First Vote				Second Vote			
	Yes	No	Not Voting	Cohesion	Yes	No	Not Voting	Cohesion
Urban Reps.	24	5	0	65.5	21	3	5	44.8
Rural Reps.	4	9	1	38.5	3	7	4	40.0
Minority Dems.	0	17	0	100	0	13	4	100
Totals	28	31	1		24	23	13	

1. Combined Republican Cohesion=28.4 (Affirmative)
2. Combined rural Republican and minority Democratic likeness = 69.6 (Negative)

With the urban Republicans splitting in support for the Cavicchia Plan, the next alternative available was the senate-passed Equal Proportions Plan. The strategy now was to maintain overall Republican party cohesion in order to overcome the objections expressed by Essex County. However, party discipline was impossible to achieve among all Republicans. Again, the urban Republicans divided in

[39] Derge, *op. cit.*, p. 1065.

both supporting and opposing the senate plan. With the Bergen and Union delegations splitting their votes and Passaic joining Essex in opposing, the Equal Proportions Plan failed to achieve an effective majority in the assembly.[40] Thus, the rural county strategy did not pay off in getting a bloc vote for the Equal Proportions Plan. The same urban Republican division persisted throughout both plans.

TABLE 4.8. Essex Republicans joined with minority to defeat the senate-passed Equal Proportions Plan, 1953

County Groups and Party	First Vote Yes	No	Not Voting	Cohesion	Second Vote Yes	No	Not Voting	Cohesion
Non-Essex Urban Reps.	12	5	0	41.2	9	1	7	5.9
Rural Reps.	13	0	1	84.6	10	0	4	100
Essex County	0	12	0	100	0	12	0	100
Minority Dems.	0	17	0	100	0	14	3	100
Totals	25	34	1		19	27	14	

1. Combined Essex-Democratic Likeness = 100 (Negative)
2. Combined Rural-Non-Essex Urban Republican Cohesion=44.4 (Affirmative)

Neither the Cavicchia Plan nor the Equal Proportions Plan could pass the assembly because the necessary conditions for achieving an effective majority among assembly Republicans were simply not present in 1953. The urban Republicans did not vote as an effective bloc for either plan even though they had the potential votes to pass both plans. The rural Republicans could pass a plan in the sen-

[40] Sources: *NJAM*, 177th, February 2, 1953; and *Ibid.*, February 16, 1953, p. 285.

ate, but could not get enough outside votes to pass the same plan in the assembly. Essex County could therefore block any two-seat loss as long as overall Republican party voting cohesion remained low. The Democrats took an essentially negative position on all Republican-sponsored plans and welcomed the negative votes from Republican counties that rendered Republican plans ineffectual. Republicans began to realize at the end of 1953 that Essex County exercised a veto power over Republican plans. New efforts focused on returning Essex County to Republican ranks so that an effective solution could be found.

Efforts to compromise with Essex County in 1954

The November, 1953 elections resulted in a victory for Democratic Governor Robert B. Meyner, who carried 12 of 21 counties with a 153,642 plurality.[41] Meyner's election, which represented the first breakthrough on Republican control of the governorship in ten years,[42] had only a slight impact on Republican control of the legislature. Four additional Democrats were elected to the assembly, including the three-member Camden County delegation and the Salem representative,[43] while the Sussex County seat switched from Democratic to Republican representation. Thus, the 1954 legislative alignment was 40 Republicans to 20 Democrats in the assembly and 17 Republicans and four Democrats in the senate.

Republican strategists attempted to take into account both the party change in Camden County and the prior Essex County opposition to a two-seat loss by proposing the

---

41 Source: *N.J. Legislative Manual* (1954), p. 638.

42 The last Democratic governor was Charles Edison (1941–1943). He was followed by Walter E. Edge (1944–1946), and Alfred E. Driscoll (1947–1949; 1950–1953).

43 The average assembly vote for the three Camden Democrats (60,818) was closely correlated with Meyner's vote of 68,183. The same was true for Salem county. Source: *N.J. Legislative Manual* (1954), p. 574, 638.

so-called "Arithmetical Eliminations" plan in 1954. During a Republican party strategy conference in April, 1954, Essex County opposition to a two-seat loss by proposing the it was decided that Burlington, Monmouth, and Union counties should each gain one seat, while Essex County would lose one and Hudson County two seats.[44] As with the Equal Proportions Plan of 1953, the new plan would give the Republicans two additional assembly seats, but Essex would be reduced by only one seat. In comparison with the two 1953 plans, the new plan was more heavily weighted toward rural county interests. Union County was the only urban county "gainer," while one southern (Burlington) and one seashore (Monmouth) rural county gained seats. There was also a regional shift in the new plan with the urban northeastern counties giving way to the rural southern and seashore counties. But Republican strategists still felt Essex County was the key, since Essex had supported the loss of one seat in the Cavicchia plans of 1952 and 1953. With 12 favorable Essex votes, the rural Republicans felt they could pass the new plan without difficulty.

Two major developments resulted when the Arithmetical Eliminations Plan was introduced in the senate.[45] First, the senate majority leader, Bruce A. Wallace, a Republican representing Camden County, objected to the plan because it did not include an additional seat for Camden.[46] Other Republican leaders argued that Camden County should not gain a new seat since the first major consideration was to devise a plan that "rewarded" Republican counties only.[47] Senator Wallace thereupon made

---

44 Newark *Evening News,* April 10, 1954.

45 By Senator Kenneth C. Hand (Republican–Union) on April 12, 1954. Source: Newark *Evening News,* April 13, 1954.

46 Both the Cavicchia Plan and the Equal Proportions Plan had included one-seat gains for Camden County, when the Camden Assembly delegation was Republican.

47 Newark *Evening News,* April 10, 1954.

every effort to delay a floor vote on the Arithmetical Eliminations Plan in the senate.[48]

The second major development focused on gaining the support of the Essex County delegation for the new plan. The crucial question for Republican legislative leaders was: Would Essex County agree to a "compromise" initiated by other Republican leaders? Essex Senator Mark Anton answered this question with a loud "no." According to Senator Anton, the Essex County position was now as follows: "Now we should recognize the increasing population of counties *without depriving* any county of its existing membership."[49] (Emphasis added) Anton proposed that the state constitution be amended to increase the size of the assembly from 60 to 67 members.[50] By doing this, 14 counties would retain their existing representation, while seven counties, including Essex, would each gain a new seat.[51] Since five of the seven "gaining" counties were urban, the net effect of Anton's plan was to increase the assembly voting power of the urban counties at the expense of the rural counties.[52]

Senate Republicans viewed Anton's proposal simply as a statement of Essex policy on reapportionment without consideration as a serious alternative. The plan was quickly buried in the senate judiciary committee.[53] Republican

---

[48] Newark *Evening News,* May 11, 1954. Wallace came out flatly for the Equal Proportions Plan of 1953, which gave Camden County a new seat and reduced Essex County by two seats.

[49] Newark *Evening News,* February 14, 1954.

[50] *Ibid.* Unlike the Cavicchia Plan, the Equal Proportions Plan, and the Arithmetical Eliminations Plan, Anton's proposal did not include a mathematical formula for reapportionment.

[51] The other six "gainers" were Bergen, Burlington, Camden, Middlesex, Monmouth, and Union counties.

[52] Also, since five of the "gainers" were Republican in 1954, the Republicans would gain a net total of three seats.

[53] Newark *Evening News,* May 16, 1954.

leaders reconvened for another strategy conference and decided to override Majority Leader Wallace's delaying tactics and vote on the Arithmetical Eliminations plan.[54] In a 14–6 roll-call, 11 rural Republicans joined with urban Republicans from Bergen, Passaic, and Union counties to pass the plan.[55] The supposed "compromise" for Essex County failed as the Essex and Camden Republicans joined with four minority Democrats in opposition.

The Essex County position remained consistent in the assembly. With the Republican majority reduced to 40 members (as a result of the change in the Camden delegation), Essex County now had sufficient votes to reduce the Republican majority to 28 by casting its 12 votes with the minority Democrats. Any tactical maneuvering by assembly Republicans would therefore have to focus on attracting three outside Democratic votes to reach the required 31 votes needed for a majority. This failed and the plan lost on a roll-call vote of 19–28.[56] Essex County simply cast its 12 votes with the minority Democrats to defeat the plan. Republicans favoring the plan did not cast all available 28 votes. The conclusion is that no unified position existed to Essex County opposition.

As shown in Table 4.9, reapportionment actions in 1954 were an exercise in futility. The Senate Republicans had voting power to overcome Essex resistance, while the same rural Republicans could not overcome Essex bloc opposition in the assembly. Two alternatives to rectify this situation were either (1) seek a new "compromise" with Essex County; or (2) develop a plan to attract three outside Democratic votes, in assuming that the remaining 28 assembly Republicans would vote as a solid unit in a direct confrontation with Essex county.

---

54 *Ibid.*, April 23, 1954.
55 *NJSJ*, 110th, May 24, 1954, pp. 545–546.
56 *NJAM*, 178th, June 21, 1954, p. 914.

TABLE 4.9. Rural Republicans could pass Arithmetical Elimination Plan in senate while Essex County defeated plan in assembly, 1954

County Groups and Party	Senate				General Assembly			
	Yes	No	Not Voting	Cohesion	Yes	No	Not Voting	Cohesion
Rural Reps	11	0	1	100	9	0	5	63.6
Non-Essex Urban Reps.	3	1	0	50	9	0	5	100
Essex County	0	1	0	100	0	11	1	100
Minority Dems.	0	4	0	100	1	17	2	89.5
Totals	14	6	1		19	28	13	

1. Combined Rural-Non-Essex Cohesion = 80.
2. Combined Essex-Democrat-Cohesion = 93.3

Republican attempt to lure Camden County Democrats, 1955

Two reapportionment efforts were made in 1955. First, the Republican assembly leadership tested the ability of Assemblyman William O. Barnes (Republican—Essex), the newly elected majority leader, to exert influence within the Essex delegation to gain at least three affirmative votes for the Arithmetical Elimination Plan.[57] If Barnes were successful there would be no reason for developing a new plan that cut across party lines to overcome Essex County objections.

Barnes met with the Essex delegation but encountered resistance. Not only could he not change any votes, but

[57] Newark *Evening News,* January 22, 1955.

Barnes himself was convinced not to support the plan.[58] The majority leader then agreed to permit a vote on the plan. If a majority of the Republicans supported it, he would also vote affirmatively as an expression of party loyalty. However, as an Essex assemblyman, he would argue against the plan. The schizophrenic position of Mr. Barnes was readily understandable in view of the different pressures placed on an individual in a legislative leadership capacity.[59] Barnes had to show divided loyalties or else face strong opposition from Essex County on other equally important matters of legislative business.

The Republicans decided to take another roll-call vote on the Arithmetical Eliminations Plan even though the Essex position was known in advance. By a vote of 24–29,[60] the plan was defeated in the same manner as 1954: Essex County joined with the Democrats in opposition to the remaining assembly Republicans. Rural Republican cohesion increased to 85.7 over the 1954 cohesion of 63.6, but Passaic County still refused to support the plan and cast its urban votes with Essex in opposition along with the solid bloc vote of the minority Democrats.

Not only had Majority Leader Barnes failed to change any Essex votes for the Arithmetical Eliminations Plan, but he also encountered a challenge to his leadership within the Essex delegation. J. Peter Lassans, speaking for the Essex delegation, stated that support would be given to the Hudson Democrats in opposing seat losses.[61] This marked the formal tie of Essex and Hudson counties as an anti-reapportionment bloc. The Essex-Hudson alliance was formidable, since together they controlled 21 votes, representing 35 percent of all assembly votes. Also, with

58 *Ibid.*

59 See John C. Wahlke, *et al., The Legislative System* (New York: John Wiley and Sons, Inc., 1962), pp. 191–192; 384–385.

60 *NJAM,* 179th, January 17, 1955, p. 77.

61 Newark *Evening News,* January 16, 1955.

the majority Democrats voting as a solid bloc of 20 votes, the Essex-Hudson tie represented in effect 53.3 percent or a majority in opposition to other Republican plans.

The Republicans held another strategy conference during which they decided to lure the three votes of the Camden County Democrats through a reintroduced Equal Proportions Plan.[62] This was the same plan that lost in 1953 under which two seats were taken from both Essex and Hudson counties with a four seat distribution to Burlington, Camden, Monmouth, and Union counties. The Republicans had decided to offer a plan that cut across party lines in order to overcome Essex objections. The Republicans were convinced that Camden County could not afford to turn down this offer.[63]

The Republican party state chairman, Samuel L. Bodine, made a personal telephone call to Camden County's Democratic chairman, George E. Brunner, urging him to accept the plan. [64] Obviously, the Camden Democrats faced a dilemma. The problem was twofold: Camden could accept the seat to bolster its own position, while the Republicans were gaining an additional seat; or, Camden could refuse the offer by arguing that it was not truly bipartisan. The Democrats should not assist the Republicans when they held substantial voting pluralities in both chambers.[65] The plan was a trap to lure Camden County away from the solid front of Democratic party opposition to all Republican plans.

The Camden Democrats pursued the second course of action outlined above. They refused the Republican "deal" on the grounds that the Cavicchia Plan of 1952 and 1953 was more favorable.[66] This plan gave the Hudson Demo-

---

[62] Newark *Evening News,* January 22, 1955.
[63] *Ibid.*
[64] *Ibid.,* January 27, 1955.
[65] Newark *Evening News,* January 30, 1955.
[66] *Ibid.*

cratic seat loss to Camden, while Atlantic County also had to relinquish a seat to Monmouth County (as well as Essex County losing a seat to Union County). Camden County indeed wanted a seating gain, but it did not favor a plan that increased Republican voting strength.

The reintroduced Equal Proportions Plan therefore failed to attain the necessary 31 votes for passage and was defeated in a 27–32 roll-call.[67] The Democrats and Essex Republicans lined up against the remaining assembly Republicans. Thus, the Essex-Democratic coalition was a

TABLE 4.10. Alignment of assembly voting blocs emphasizes Reapportionment deadlock, 1955

Affirmative Bloc Republicans		Negative Bloc	
Gaining Counties	Stationary Counties	Gaining Democrats	Losing Counties Republicans
Burlington (1)	Atlantic (2)	Camden (3)	Essex (12)
Monmouth (2)	Bergen (6)		
Union (4)	Cape May (1)		*Dem.*
	Cumberland (1)		Hudson (9)
	Gloucester (1)		
	Hunterdon (1)	*Stationary Dem.*	
	Morris (2)	Mercer (3)	
	Ocean (1)	Middlesex (3)	
	Passaic (4)	Salem (1)	
	Somerset (1)	Warren (1)	
	Sussex (1)		
Total Votes = 28		Total Votes = 32	
1. Arithmetical Eliminations Plan Voting Cohesion = 80 Affirmative		1. Arithmetical Eliminations Plan Voting Cohesion = 93.3 Negative	
2. Equal Proportions Plan Voting Cohesion = 92.8 Affirmative		2. Equal Proportions Plan Voting Cohesion = 100 Negative	

[67] *NJAM*, 179th, January 31, 1955, p. 147.

major force in nullifying any attempts to change the *status quo*. The reapportionment problem had now reached the stage of hopeless deadlock.

Senate Republicans focus on Equal Proportions Plans, 1956–1957

With the assembly hopelessly deadlocked on the apportionment issue, the senate focused attention on Equal Proportions Plans based on a new objective: Instead of reapportioning on the basis of the 1950 census, the problem should be solved after the 1960 census. The strategic consideration, as viewed by Senator Albert McCay (Republican–Burlington), was to "let the chips fall where they may."[68] The argument was that no one could accurately predict the precise outcome of a plan based on the 1960 census. However, based on the proposed four-seat shift under previous Equal Proportions plans (that is, Essex and Hudson counties relinquishing four seats to Burlington, Camden, Monmouth, and Union Counties), Senator James F. Murray considered the Republican actions as "politically punitive" against Essex and Hudson counties. Furthermore, the Essex County assembly delegation stated that it only supported a plan that would "apply to all counties equally and not give a political advantage to one group of counties over another."[70]

No efforts were made to bring either the Hudson Democrats or the Essex Republicans in on the design of the new plan. Senate Republicans assumed, apparently, that the two counties would not object to an impartial plan as long as the Republicans defined "fairness" in the plan. "Fairness" included the following elements: (1) No changes

[68] Newark *Evening News*, May 29, 1956.
[69] *Ibid.*, January 31, 1956.
[70] *Ibid.*, February 7, 1956.

until the 1960 census: (2) Making reapportionment "automatic" by delegating responsibility to the secretary of state or some other administrative official, who would put into effect a plan based on a mathematical formula designated by the legislature. Senate Republicans were convinced that reapportionment had to be removed from the realm of partisan controversy to prevent a replication of the existing problem in the future. Thus, in reality, the "chips falling" strategy involved legislative delay until 1960 and delegation to "objective" determination.[71]

During 1956 and 1957, the Senate Republicans passed three variations of Equal Proportions Plans on five separate occasions. The variations were: (1) Reapportioning immediately and applying the same formula to the 1960 census;[72] (2) Retaining the present apportionment, but instituting an automatic system after the 1960 census; [73] and (3) Amending the state constitution in order to make Equal Proportions mandatory after the 1960 census.[74] The primary sponsors of these plans were Senators Kenneth C. Hand (Republican–Union) and his successor, Robert C.

[71] See, for example, Robert C. Wood, *Suburbia* (Boston: Houghton Mifflin Co., 1958), pp. 153–161.

[72] See Senate Bill 5 (1956) and Senate Concurrent Resolution 31 (1957).

[73] See Senate Bills 74 (1956) and 32 (1957).

[74] See Senate Concurrent Resolution 23 (1957). Public hearings were held in 1957 by the Senate Judiciary Committee on Senate Concurrent Resolution 23. At these hearings, members of the Rutgers University Bureau of Government Research testified in favor of a plan which called for automatic Assembly reapportionment by the Equal Proportions method following the 1960 census. In addition, the Executive Vice-President of the State CIO Council, Mr. Joel R. Jacobson, was opposed to S.C.R. 23. The labor union representative argued for a system of assembly districts which would cut across county lines and provide fairer representation to the people of the state. See: Senate Judiciary Committee, *Public hearings on Senate Concurrent Resolutions Nos. 22 and 23*, May 22, 1957, p. 34, and "Statement by Bureau of Government Research, Rutgers –State University," pp. 12–13.

Crane (Republican–Union). Naturally, Union County expected to gain a new seat under every proposed variation.

Senate Republican voting cohesion, as shown in Table 4.11 below, was remarkably high on all five roll-calls. Only two abstaining (and negative) Republican votes were recorded among 53 votes cast for a combined cohesion of 92.8. The Democrats solidly opposed all five variations.[75]

TABLE 4.11. Senate voting cohesion on Equal Proportions Plans, 1956–1957

County Groups and Party	Equal Proportions 1950 Census Two Votes[a]			Equal Proportions 1960 Census Three Votes[b]			
	Yes	No	Cohesion	Yes	No	Not Voting	Cohesion
Rural Reps.	20	0	100	30	0	3	93.6
Urban Reps.	6	0	100	7	0	2	75
Minority Dems.	0	14	100	0	11	10	100
Totals	26	14		37	11	15	

a. Votes on S. 5 and S. 31.
b. Votes on S. 74 S. 32, and SCR 23.

Assembly response to senate-passed Equal Proportions Plans was delayed until a special legislative session in December, 1957. By this time, the assembly Republicans were attempting to act after the November elections had produced a dramatic shift of 22 seats from Republicans to

[75] The votes were as follows:
S. 5 (1956) 14 yea, 5 nay, 2 abstain
S. 31 (1957) 12 yea, 7 nay, 2 absent
S. 74 (1956) 12 yea, 1 nay, 7 abstain, 1 absent
S. 32 (1957) 12 yea, 7 nay, 2 absent
SCR 23 (1957) 13 yea, 3 nay, 5 abstain
Sources: *NJSJ*, 112th, February 6, 1956, p. 92 for S. 5; *Ibid.*, 113th, January 28, 1957, p. 124 for S. 31; *Ibid.*, 112th, May 8, 1956, p. 657 for S. 74; *Ibid.*, 113th, January 28, 1957, p. 129 for S. 32; and *Ibid.*, June 12, 1957, p. 646 for SCR 23.

Democrats.[76] The 1958 assembly would be controlled by the Democrats for the first time since 1937. Under these conditions, it might have been expected that the Essex Republicans (who were to be replaced by 12 Democrats in 1958) would support Senator Crane's constitutional amendment establishing an automatic Equal Proportions system after the 1960 census.[77] However, this was not the case. Essex County Republicans still opposed two-seat losses under any plan and continued to vote with the minority Democrats to defeat it. County self-interest was also evident in the vote of the Union delegation, which was changing from Republican to Democratic in 1958. Union Republicans supported Crane's amendment. Table 4.12 shows that the county delegation voting positions remained consistent even with a change in party affiliation imminent.[78]

Observations on the reapportionment deadlock, 1952–1957

The year 1957 marked the end of the first phase of the reapportionment struggle, a period of Republican party control of both the senate and the general assembly. Republicans, while continually passing plans in the senate, could not find an effective 31-vote majority in the assembly. The major difficulty in the assembly was overcoming the negative position of Republican delegations which sup-

---

[76] Democratic party successes in the assembly were directly attributable to Governor Meyner's re-election. The 22 seats gained by the Democrats were: Cumberland (1), Passaic (4), Essex (12), Gloucester (1) and Union (4).

[77] The vote was on Senate Concurrent Resolution 23. See p. 156, *Supra,* footnote 75.

[78] County self-interest is a predominant theme in state legislative reapportionment. See, for example, Royce Hanson, *The Political Thicket* (Englewood Cliffs, New Jersey: Prentice-Hall, Inc., 1966), pp. 35–36.

TABLE 4.12. Essex Republicans joined with Democrats to defeat Equal Proportions Plan based on 1960 Census[79]

County Groups	Yes	No	Not Voting	Cohesion	Combined Cohesion
Rural Republicans	8	0	6	77.8	
					76.5
Urban Republicans Minus Essex	7	0	5	55.5	
Essex Republicans	0	12	0	100	
					100
Minority Democrats	0	12	8	100	
Totals	15	24	19		

ported a retention of the *status quo*.[80] Essex Republicans, controlling 20 percent of all potential assembly votes, sided with the Democrats in opposing losses of two seats. Essex recalcitrance was the most visible aspect of the deadlock and stifled opportunities for change, especially under the Equal Proportions and Arithmetical Eliminations Plans. Rural county determination to maintain the *status quo* was evident in the thrice-defeated Cavicchia Plan, where Atlantic County led the rural Republicans to defeat the proposal.

When the majority party tried to surmount Essex County obstructionism, they were not successful. The so-called "bipartisan" approach of 1955 failed because Cam-

[79] Source: *NJAM*, 181st, December 9, 1957, p. 1025.

[80] See Hanson, *op. cit.*, p. 35, who states: "Rural desperation, an urban member's hypocrisy, and the eternal problem of securing the required majority of votes to pass the new arrangement provide the basis for what appear to be the unwritten rules of legislative reapportionment. As such, the factors mentioned above help explain the lack of substantial change which has contributed almost as much to the decline of representative government as has the outright failure of the legislature to act on reapportionment."

den Democrats were not convinced to break minority party ranks and join the majority party. The essential difficulty with the 1955 plan was that the minority Democrats, as with all other plans in both chambers, were never once brought into the preliminary discussions in developing plans. The majority party sought a solution, but on their own terms. The minority party therefore solidly opposed all majority party plans.

While Essex blocked two proposals, it could not at the same time develop an effective voting bloc to enact the Cavicchia Plan in 1952 and 1953. The urban Republican delegations were seriously divided in sentiment for this plan. There was no evidence of strong bloc leadership to mobilize effective voting power among the urban Republicans. These counties were therefore far more effective in preventing action than in mobilizing support for change.[81]

Rural-urban differences also contributed to legislative inaction. In the senate, the rural Republicans, with a numerical majority, easily passed plans without requiring the assistance of their urban counterparts or the minority Democrats. But a strong rural Republican bloc vote in the assembly was not enough to pass the same plan, the Equal Proportions Plan. Without affirmative legislative leadership, the Essex Republicans broke party ranks and joined forces with the Hudson Democrats. Hudson was able to maintain a solid opposition bloc vote among the other minority Democrats. Under these conditions, as long as Essex voted with the Democrats, no plan could pass the assembly. The Essex-Hudson bloc was more effective in opposition because neither the remaining urban Republicans nor the rural Republicans voted with high cohesion to show a united front to Essex-Hudson resistance.

---

[81] See Key, *op. cit.*, pp. 74–84.

By the end of 1957 it was evident that no plan could pass unless a bipartisan approach was adopted. Such a plan would require the prior approval of the counties that were to lose seats, both Democrats and Republicans.

Increasing the size of the assembly to 67

Senator Robert C. Crane (Republican–Union) continued to sponsor Equal Proportions variations through 1958 and 1959 even though the Democrats had taken control of the assembly and the Union delegation was now Democratic. Crane added a new feature to Equal Proportions in 1958. He proposed that the size of the assembly be increased from 60 to 67 members so that the Equal Proportions formula would not reduce any existing county delegations after the 1960 census.[82] Crane was attempting to overcome the objections of Essex and Hudson.[83] However, Crane ran into opposition within the ranks of the senate Republicans. The rural counties argued against increasing the size of the assembly. They did not want the voting power of the urban counties increased and they foresaw both perpetuation of Democratic party control and endless changes in total assembly membership. Crane's plan was

[82] Senate Concurrent Resolution 13 introduced on February 17, 1958. The plan retained all of the existing Essex and Hudson seats and added seats for Bergen, Burlington, Camden, Middlesex, Monmouth, Passaic, and Union counties. Public hearings were held on Senator Crane's proposals in 1958. At the hearings, Dr. Stanley H. Friedelbaum, representing the Rutgers University Bureau of Government Research, testified in favor of using the Equal Proportions method for reapportioning the assembly. The Bureau supported both of Crane's bills. The most important considerations, in Dr. Friedelbaum's view, were that the Equal Proportions method be adopted in future apportionments and that the responsibility for reapportionment be given to a designated ministerial officer. See: Senate Committee on Revision and Amendment of Laws, *Public hearings on Senate Concurrent Resolutions Nos. 9 and 13,* March 19, 1958, pp. 11–12.

[83] Newark *Evening News,* February 22, 1958.

never voted out of the senate caucus. Instead the rural Republicans again passed a "straight" Equal Proportions Plan by a vote of 12–0.[84] Seven Democrats registered their objections by abstaining. The same situation persisted in 1959. Again the senate Republicans passed an Equal Proportions Plan[85] and the assembly Democrats refused to take action.

It was obvious by the end of 1959 that any apportionment solution would have to be based on the 1960 census. Also, the Democrats would have to participate in designing the new plan. The keys to finding a solution rested with the Democratic party leadership and the positions of Essex and Hudson counties.

Forces for reapportionment begin to mobilize

Three significant developments occurred in 1960. First, the estimated census figures for 1960 indicated that a six-seating shift (rather than a four-seat change under the 1950 census) would be required under an Equal Proportions Plan.[86] Essex and Hudson counties, having the least population gains since 1950, would have to yield three seats each to Bergen, Burlington, Camden, Middlesex, Monmouth, and Union counties.[87] Second, the November, 1959 elections resulted in an eight-seat gain for the assembly Republicans. Ten assembly seats changed after these elections, with the Republicans gaining in Essex (seven seats), Gloucester (one seat), and Union (one seat), while the Democrats gained the Burlington County seat.[88] Thus, the 1960 assembly lineup stood at 34 Democrats and 26 Repub-

---

[84] *NJSJ*, 114th, June 9, 1958, pp. 685–686.

[85] *Ibid.*, 115th, April 13, 1959, p. 424. The vote was 13 Republicans against 6 Democrats.

[86] Newark *Evening News*, February 9, 1960.

[87] *Ibid.*

[88] *N.J. Legislative Manual* (1960), pp. 614–684.

licans. The effects of the new Equal Proportions Plan on the census projections and the political composition of the assembly were as follows: Essex and Hudson, the two largest assembly delegations would be yielding seats to four urban and two rural counties. Bergen County (urban northeastern), a Republican stronghold,[89] would replace Hudson County as the second largest delegation with seven seats. Four seats would be shifted from the urban northeast to the central (Middlesex–Democratic), southern (Burlington and Camden, both Democratic), and seashore (Monmouth–Republican) counties. In assuming that the existing party affiliations of the eight counties would remain the same in 1961, the six seat shift would result in three gains for Democratic counties, two gains for Republican counties, and an uncertain result for one county.

TABLE 4.13. Effects of an Equal Proportions Plan based on the 1960 census projections

Gaining Counties			Losing Counties
Bergen	(Republican)	Urban	Essex (7 Rep.–5 Dem.)
Union	(Competitive)	Northeastern	Hudson (Democrat)
Middlesex	(Democrat)	Urban Central	Urban Northeastern
Burlington	(Democrat)	Rural Southern	
Camden	(Democrat)	Urban Southern	
Monmouth	(Republican)	Rural Seashore	
Total = Gain 6 Seats			Total = Loss 6 Seats

The third major development of 1960 centered on Governor Meyner's attempts to block the selections of LeRoy J. D'Aloia (Democrat–Essex) and Maurice V. Brady (Democrat–Hudson) as assembly majority leader and speaker, respectively. Meyner argued that Essex and Hudson coun-

[89] Prior to 1960, Bergen county had solid Republican delegations for 44 consecutive years.

ties should not continue to monopolize the legislative leadership positions when they were certain to oppose reapportionment. Meyner was convinced that Essex and Hudson must lose seats under a "fair" plan, the Equal Proportions proposal.[90] The "big county bosses," Dennis F. Carey (Essex) and John V. Kenny (Hudson), would not permit this through their direct control over Essex and Hudson assemblymen.[91]

The reaction to Meyner's attempts to intervene in the selection of assembly leadership prompted an anti-Meyner urban northeastern coalition consisting of the 20 votes of Essex (7), Hudson (9), and Passaic (4) counties. These three county delegations forced the selections of D'Aloia and Brady.[92]

Passaic County, led by Senator Anthony J. Grossi, apparently had second thoughts about supporting Essex and Hudson counties in the reapportionment fight. Even though the Passaic County delegation had insisted that the governor should not intervene in the selection of assembly leaders, it wanted to be free of the influence of Essex and Hudson counties in deciding the apportionment dispute,[93] Senator Grossi therefore instructed the two Passaic Democrats on the assembly judiciary committee to vote for an Equal Proportions Plan based on the 1960 census. The two Passaic votes added to those of Republican assemblymen from Atlantic and Monmouth counties produced a 4–2 majority over the objections of the Essex and Hudson committee members.[94]

The Passaic bolt had an immediate impact on the Essex-

---

[90] Interview with Governor Meyner, May 12, 1965.

[91] *Ibid.*

[92] Newark *Evening News*, February 9, 1960.

[93] Newark *Evening News*, February 9, 1960. Passaic county did not gain a seat under the reapportionment plan. The major consideration was focused on Passaic's independence from Essex-Hudson control.

[94] *Ibid.*

Hudson leadership team. Under assembly rules, the speaker was obligated to permit the full assembly to vote on committee-reported bills.[95] If this were done, Passaic County with its four votes could cross party lines and, together with one additional anti-Essex-Hudson Democrat, assist the minority Republicans in passing an Equal Proportions Plan.

The Essex-Hudson bloc therefore decided on a strategy under which the full assembly would be prevented from voting. First, Speaker Brady employed stalling tactics. He argued that the assembly should vote on several alternative plans and make a choice among them.[96] However, this was clearly impossible since the Essex-Hudson bloc now made certain that no additional reapportionment bills would be reported out of committee. With the pressure mounting for an assembly vote, Brady then shifted to a second tactic: He resorted to outright obstruction. The maneuver was to appeal for Democratic party loyalty in supporting the prerogative of the assembly speaker to permit floor votes.[97]

The Republicans made two assaults on Brady's position. The first effort was to show the Democrats that the speaker was preventing them from voting on a bill that most Republicans and Democrats favored. On March 21, Assemblyman Alfred N. Beadleston (Republican–Monmouth) attempted to test Brady's control. He moved for a floor vote, but Brady ruled him out of order. Beadleston then requested to speak on a point of personal privilege and charged Brady with "gagging" discussion on the bill.[98] Then Assemblyman William V. Evans (Republican-Bergen) tested Brady's ruling by requesting to speak because the "integrity of the body" was involved in preventing an assembly vote.[99] Brady also ruled Evans out of

[95] *Ibid.*

[96] Newark *Evening News,* February 12, 1960.

[97] *Ibid.,* February 22, 1960.

[98] *Ibid.*

[99] Newark *Evening News,* March 22, 1960.

order. Evans appealed to the assembly to overrule Brady, but the speaker was sustained by a 33–21 roll-call vote.[100] With the exception of one Democrat from Union County, this was a straight party line vote. The Democrats lined up in support of Brady while the Republicans unanimously voted against the speaker.[101]

Realizing that many Democrats wanted action, the Essex-Hudson leaders proposed that a vote be taken on the 67-member plan, a proposal that was not unfavorable to Essex-Hudson interests.[102] But the 67–member plan required a two-thirds assembly majority since it was a proposed constitutional amendment. The plan seemed impossible to pass because of two reasons: The senate rural Republicans were firmly opposed to increasing assembly membership and the assembly itself had yet to form even a 31-vote majority in eight years of prior efforts to reapportion.

While Essex and Hudson were considering a floor vote on the 67-member plan, the assembly Republicans made a second effort to get a vote on the Equal Proportions Plan. On April 4, Minority Leader Pierce Deamer (Republican–Bergen) tried to push through a rules change to permit immediate assembly consideration of all committee-reported bills if the sponsors requested a floor vote.[103] However, this maneuver failed when the Democrats lined lined up solidly with Speaker Brady and, along with the

---

100 *NJAM,* 184th, March 21, 1960, pp. 373–374.

101 *Ibid.* One Republican was absent (Bate of Essex) and five abstained. An abstention on this crucial roll-call was certainly evidence of opposition to Speaker Brady.

102 Newark *Evening News,* April 5, 1960.

103 *NJAM,* 184th, April 4, 1960, p. 479. Deamer's proposal read in part: "Any bill, joint resolution or concurrent resolution, which is ready for third reading in this House, shall be placed upon the calendar forthwith by the Speaker upon the request made in open meeting of the sponsor . . . and any bill . . . so placed upon the calendar shall be continued upon the calendar from day to day until acted upon."

seven abstentions of the Essex Republicans, Deamer's proposal lost by a 30–18 roll-call vote.[104]

The Democratic party speaker won both encounters with the Republicans because the majority party maintained loyalty to their titular assembly leader. Brady next moved toward his third victory of the 1960 session: He permitted a vote on the 67-member plan, knowing full well that the plan would fall short of the necessary two-thirds majority of all members. The Hudson delegation would make certain of this result by refusing to vote for the plan.[105]

The 67-member plan passed by a vote of 36–15 with seven abstentions and two absences.[106] As shown in Table 4.14, 40 affirmative votes were not possible as long as the Hudson Democrats and most of the rural Republicans withheld approval. With a 34–26 advantage, the Democrats needed either a solid party vote and six Republican votes (which were available from the Essex delegation) ; or, with Hudson opposition, a bipartisan vote consisting of 25 Democrats and 15 Republicans. But to get 15 Republican votes the urban and rural Republicans had to agree on increasing the size of the assembly. The rural Republicans had consistently refused to consider this as an acceptable alternative. Therefore, Speaker Brady knew in advance that the 67-member plan could not get the required two-thirds majority. The combined opposition of the Hudson Democrats and the rural Republicans resulted in a four-vote deficit. Even though the assembly passed the first apportionment plan since 1941, its action was in fact an exercise in carefully preconceived legislative futility.

1960 was a pivotal year in the apportionment struggle. Assembly actions were affected by three key developments:

---

[104] *Ibid.*

[105] Newark *Evening News,* May 10, 1960.

[106] *NJAM,* 184th, May 9, 1960, pp. 705–706. The abstentions were recorded in Hudson County; the absences in Hudson and Cumberland counties.

TABLE 4.14. Hudson Democrats and Rural Republicans combined to prevent formation of a two-thirds majority on 67-member plan

County Groups and Party	Yes	No	Not Voting	Cohesion	Inter-Group Likeness
Essex Dems.	5	0	0	100	
Other Urban Dems. Minus Hudson	16	0	0	100	100 Affirmative
Rural Dems.	3	0	1	100	
Essex Reps.	7	0	0	100	
Other Urban Reps.	2	5	0	42.8	
Rural Reps.	2	10	0	66.7	88.1 Negative
Hudson Dems.	1	0	8	75.0	
Totals	36	15	9		

(1) The split between Governor Meyner and the county leaders of Essex and Hudson over the selections of assembly leaders; (2) The growing dissatisfaction of both Democrats and Republicans to Essex-Hudson opposition evidenced by the Passaic County bolt; and (3) The realization by both Democrats and Republicans that further inaction was intolerable. Twenty years had passed since the assembly was last reapportioned. A number of counties had gained population but did not have fair representation. Further efforts would have to focus on breaking the Essex-Hudson bloc through developing a bipartisan solution to the problem.

A reapportionment solution is found, 1961

Governor Meyner emphasized the necessity for breaking the deadlock in his message to the legislature in January, 1961, by stating, in part:[107]

[107] Source, *NJAM*, 185th, January 10, 1961, pp. 16–17.

"One item on the 1961 legislative agenda stands out above all others—fair representation of the people. Our population is nearly 2,000,000 greater than it was when the General Assembly seats were last apportioned twenty years ago . . . This year, the parties share control of the State Government . . . I urge you to use this opportunity to reach a bipartisan solution on reapportionment in 1961."

If the legislature did not act, Meyner was aware of the possibility of a court-ordered reapportionment. In 1958, the owner and publisher of the Asbury Park *Press* (Monmouth County) had filed a court suit to force the legislature to reapportion on the basis of the 1950 census.[108] The superior court refused to decide the issue and stated that the matter was solely a legislative responsibility.[109] The *Press* had then appealed to the state supreme court, which decided the case on June 7, 1960.[110]

The decision by the state court represented an historic prelude to the landmark case of *Baker v. Carr,*[111] decided by the United States Supreme Court in 1962. In a unanimous opinion, the state court held that it could review constitutional questions arising under legislative apportionment. The court had the right to guarantee equal protection of the laws to New Jersey citizens when they were denied proper representation in the assembly. In effect, equal protection was denied when the full value of a cit-

108 Asbury Park *Press,* August 26, 1958.

109 *Asbury Park Press, Inc. v. J. Russell Woolley.* Appendix to Brief for Appellants. *New Jersey Supreme Court Briefs,* Vol. 570 (1959–1960), Decided March 26, 1959.

110 In the case of *Asbury Park Press, Inc. v. Woolley,* 33 N.J. 1.

111 369 U.S. 186 (1962). Both the *Asbury* and *Baker* decisions represented a departure from Justice Frankfurter's position that the Courts should not enter the political thicket of reapportionment. In Frankfurter's view, apportionment questions should be decided by legislatures and not the courts. See: *Colegrove v. Green,* 328 U.S. 549 (1946).

izen's vote was not reflected in the number of representatives he could elect:[112]

> Inaction which causes an apportionment act to have unequal and arbitary effects throughout the State is just as much a denial of equality as if a positive statute had been passed to accomplish the result. In our view, such deprivation not only offends against the *State Constitution* but may very well deny equal protection of the laws in violation of the *Fourteenth Amendment of the United States Constitution.*[113]

The court rejected the defendants' claim that it lacked jurisdiction. When the legislature refused to act, it was the duty of the court to guarantee a remedy. The court had the power to design remedies in its role as constitutional guardian.[114] Such remedies did not violate the separation of powers between the legislative and judicial branches of state government.[115]

Finally, the court held that the legislature should assume its proper responsibilities to reapportion in 1961 on the basis of the 1960 census figures for New Jersey counties.[116] The court would not design an apportionment plan at the present time, nor would it specify that remedies were available to end the legislative deadlock.[117] Instead, the court retained jurisdiction over the matter until the legislature tried again in 1961 to enact its own reapportionment plan.[118]

---

112 This later became known as the "one man, one vote" principle. See: *Reynolds v. Sims,* 377 U.S. 533 (1964) and *Jackman v. Bodine,* 43 N.J. 453 (1964). Also, see Chapter V, below.

113 33 N.J. 11 (1960)

114 *Ibid.,* p. 12.

115 *Ibid.,* p. 14.

116 *Ibid.,* p. 19.

117 *Ibid.*

118 *Ibid.,* p. 21. By retaining jurisdiction, the court was reserving the right to review legislative intentions to reapportion before the 1961 primary elections. In effect, a new limiting condition was

In meeting the court's demand for action, Meyner and the assembly Democrats were still confronted with the Essex-Hudson opposition. LeRoy J. D'Aloia (Democrat—Essex) had succeeded Brady as assembly speaker. D'Aloia was opposed to all solutions except the 67-member plan, which had not passed both chambers in 1960.[119] The speaker made certain that no proposals would be voted out of assembly committees by referring all bills to the Essex-Hudson packed labor and industrial committee.[120] Furthermore, D'Aloia argued that no floor votes would be taken unless the Democratic caucus favored such action. By controlling the caucus procedures, the speaker could overrule any new proposals. Thus Speaker D'Aloia appeared to hold all the strings and continued to exercise the same obstructionist tactics as his predecessor, Brady of Hudson County.

D'Aloia was unmoved by the pressures of Governor Meyner and the state supreme court, which now stated that the deadline for a court-imposed solution was February 1.[121] The speaker reacted to the demands for action by employing the negative tactic of recessing the assembly on January 30 after the senate had passed an Equal Proportions Plan by a vote of 17–0.[122] While Democratic Majority Leader John W. Davis (Salem) was hastily gathering signatures to bring the senate-passed bill before the assembly, D'Aloia recognized a motion by Hudson Assemblyman Frederick H. Hauser for adjournment.[123]

---

placed on the legislature in the assembly deadlock. If the legislature refused to act, the court could demand adherence to the constitutional standard of equal protection by threatening to impose its own plan.

[119] Newark *Evening News*, January 13, 1961.

[120] *Ibid.*

[121] *Ibid.*, January 31, 1961.

[122] *NJSJ*, 117th, January 30, 1961, p. 96. On this vote, four members were absent, including the senators from Ocean and Union (both Republicans); and Cumberland and Hudson (both Democrats).

[123] Newark *Evening News*, January 31, 1961.

Governor Meyner swiftly reacted by sending a terse two-sentence telegram to the assembly, ordering all members back to "act on reapportionment."[124] The assembly therefore reconvened on February 1, the same day that the supreme court said it would hand down a reapportionment plan.

Legislative maneuvering now moved at a furious pace. The Essex-Hudson opponents needed a two-thirds majority to move the senate-passed bill from first to second reading.[125] The first maneuver was to get 40 affirmative votes, which were available from a combination of 20 Democrats and 24 Republicans. D'Aloia still maintained that 31 Democratic votes were required from the caucus before he would permit a vote. The Democrats caucused upon the insistence of Governor Meyner. At this meeting, a majority of the Democrats told D'Aloia he would be replaced by a new speaker if he did not permit a vote on the senate-passed plan. This display of naked political power finally convinced D'Aloia to permit a vote.[126] The senate bill was then moved to second reading by a vote of 44–1[127] with all Democrats and Republicans voting affirmatively and opposed to the abstentions of the Essex-Hudson Democrats.

One additional vote was needed to move the Equal Proportions bill from second to third reading, that is, a three-fourths vote. The assembly recessed at noon. Governor Meyner sent out a personal call to Assemblyman Benjamin Franklin, 3rd (Republican–Morris), who was unavoidably absent but known to favor the bill.[128] Franklin ap-

---

124 *Ibid.* As governor, Meyner could call special sessions under the state constitution if he felt the public interest demanded it. See *Constitution of 1947*, Article V, Section 1, paragraph 12.

125 *Constitution of 1947*, Article III, Section 4, paragraph 6.

126 Interview with J. Edward Crabiel (Democrat–Middlesex), June 2, 1965.

127 *NJAM*, 125th, February 1, 1961, p. 170.

128 Newark *Evening News*, February 1, 1961.

peared as the assembly was preparing to act on the crucial parliamentary procedure. He registered the required 45th vote to place the bill on final reading. Again all members voted affirmatively with the exception of the abstaining Essex-Hudson Democratic bloc.[129] The bill itself was then voted on and adopted by a roll-call vote of 44–10.[130] The muted voices of Speaker D'Aloia and the Hudson Democrats registered the negative votes.

The two procedural maneuvers and the final roll-call indicated that a variety of pressures had finally overcome Essex-Hudson objections. The pressures exerted by Governor Meyner, the state supreme court, and especially the Democrats and Republicans in the assembly who finally agreed on an Equal Proportions Plan all resulted in effectively isolating the obstructionist Essex-Hudson bloc.

TABLE 4.15. Coalition of anti-Essex-Hudson Democrats and Republicans resulted in passage of 1961 reapportionment solution

County Groups and Party	Yes	No	Not Voting	Cohesion	Inter-Group Likeness
Urban Democrats Minus Essex, Hudson	15	1	0	87.5	
Rural Democrats	4	0	0	100	93.7 Affirmative
Urban Republicans	14	0	0	100	
Rural Republicans	11	0	1	100	
Essex Democrats	0	1	4	100	
Hudson Democrats	0	8	1	100	100 Negative
Totals	44	10	6		

129 *NJAM*, 125th, February 1, 1961, pp. 171–172.
130 *Ibid.*, p. 172.

Why was the assembly able to pass an Equal Proportions Plan in 1961 when all other previous attempts had failed? Two major reasons seem evident. First, the senate Republicans consistently demanded this plan and adamantly rejected any other alternatives that would preserve the Essex-Hudson power position. Senate insistence on one particular plan effectively limited assembly strategies in developing viable alternatives. This can be shown by comparing the average voting cohesion of the senate blocs in the first and second stages of the apportionment deadlock. From 1953 to 1957, the senate passed Equal Proportions Plans on six separate occasions, while the same action was taken four times from 1958 through 1961. The ten stationary rural Republican counties, controlling the largest bloc of votes in both periods, were nearly unanimous in supporting this plan. When their votes were added to the "gaining" rural Republicans and the "gaining" urban Republicans, a continuously solid bloc of counties was formed. In contrast, the minority Democrats were moving from a solid opposition bloc in the first period to a growing supporting bloc in the second period. By 1961, all the minority Democrats, except Hudson County, voted unanimously in favor of the plan.

TABLE 4.16. Senate Republicans consistently favored Equal Proportions Plan, 1953–1961

Republicans	% of Votes	Average Cohesion 1953–1957	Average Cohesion 1958–1961
Rural Stationary	42.5%	97.2+	100+
Rural Gaining	8.2%	100 +	100+
Urban Gaining	9.6%	100 +	100+
Urban Stationary	2.7%	50 +	(Not applicable)
Urban Losing	.7%	100 —	(Not applicable)
Totals	63.7%		

The second reason for the success of the Equal Proportions Plan in 1961 can be found in assembly voting patterns. Prior to the final vote, the urban counties, both Republican and Democratic, opposed the plan. In order to get a majority, it was necessary to form a bipartisan alliance consisting of the "gaining" and "stationary" Democrats and the minority urban Republicans. The key votes were available from the seven Republicans representing Essex County. When they broke away from their five Democratic counterparts, the "winning" combination was found, as shown in Table 4.17 below:

TABLE 4.17. Assembly Democrats needed support from minority urban Republicans to pass 1961 Equal Proportions Plan

Urban Democrats				Urban Republicans			
Gaining		Stationary		Gaining		Stationary	
Camden	(3)	Mercer	(3)	Bergen	(6)	Essex	(7)
Middlesex	(3)	Passaic	(4)	Union	(1)		
Union	(3)						
Total Votes = 16				Total Votes = 14			
Cohesion = 87.5				Cohesion = 100			
Rural Democrats				**Rural Republicans**			
Gaining		Stationary		Gaining		Stationary	
Burlington	(1)	Cumberland	(1)	Monmouth	(2)	Atlantic	(2)
		Salem	(1)			Cape May	(1)
		Warren	(1)			Gloucester	(1)
						Hunterdon	(1)
						Morris	(2)
						Ocean	(1)
						Somerset	(1)
						Sussex	(1)
Total Votes = 4				Total Votes = 12			
Cohesion = 100				Cohesion = 100			

Thus, the 1958 to 1961 period was a time during which the Essex-Hudson obstructionist bloc attempted to preserve the *status quo,* but was eventually defeated by a combination of affirmative leadership exerted by Governor Meyner and the superior voting power of an anti-Essex-Hudson bipartisan coalition. When Essex and Hudson counties were reduced to 14 assembly votes and the remaining Democrats sought Republican support, the final solution was found. The anti-Essex-Hudson counteralliance had to be formed in order to isolate the Essex-Hudson bloc in the legislative struggle. However, it took ten years to develop this counteralliance and it was formed only when a crisis situation and a sense of urgency prompted final action on the apportionment problem.

Conclusions: Major areas of agreement and conflict in the apportionment struggle.

Several common themes appear consistently in the ten-year period of apportionment efforts from 1952 to 1961. The most persistent themes are (1) Party voting patterns in the senate and assembly; (2) Rural and urban county differences; (3) Regional voting patterns; and (4) The formation of coalitions and alliances. All of these themes are closely related to various strategies and tactics employed in the legislative struggle.

Party control in legislative chambers and party voting patterns

THE SENATE

Apportionment strategies in the senate were directly related to the goals sought by Republicans and Democrats. The Republicans controlled the upper chamber during the entire ten-year period. During this time, the rural Republicans determined senate policy on reapportionment. This can be shown by analyzing the various voting blocs among senate Republicans. The nucleus of Republican voting strength consisted of one urban county (Bergen) and four rural counties (Atlantic, Monmouth, Morris, and Warren) which voted for every plan. These five counties were supported by a secondary bloc of seven counties which unanimously agreed with the nucleus but did not register votes on all 11 roll-calls because of absences or changes in party composition. A third bloc of four counties showed relatively high agreement with the nucleus but cast one or two negative votes. Only one Republican county never voted with the nucleus, Essex County. And Essex County was the major source of contention in assembly apportionment disagreements. Taken together, the 17 Republican counties had a remarkably high cohesion of 88.8 during the entire ten-year period.

TABLE 4.18. Republican county voting blocs in the senate 1952–1961

Nucleus		Secondary Bloc		Periphery	
Rural	Urban	Rural	Urban	Rural	Urban
Atlantic	Bergen	Cape May	Union	Hunterdon	Passaic
Monmouth		Somerset		Ocean	Camden
Morris		Sussex			
Warren		Gloucester			
		Burlington			
		Salem			

Combined Bloc Cohesion and Likeness = 100

Likeness with Nucleus and Secondary Bloc = 61.2

Non-Bloc County
Urban
Essex (No Cohesion and Likeness with Nucleus and Secondary Bloc)

Table 4.18 shows that high senate Republican voting cohesion was directly related to the rural or urban classifications of the various counties. As repeatedly shown in prior analysis, the rural senate counties focused primary attention on the Equal Proportions and Arithmetical Eliminations Plans, while resisting both the Cavicchia and 67-member plans. The reasons for this are now clear. The Senate rural counties controlled the Senate and their strategy was simple: They could both outvote the urban counties and exclude the minority Democrats from participating in developing apportionment proposals. Further, the rural county strategy was to preserve the rural-urban balance in the assembly. When the Union County senator proposed the 67-member compromise plan, the rural counties refused to vote for it. Similarly, the rural counties blocked consideration of the Cavicchia Plan due to the opposition of Atlantic County, a leader of the voting nucleus. Thus, when the voting blocs are analyzed in terms of rural and urban differences, the superiority of the senate rural Republicans is clearly evident.

TABLE 4.19. Senate rural Republicans had both high party cohesion and more voting power, 1952–1961

County Groups and Party	% of Total Seats Held	Party Cohesion
Rural Republicans	83.9%	94.6
Urban Republicans	16.1%	67.8

Not only were the senate rural Republicans more powerful than the urban Republicans, but they were also more powerful than any combination of urban Republicans and Democrats. The Democrats were a consistent minority throughout the ten years. Only four counties had Democratic representation in the ten years (Cumberland, Hudson, Mercer, and Middlesex counties). These four counties were unanimously opposed to all Republican plans. The only plan they voted for was the final solution of 1961 (with the exception of Hudson County). The cohesion of the minority Democrats was exactly the same as the cohesion of the rural Republicans (94.6). However, Table 4.20 shows the weakness of the senate Democrats in terms of voting strength as well as the combined ineffectiveness of the urban Republicans and the minority Democrats. It was clear that the final solution had to meet the requirements of the predominant rural Republican majority.

TABLE 4.20. Rural Republicans were more powerful than both urban Republicans and minority Democrats, 1952–1961

County Groups and Party	% of Total Seats Held	Party Cohesion
Rural Republicans	57.1%	94.6
Urban Republicans	11.4%	67.8
Minority Democrats	31.5%	94.6

THE ASSEMBLY

Both Republicans and Democrats had difficulty in finding an effective 31-vote majority to pass an apportionment plan. During the period of Republican control (1952–1957), no plans passed the assembly. From 1958 to 1961, the Democrats were able to pass the 67-member plan, but this was unacceptable to the senate Republicans. The final solution of 1961 had to take into account the inability of party control *per se* to develop an effective 31-vote majority.

Two approaches may be employed to show the difficulties of translating party control into an effective and cohesive assembly majority; (1) Voting cohesion in the various assembly blocs as it is related to political party composition; and (2) Comparing majority party cohesion during the two periods of party control.

The most cohesive Republican bloc consisted of ten rural counties (Bloc 1), only one of which was affected by any plan (Atlantic County by the Cavicchia Plan). Bloc 2 is composed of four counties which stood to gain seats under most proposed plans. Voting cohesion here was slightly lower than in Bloc 1 due to the disagreement among gaining counties when proposed plans did not include all of them. Bloc 3 has the lowest voting cohesion and consists of the three urban counties which could not develop a consistent position on any one plan. Bloc 3 is the key to Republican failures for this bloc is both low in party cohesion and controls the most assembly votes.

TABLE 4.21. Republican county voting blocs in the assembly, 1952–1961

Bloc 1 Rural	Bloc 2 Gaining Counties	Bloc 3 Urban Northeastern
Atlantic	Burlington	Essex
Cape May	Monmouth	Bergen
Gloucester	Camden	Passaic
Morris		
Ocean		
Hunterdon		
Salem		
Somerset		
Sussex		Group Cohesion = 55.2
Cumberland		Likeness with Blocs
Combined Likeness =91.9		1 and 2 = 44.5

The Democrats are also divided into three voting blocs. Again the problem is with Bloc 3, consisting of Essex and Hudson counties. Essex and Hudson have low party cohesion but substantially higher cohesion when they vote together to oppose party plans. Bloc 3 is important because together Essex and Hudson controlled more votes than either Bloc 1 or Bloc 2.

When party voting is compared during the periods of Republican and Democratic party control, the major finding is that the minority party is much more cohesive than the majority. A negative position by the minority forced the majority to develop a bipartisan plan. Collective Demo-

TABLE 4.22. Democratic county voting blocs in the assembly, 1952–1961

Bloc 1		Bloc 2		Bloc 3
Stationary Counties		Gaining Counties		Losing Counties
Rural	Urban	Rural	Urban	Urban
Cumberland	Mercer	Burlington	Camden	Essex
Salem	Passaic		Middlesex	Hudson
Sussex			Union	
Warren				
Gloucester				
Combined Likeness = 99			Likeness with Blocs 1 and 2 = 76.9	

cratic party resistance and the obstruction of the Essex Republicans led to the formation of a most effective counterbloc to all Republican party proposals. Essex County would yield only one seat and the Democrats refused to assist the Republicans when they were not brought into direct consultation. Additional Republican difficulties included rural-urban differences and low cohesion among the urban counties. Thus, even though the Republicans controlled 36 percent more seats than the Democrats from 1952 to 1957, party control in itself was ineffective in resolving the apportionment struggle. In reality Republican party control represented a combination of divergent interests, none of which could agree on a final plan.[131]

When the Democrats controlled the assembly from 1958 to 1961, the minority Republicans were more cohesive than the Democrats. Faced with the Essex-Hudson bloc, the Democrats could not pass a plan until 1960. This was the 67-member plan which was firmly opposed by Hudson County. As long as the Democrats tried to develop a solution within party ranks, all their efforts were reduced to appeasing the Essex-Hudson bloc. After the 1959 elections

[131] See Key, *op. cit.*, pp. 228–230.

this bloc was reduced to 14 votes, but Essex and Hudson were still able to enlist outside urban county support to control the leadership positions. Thus, the Democrats still were unable to pass a plan without rebuking the Essex-Hudson leadership team and crossing party lines.

Thus, in conclusion, Table 4.23 shows the two major limiting conditions on the ten-year apportionment battle. First, high cohesion among the senate Republicans forced the non-cohesive assembly majorities to focus on a plan that met senate requirements.[132] Secondly, higher voting cohesion by the assembly minority parties forced the assembly majority parties to seek a bipartisan solution.[133]

TABLE 4.23. Party voting cohesion in the New Jersey Legislature, 1952–1961

Legislative Voting Groups	Voting Cohesion On All Roll-Calls High	Moderate	Low
Minority Assembly Democrats	98.8		
Minority Senate Democrats	94.6		
Majority Senate Republicans	88.8		
Minority Assembly Republicans		76	
Majority Assembly Democrats			51.6
Majority Assembly Republicans			23.2

Formation of coalitions and alliances: Bipartisanship is the key

To reemphasize the assembly difficulties in developing an acceptable plan, Table 4.24 shows that during the first period of Republican control (1952–1957) the Essex

[132] This finding appears to refute one of the major reapportionment rules that the chamber most affected by a plan exercises control over the formation of the plan. See Steiner and Gove, *op. cit.*, p. 117; and Hanson, *op. cit.*, pp. 35–36.

[133] The necessity for bipartisanship similarly refutes the rule that the minority party is suppressed in a reapportionment. See Hanson, *op. cit.*, p. 37.

County alliance with the Democrats was more effective than any other group that could be formed in Republican ranks.

TABLE 4.24. Coalitions and alliances during Republican assembly control, 1952–1957

County Groups and Party	% of Total Assembly Votes	Party Cohesion On All Roll-Calls		
		High	Moderate	Low
Republicans:				
Gaining	13.1%		72.6	
Stationary	33.6%			40.2
Losing	21.3%			27.2
Democrats	32.0%	98.8		

When Essex County joined the Democrats, the combined voting power of this alliance was greater than that of the Republicans. The voting power of the Essex-Democratic alliance was translated into moderate voting cohesion in contrast to the low cohesion of all Republicans without Essex County. Thus, Essex and the Democrats, comprising 52 percent of the assembly votes, had a combined cohesion of 71.6, while the remaining Republicans with 48 percent of the votes had a cohesion of only 48. Thus, the Republicans were split as a party; the urban Republican counties were divided among themselves; and the Essex-Democratic voting alliance was more effective than any combination of Republicans.

The Democrats encountered the same resistance from Essex and Hudson counties when they controlled the assembly. Bipartisanship was the key to overcoming the Essex-Hudson bloc. Only when the Democrats unanimously opposed Essex and Hudson and crossed party lines to join with the Republicans was a solution possible. The Democrats had finally acceded to the senate-backed Equal Proportions Plan by 1961 as the only available alternative.

When Essex-Hudson votes were reduced to 14 and the blocking strategy of crossing party lines was no longer possible, the affirmative strategy was to isolate Hudson and Essex and pass the Equal Proportions Plan.

TABLE 4.25. Bipartisanship is the key to solving the deadlock, 1958–1961

County Groups and Party	% of Total Assembly Votes	Party Cohesion On All Roll-Calls			
		High	Moderate	Low	Blocking
Democrats Minus Essex and Hudson	33.4%	96.6			
Republicans	43.3%		76		
Essex-Hudson Dems.	23.3%				92.6

Conclusions

The ten-year protracted conflict to reapportion the New Jersey Assembly revealed that entrenched legislative groups could effectively block action over a long period of time. The narrow defeat of the Cavicchia Plan in 1952 paved the way for a direct confrontation between the senate Republicans and the assembly Essex-Hudson bloc. No solution was possible without an accommodation with either of these groups. In a sense, the senate Republicans "won" in the end by forcing the Equal Proportions Plan on the assembly. But even more significant was the addition of a new limiting condition on legislative actions in reapportionment, the direct intervention of the courts. By 1961, the New Jersey assembly had not been reapportioned for 20 years, representing the longest delay in the state's history. Essex and Hudson counties had to "lose" under these conditions. The reapportionment battle could not be "won" by a negative approach without alternative courses of action. Thus, the necessity for a solution finally forced a bipartisan combination which overrode outright obstruction. In the future, the various legislative groups were fully aware that reapportionment was not solely their own province. Instead, a "fair" reapportionment had to take into consideration the element of fair representation. If the legislature refused to distribute seats in accordance with a population principle, the courts would enter the struggle and make certain that this was done.

5

Legislative Response To "One Man, One Vote," 1964–1965

THE "ONE MAN, ONE VOTE" RULING OF THE UNITED STATES Supreme Court in 1964 prompted a nationwide reapportionment revolution.[1] The population equality standard had an immediate impact on the New Jersey Legislature. The state supreme court ordered a change for the state senate.[2] The legislature was required to alter the senate basis of representation. This represented a notable departure from past tradition. The temporary plan of 1965 resulted in the first senate realignment since 1776. From 1776 to 1964, an interval of 188 years, senators represented counties and only one senator was elected from each county. Previous attempts to change the one-senator-per-county system had failed most notably in 1844 and 1947. The second state constitution of 1844 had continued the

[1] In the case of *Reynolds v. Sims,* 377 U.S. 533 (1964).
[2] In the case of *Jackman v. Bodine,* 43 N.J. 453 (1964).

one-senator system written into the 1776 constitution. From 1941 to 1946, all efforts to revise the state constitution were directly related to the issue of senate representation. The *quid pro quo* of the 1947 constitution was a non-reapportionment restriction.

With both the long tradition of equal county senate representation and entrenched resistance to change, the 1964–1965 legislature faced strong internal and external pressures in devising an acceptable solution. Rural senators, who benefited from county equality, tried at first to preserve the *status quo*. When this failed, another effort was directed toward combining legislative reapportionment with congressional redistricting as a partisan maneuver to put the Democrats on the defensive. In contrast, the Democratic party governor and most urban assemblymen favored implementation of the state supreme court ruling, which focused on the senate.

The various responses by contending legislative groups encompassed rationally calculated objectives leading toward a maximization of political power. The 1964–1965 case is characterized by the complexity of maneuvers within a relatively short time period. Having been forced to act quickly, the legislature had to devise a solution acceptable to court guidelines and internal pressures. The final agreement represented only a "temporary" solution, serving as a prelude to final action on a reapportionment plan.

The legislative political environment, 1964–1965

The 1964–1965 legislative response to reapportionment was bounded by three major limiting conditions. First, the state supreme court forced legislative action. Without court involvement, the legislature would not have responded to the "one man, one vote" requirement.[3] Sec-

[3] See, for example, Gordon E. Baker, *The Reapportionment Revolution* (New York: Random House, 1966), pp. 111–141.

ondly, the senate, led by the rural Republicans, wanted to devise a solution that most favorably protected their interests. Basically, the senate wanted to retain control over its own apportionment problem without outside interference or participation by the governor.[4] Thirdly, the governor, who was a Democrat, wanted to force a solution for maximum political advantage. With senate reapportionment high on his list of legislative priorities, Governor Hughes did not hesitate to enter the struggle.[5] Due to the close party division in the assembly, Hughes saw a chance for the Democrats to gain two-house control in the near future through Senate reapportionment.[6]

Both the governor and the senate were limited by a high degree of two-party competition throughout the struggle. Governor Hughes had won a narrow electoral victory in November, 1961, when he carried only 11 of the state's 21 counties with 50.8 percent of the popular vote.[7] Hughes' vote plurality of 35,000 was primarily attributable to the urban county vote in Camden, Essex, Hudson, Mercer, Middlesex, and Passaic counties.[8] The Democrats also increased their 1960–1961 assembly advantage from 34 to 38 seats with gains in Burlington, Camden, Essex, Middlesex, and Union counties. The senate remained at a close 11–10 margin for the Republicans.

By the next legislative elections, however, the Republicans reasserted two-chamber control for the first time since 1957. Twelve assembly seats changed party affiliation in

---

[4] See Royce Hanson, *The Political Thicket* (Englewood Cliffs, New Jersey: Prentice-Hall, Inc., 1966), pp. 35–36; and Gilbert Y. Steiner and Samuel K. Gove, *Legislative Politics in Illinois* (Urbana: University of Illinois Press, 1960), p. 117.

[5] This contrasts with the usual passive role of the governor in such struggles. See Malcolm E. Jewell, Ed., *The Politics of Reapportionment* (New York: Atherton Press, 1962), p. 31.

[6] The governor's objective was to end divided party control. See Jewell, Ed., *op. cit.*, p. 20.

[7] Source: *N.J. Legislative Manual* (1962), p. 742.

[8] *Ibid.*

1964 in Burlington, Camden, Essex, and Union counties. This resulted in a 33–27 Republican assembly advantage. The Republicans also increased senate control to 15–6 with gains in Burlington, Camden, Essex, and Gloucester counties.

Legislative competition was further evident in the party composition of assembly and senate county delegations. In the assembly, nine solidly Republican counties opposed seven solidly Democratic counties in the 1964–1965 session. The remaining five counties were competitive, due either to divided delegations or switches in party affiliation from one session to the next. The competitive counties clearly constituted a "swing" bloc, since neither the solidly Republican nor Democratic counties controlled an outright voting majority. In fact, as shown in Table 5.1, the competitive counties controlled 23 votes, while the solidly Republican group had 17 and the solidly Democratic counties had 20 votes. Thus, a near equilibrium of voting balance existed in the 1964–1965 assembly. Under these conditions, the assembly was not in a position to exercise initiative on the apportionment issue without strong leadership focused on developing a bipartisan coalition.

TABLE 5.1. Party composition of assembly county delegations indicated a high degree of competition, 1964–1965

Solidly Republican		Competitive		Solidly Democratic	
Atlantic	2	Burlington	2	Cumberland	1
Bergen	7	Camden	4	Hudson	6
Cape May	1	Essex	9	Mercer	3
Gloucester	1	Monmouth	3	Middlesex	4
Hunterdon	1	Union	5	Passaic	4
Morris	2			Salem	1
Ocean	1			Warren	1
Somerset	1				
Sussex	1				
Total	17 votes	Total	23 votes	Total	20 votes

While the assembly lacked either a clear party majority among solid county delegations or a solid bloc of urban counties that could control reapportionment, the senate, in contrast, was characterized by solidly Republican and rural county control. Republicans were represented in 11 counties, consisting of nine rural and two urban counties. The ten remaining counties were spit among six solidly Democratic and four competitive counties as shown in Table 5.2. In order to maintain control over apportionment measures, the rural Republicans constituted a majority in the senate caucus. No bills were released to the senate floor unless the rural county bloc voted for them in caucus.[9]

TABLE 5.2. Party composition of senate counties reflected a rural Republican advantage, 1964–1965

Solidly Republican		Competitive	Solidly Democratic
Atlantic	Ocean	Burlington	Cumberland
Bergen	Somerset	Camden	Hudson
Cape May	Sussex	Essex	Mercer
Hunterdon	Union	Gloucester	Middlesex
Monmouth	Warren		Passaic
Morris			Salem

Initial attempts to nullify and circumvent the court ruling

The landmark United States Supreme Court decision in *Reynolds v. Sims* on June 15, 1964,[10] provided the impetus

[9] See Dayton David McKean, *Pressures on the Legislature of New Jersey* (New York: Columbia University Press, 1938), pp. 30–40; Bennett M. Rich, *The Government and Administration of New Jersey* (New York: Thomas Y. Crowell Co., 1957), pp. 52–56; and Belle Zeller, Ed., *American State Legislatures* (New York: Thomas Y. Crowell Co., 1954), p. 207.

[10] 377 U.S. 533 (1964). The *Reynolds* decision represented a clarification of *Baker v. Carr,* 369 U.S. 186 (1962) in which the Court had stated that the Fourteenth Amendment of the United States Constitution provided manageable standards for determining

for New Jersey responses to reapportionment. The Court established the "one man, one vote" standard for electing representatives in bicameral state legislatures. Legislators had to represent equal numbers of voters. The so-called "federal analogy"[11] was rejected for state representation. Substantial population equality became the rule. State senates could no longer represent geographical areas comparable to equal state representation in the United States Senate.

The *Reynolds* decision, as applied to New Jersey, meant that the one-senator-per-county system was unconstitutional under the Equal Protection and Due Process clauses of the Fourteenth Amendment of the United States Constitution. There was also some indication that guaranteed county representation in the assembly did not meet the "one man, one vote" test.[12]

The Court's entry into the reapportionment thicket represented a direct threat to legislative control over apportionment problems. However, the New Jersey Legislature had already experienced state supreme court willingness to force legislative action in the 1952–1961 reapportionment case.[13] The new Supreme Court guidelines had been predicted by the state court in 1960.

Initial legislative response to the *Reynolds* ruling came from a group of Republican assemblymen, who saw "one man, one vote" resulting in a Democratic party takeover of both legislative chambers. Based on recent Statewide electoral patterns (as shown in Table 5.1), two-party competition was becoming increasingly evident. The Democrats could regain control of the assembly by winning in a few strategic counties (that is, the "swing bloc" of competitive

---

constitutionally apportioned state legislatures. "One man, one vote" was now the specified constitutional test.

[11] *Ibid.*

[12] *Constitution of 1947*, Article IV, Section 3.

[13] In the case of *Asbury Park Press, Inc. v. Woolley*, 33 N.J. 1 (1960).

counties shown in Table 5.1, Burlington, Camden, Essex, Monmouth, and Union). Senate control might also shift to the Democrats if a population basis of representation was adopted. In contrast, the traditional pattern of Republican legislative control was based on an urban-rural assembly alliance and rural county predominance in the senate.

Assembly Republicans, led by Speaker Marion West Higgins and State Party Chairman Webster B. Todd, sought to have the lower chamber go on record in opposition to the *Reynolds* decision. To show their dissatisfaction with "one man, one vote," these Republicans wanted to petition the United States Congress to convene a constitutional convention for the purpose of writing a new constitutional amendment. The amendment would allow apportionment of one state legislative chamber on a basis other than population.[14]

The Republican leadership sought to gain as many co-sponsors of the anti-*Reynolds* petition as possible. This would show both widespread rural and urban county support and ensure passage of the resolution at the roll-call stage. The assembly speaker convinced 18 of the 32 Republican assemblymen to join in sponsoring Assembly Concurrent Resolution 51.[15] The 19 co-sponsors, as shown below, then sought 12 additional votes to obtain a 31-member majority.

The 19 co-sponsors attracted only nine additional votes and the plan failed to pass the Assembly in a 28–25 roll-

---

[14] Petitioning the Congress to nullify Supreme Court entry into state legislative apportionment had begun in other states as early as 1963 following the decision in *Baker v. Carr*. See *The New York Times*, April 14, 1963. Similarly the Council of State Governments had passed a resolution opposing the *Reynolds* decision and called for a constitutional amendment in 1964. See *The New York Times*, December 6, 1964.

[15] Source: *Minutes and Proceedings of the One Hundred and Eighty-Eighth General Assembly of the State of New Jersey*, November 30, 1964, p. 1147. Hereinafter cited as *NJAM*.

TABLE 5.3. 19 Republicans joined in sponsoring the anti-Reynolds Resolution

Urban Republicans		Rural Republicans	
Bergen	3	Atlantic	2
Camden	2	Burlington	2
Essex	1	Hunterdon	1
Union	4	Monmouth	1
		Morris	1
		Ocean	1
		Somerset	1
	10		9

call.[16] Two major reasons explained the defeat of the anti-Court resolution. First, the vote took place after the state supreme court had decided to apply the "one man, one vote" standard to the legislature based on the *Reynolds* decision. The legislature was thus being forced into a position of implementing the state court ruling, while others were asking for support to oppose the population equality standard. Second, the Essex County delegation bolted from the party leadership and voted with a nearly solid bloc of Democrats. The Essex vote reflected both the past independence of this important urban northeastern county in reapportionment matters and the close nature of party competition in the county in the 1964–1965 session. The Essex delegation was split between five Republicans and four Democrats, while the Essex senator was Republican.

The voting alignment appeared to substantiate Republican party claims regarding the expected beneficiaries of the "one man, one vote" ruling. As shown below, the urban Democrats were unanimously opposed to the resolution, while the urban Republicans, with the lone exception of

16 *Ibid.*

the Essex delegation, were solidly in favor. But the assembly Republicans could not exercise initiative on the apportionment issue as long as the urban county delegations were split.[17]

TABLE 5.4. Assembly Republicans failed to pass resolution nullifying the "one man, one vote" ruling

County Groups and Party	Yes	No	Not Voting	Cohesion	Party Cohesion
Urban Reps. Minus Essex	15	0	0	100	All Republicans = 62.5 Affirmative
Rural Reps.	11	0	1	83.3	
Rural Dems.	2	0	1	33.3	
Essex Reps.	0	4	1	100	All Democrats = 84.6 Negative
Urban Dems.	0	21	4	100	
Totals	28	25	7		

Senate Republicans employed a different strategy in attempting to circumvent application of the "one man, one vote" standard. Instead of seeking to nullify the Court's decision by a constitutional amendment, the alternative strategy was to avoid the effects of reapportionment by instituting a system of "weighted voting." The setting for senate Republican objectives was determined by the pending litigation in the case of *Jackman v. Bodine.*[18] The *Jackman* suit was brought by two labor union representatives against the county clerks of Sussex, Salem, Hunterdon, Cape May, and Warren counties; the secretary of state; the president of the senate; and the speaker of the general assembly. The plaintiffs contended that the existing senate

[17] See David R. Derge, "Metropolitan and Outstate Alignments in Illinois and Missouri Legislative Delegations," *American Political Science Review,* Vol. 52, No. 4 (December, 1958), p. 1065.

[18] 43 N.J. 453 (1964).

and assembly apportionment systems violated the Fourteenth Amendment of the United States Constitution. After an adverse ruling in the superior court, the plaintiffs had appealed to the state supreme court.[19]

The senate Republicans were certain that the highest state court would apply the "one man, one vote" standard to the senate.[20] Anticipating such a ruling, senate leaders sought to withstand the full impact of reapportionment. "Weighted voting" seemed to be the answer. This technique was proposed by Walter H. Jones, the Republican leader of Bergen County.[21] Weighted voting consisted of assigning a proportionate number of votes to incumbent senators on the basis of the 1960 census figures for counties. Under the system, Cape May, the smallest county, would have one vote, while Essex, the most populous county, would have 19.1 votes.[22]

The problem with weighted voting depended upon its application at the various stages of senate decision-making. If the system prevailed only at the roll-call stage, the rural Republicans would still retain control over caucus proceedings. Control of the caucus in effect meant control of the senate. It became obvious that weighted voting was simply a diversionary maneuver when the rural Republicans went on record against full-scale implementation of the system in the caucus.[23]

Senate Majority Leader William F. Ozzard (Republican—Somerset) sought to institute weighted voting over the objections of both urban Republicans and Democrats. Ozzard employed the tactic of utilizing senate rules of procedure for adopting the new system. A rules change required only a simple majority of senators present and

[19] In *Jackman v. Bodine,* 78 N.J. Super. 418 (February 27, 1963).
[20] This was evident in a strategy conference called by Republican leaders in October. See *The New York Times,* October 16, 1964.
[21] *Ibid.*
[22] *Ibid.*
[23] Newark *Evening News,* November 8, 1964.

voting in contrast to the ordinary two-chamber and governor approval for bills. Ozzard and other rural senators considered weighted voting as an internal procedural senate problem which did not require outside participation.[24]

The senate Republican leadership faced internal party opposition to weighted voting. Senators Pierce H. Deamer, Jr. (Bergen) and Wayne Dumont (Warren) objected to the rules change procedure and argued for two-chamber participation in adopting the plan.[25] If assembly Republicans agreed to the plan, Governor Hughes would be confronted by a united majority party. The dispute could then be taken to the Supreme Court as proof of legislative intentions in meeting the "one man, one vote" requirement. A second objection was raised by urban Republicans who argued that the rural counties were forcing the urban counties to accept a plan that did not result in a true senate reapportionment.[26]

Majority Leader Ozzard ignored these claims and sought the 11 votes necessary for adoption. Ozzard had to get the nearly solid backing of other rural Republicans and some outside urban support to achieve a favorable majority. On the roll-call, nine rural and two urban Republicans voted affirmatively.[27] Only the Warren County senator voted against the plan within rural Republican ranks, while the Camden senator voted affirmatively and split off from the Bergen, Essex, and Union urban Republicans. Senator Scholz of Camden supported weighted voting to protect

[24] *Ibid.*, November 6, 1964.

[25] Newark *Evening News*, November 6, 1964.

[26] *Ibid.*, November 11, 1964. Senators Sarcone (Essex) and Stamler (Union) supported the plan as only a temporary measure prior to a true reapportionment. They also wanted weighted voting to apply in the caucus.

[27] Source: *Journal of the One Hundred and Twentieth Senate of the State of New Jersey being the One Hundred and Eighty-Eighth Session of the Legislature*, November 16, 1964, p. 839. Hereinafter cited as *NJSJ*.

Republican party interests in his closely competitive county. Bergen's Senator Deamer joined the Essex-Union opposition because he was leading a revolt against the county party leader, Walter H. Jones, author of the weighted voting plan.[28]

The voting pattern demonstrated a nearly solid bloc of rural Republicans opposing a coalition of northeast urban Republicans and minority Democrats.[29] The adoption of weighted voting thus indicated that "minority will" was necessary to institute the plan. The rural Republicans were engaging in a power play to preserve rural control in the caucus. Table 5.5 summarizes the voting blocs that developed in the weighted voting plan correlated with the projected weighted votes for each senator. The inescapable conclusion is that the rural Republicans did not want to yield control to the urban counties in a senate reapportionment.[30]

TABLE 5.5. Rural Republicans succeed in adopting weighted voting in the senate

County Groups and Party	Yes	No	Not Voting	Cohesion	"Weighted Votes" Yes	No	Uncast
Rural Reps.	10	1	0	81.8	31.3	1.3	0
Urban Reps.	1	3	0	50	8.1	45.6	0
Minority Dems.	0	5	1	100	0	30.4	8.4
Totals	11	9	1		39.4	77.3	8.4

As indicated previously, the adoption of weighted voting was intended to anticipate the state supreme court's ruling

[28] Newark *Evening News,* November 9, 1964.

[29] The solid Democratic vote was in contrast to the rural Democratic support for the constitutional amendment in the assembly. *Supra,* p. 193.

[30] See Malcolm E. Jewell, *The State Legislature* (New York: Random House, 1962), p. 18. Jewell observes that a possible strategy for maintaining legislative control is to develop a plan that "would preserve rural control in one or both branches of the legislature."

in *Jackman v. Bodine.* On November 25, 1964, the court established three guidelines for the legislature in meeting the "one man, one vote" standard. First, a temporary reapportionment plan had to be instituted prior to the November, 1965 general elections. Second, the legislature should adopt the temporary plan in time for the 1965 primary elections. Third, a permanent plan was to be put into effect by the November, 1967 general elections.[31] Did weighted voting meet the requirement for a temporary senate reapportionment? The court summarily rejected weighted voting in a separate *per curiam* decision delivered on December 15, 1964.[32] The court was critical of the method of adopting weighted voting by a simple change of senate rules and refused to rule on the applicability of the plan in meeting court guidelines.

With the defeat of weighted voting, the Republican efforts to nullify and circumvent "one man, one vote" ended in failure. In the assembly, the Republicans could not get the required support of Essex County to oppose the *Reynolds* decision. Legislative self-determination had not particularly benefited Essex County in the most recent reapportionment case. Furthermore, Essex was part of the northeastern bloc of counties that continually was subordinated to the power of the senate rural counties. The rural Republicans either misjudged the attitude of the state court or were engaging in a futile effort to preserve power under the weighted voting plan. When the court rejected weighted voting, the Democrats seized the initiative and sought quick adoption of a temporary senate reapportionment.

The Republicans now had to design a new strategy to withstand the demands of the Democrats, led by Governor Hughes, to meet court guidelines. Continuing to assert that reapportionment was an internal legislative matter,

---

[31] 43 N.J. 453 (November 25, 1964).
[32] *Jackman v. Bodine,* 43 N.J. 491 (1964).

the Republicans moved to the next phase of the apportionment struggle. The new maneuver was to challenge Democratic party control in the state's 15 congressional districts. New Jersey congressional districts had not been redrawn since 1931.[33] The 1964 elections had resulted in an 11–4 Democratic party advantage in the state's congressional delegation.[34] If a new plan could focus upon changing congressional district lines together with new assembly and senate bases of representation, the Republicans felt they would be in a good position to withstand the Democratic party calculations of an electoral sweep in 1965. The Republicans therefore supported a "1–2–4 plan," which was first proposed by former Assemblyman Wesley L. Lance (Republican–Hunterdon).[35]

The 1–2–4 plan had three major provisions, as viewed by Lance: First, the state's approximate six million population would be divided by 15 congressional districts so that each district would have about 400,000 people per representative. Secondly, each congressional district would be split in half to form 30 senate seats representing 200,000 people each. Finally, each senate district would be split in half, resulting in 60 assemblymen with 100,000 people in each assembly district.[36]

The Republicans therefore wanted to attack the gross inequalities in the existing congressional districts, while retaining county representation in the legislature. In effect, the 1–2–4 plan sought to reduce representation inequality for congressmen and state senators, while improving the

[33] See Ernest C. Reock, Jr. and Stanley H. Friedelbaum, *Congressional Districting in New Jersey* (New Brunswick: Bureau of Government Research, Rutgers – The State University, 1956), p. 18.

[34] *The New York Times,* November 5, 1964.

[35] Interview with Mr. Lance, May 6, 1965.

[36] Source: *Legislative Reapportionment Alternatives and Their Impact on New Jersey Citizens* (New Brunswick: Proceedings of Rutgers Policy Forum, Extension Service, College of Agriculture, Rutgers – The State University, January 12, 1965), p. 50.

TABLE 5.6. Existing population inequalities in New Jersey congressional disetricts and state senate.[37]

Congressional District	Counties	1960 Pop.	Relative Deviations in Population As Compared With The Ideal Population Per Seat	
			Cong. Dist.	Senate
1	Camden	392,035	+44.8%	+ 35.7%
	Gloucester	134,840		− 53.3%
	Salem	58,711		− 79.7%
2	Atlantic	160,880	−21.8%	− 44.3%
	Cape May	48,555		− 83.2%
	Cumberland	106,850		− 63.0%
3	Monmouth	334,401	+ 9.4%	+ 15.7%
	Ocean	108,241		− 62.5%
4	Burlington	224,499	+21.4%	− 22.3%
	Mercer	266,392		− 7.8%
5	Morris	261,620	+ .3%	− 9.4%
	Somerset	143,913		− 50.2%
6	Union	504,255	+24.7%	+ 74.5%
7	Hunterdon	54,107	+37.4%	− 81.3%
	Sussex	49,255		− 82.9%
	Warren	63,220		− 78.1%
	NW Bergen*	388,973		+170.1%
	NW Passaic*			+ 40.7%
8	S Passaic	394,279	− 2.5%	
9	E Bergen	451,126	+11.5%	+111.4%
	N Hudson*			
10	N Essex*	303,058	−25.1%	+219.7%
	W Hudson			
11	C Essex	308,660	−23.7%	
12	SW Essex	362,914	−10.3%	
13	S Hudson	256,977	−36.5%	
14	C Hudson	255,165	−36.9%	
15	Middlesex	433,856	+ 7.3%	+ 50.2%

* In all cases where counties are split, the % figure for Column 5 is given for the entire county.

---

37 Sources: *Report of the New Jersey Legislative Reapportionment and Congressional Redistricting Commission.* February 5,

representative basis for assemblymen. Existing population disparities in the congressional districts and senate are summarized below in Table 5.6.

Governor Hughes interpreted the *Jackman* decision quite differently. As both party leader and legislative leader of the Democrats, the governor wanted to participate directly in developing a temporary plan for the senate.[38] He moved for a special session of the legislature.[39] Hughes proposed that a jointly-appointed bipartisan study commission be established to recommend action for the 1965 legislative session.[40]

Democratic party calculations were that such a joint commission would permit two-party participation in meeting court requirements. Secondly, such a group would have access to technical information and be able to make an objective evaluation of the existing problems. Thirdly, the commission would widen the range of choices for a temporary plan rather than involving the legislative Republicans and the governor in a protracted and direct conflict.[41]

The legislative Republicans accepted the study commission proposal but argued that the governor should not participate in naming members to the group. In arguing that reapportionment was an internal legislative responsibility, the Republicans excluded the governor's participation. The Republicans assigned the commission the task of

---

1965, p. 83. Hereinafter cited as *Meyner Commission Report*; and Ernest C. Reock, Jr., *Population Inequality Among Counties in the New Jersey Legislature, 1791–1962* (New Brunswick: Bureau of Government Research, Rutgers — The State University, 1963), p. 29.

38 Interviews with Governor Richard J. Hughes and Mr. Joseph W. Katz, Special Assistant to the Governor, June 2, 1965.

39 *Special Message to the Legislature by Governor Richard J. Hughes,* November 30, 1964.

40 *Ibid.*

41 Interviews with Governor Hughes and Mr. Katz.

recommending charges in both the congressional districts and legislative reapportionment.[42]

To establish the commission without the governor's involvement, a tactical maneuver was required. The Republicans seized on the concurrent resolution device under which legislative action could be taken without the governor's signature.[43] Secondly, the Republicans united firmly on party lines to adopt the proposal at the roll-call stage.[44] The lines of conflict in the 1964–1965 reapportionment battle were firmly established: The Republicans had the votes to maintain control in responding to the court decision; Governor Hughes was at least temporarily rebuffed; and the Republicans saw the 1–2–4 plan as the technique for the most favorable optimum gain.

Republican leadership decided to make the study commission bipartisan. They also sought to have two former Governors serve as co-chairmen of the group. Both objectives would give authoritative backing and prestige to the commission's recommendations. Senate President Charles W. Sandman (Republican–Cape May) contacted former Governors Robert B. Meyner and Alfred E. Driscoll. Driscoll, a Republican, declined the invitation. He viewed the situation as intensely partisan and felt that the problem would have to be decided by the Republicans and the governor. In his view, the study commission would serve no useful purpose.[45] In contrast, Governor Meyner, a Democrat, saw a possibility for developing a solution as long as

---

[42] In Senate Concurrent Resolution 21, November 21, 1964. Reprinted in *Meyner Commission Report,* pp. 62–63.

[43] *The New York Times,* December 1, 1964. Also see *Constitution of 1947,* Article IV, Section 4, Paragraph 6; and Article V, Section 1, Paragraph 14.

[44] The votes were as follows: 14–5 in the senate and 31–22 in the assembly. Sources: *NJSJ,* 120th, November 30, 1964, p. 831; and *NJAM,* 188th, November 30, 1964, p. 1149.

[45] Interview with Governor Driscoll, May 18, 1965.

the commission remained objective and did not become embroiled in partisan disputes.[46] Meyner agreed to become chairman of the commission. Senate President Sandman and Assembly Speaker Alfred N. Beadleston (Republican–Monmouth) then appointed the remaining 11 commission members, consisting of six Republicans and five Democrats.[47]

Developing a temporary plan for the senate

The Republicans were forced to reapportion the senate in 1965. A comprehensive 1–2–4 plan was not recommended by the Meyner Commission, due to partisan divisions on important votes. Governor Hughes was determined to deal with the senate issue before congressional redistricting and assembly reapportionment. Republican leaders responded by developing a plan that sought to preserve as many incumbents as possible.

The Meyner Commission was faced with implementing the legislative mandate for a 1–2–4 plan. The complexities of design included the following elements: First, there was the problem of congressional districts in Essex, Hudson, and Union counties. The three urban northeastern counties included six districts, represented by five Democrats

---

[46] Interview with Governor Meyner, May 12, 1965.

[47] Sources: *Meyner Commission Report,* p. 1; Newark *Evening News,* December 3, 1964; and *The New York Times,* December 11, 1964. The six Republicans were: Mark Anton, a former Essex senator; Beadleston, assembly speaker; David L. Horuvitz, former Cumberland County judge; J. Edward Knight, former Monmouth County judge; William E. Ozzard, senate majority leader; and Harry L. Towe, former Bergen County congressman. The five Democrats were: Senator John A. Lynch of Middlesex County; Assemblyman William V. Musto of Hudson County; Charles H. Roemer, former Paterson City attorney (Passaic County); William A. Wachenfeld, former state supreme court justice (Essex County); and Bartholomew A. Sheehan, former Camden County judge.

and one Republican.[48] The major consideration was proper representation for the Democratic cities and the Republican-dominated suburbs. Secondly, in proposing senate districts, the commission was confronted with the objections of Bergen County's Republican leader, Walter H. Jones, who opposed senate districts and favored at-large elections within the newly aligned congressional districts.[49] Thirdly, the commission divided over including new assembly districts within a 1–2–4 plan, or proposing separate assembly districts under the Equal Proportions formula.[50]

The six Republicans on the commission designed a congressional redistricting plan which attracted the support of Hudson County Democrat William V. Musto.[51] The objective of this plan was to retain Hudson control over two districts (the 13th and 14th) in return for reducing Democratic party strength in Essex and Union counties (the 6th, 10th, 11th, and 12th districts). The seven-member majority recommended that the city of Elizabeth (in Union County) be combined with the existing 13th district, consisting of Hudson County's Jersey City and Bayonne.[52] The remainder of Union County would constitute the 6th district and presumably retain incumbent Dwyer, the Republican congresswoman. Thirdly, the other part of Hudson County (presently forming the 14th district)

---

48 Source: *The New York Times,* November 5, 1964. Following the 1964 elections, the congressmen represented in the 6th, 10th, 11th, 12th, 13th and 14th Districts were:

Florence P. Dwyer, Rep.	6th—Union
Peter W. Rodino, Jr., Dem.	10th—Essex
Joseph G. Minish, Dem.	11th—Essex
Paul J. Krebs, Dem.	12th—Essex
Cornelius E. Gallagher, Dem.	13th—Hudson
Dominic V. Daniels, Dem.	14th—Hudson

49 Newark *Evening News,* January 27, 1965.

50 *Ibid.,* January 7, 1965.

51 *Meyner Commission Report,* pp. 1–2.

52 *Ibid.,* p. 21.

would become the new 10th by adding the Essex suburbs of Belleville, Bloomfield, and Nutley. Fourth, the city of Newark was designated as the new 11th district (and conceded to the Democrats) . Finally, the rest of Essex County (that is, all but the portions annexed to the 10th and the city of Newark in the 11th) would consist of the 12th district.[53] The plan appeared to aim for a new party line-up of three Democrats and two Republicans in five districts, as compared with five Democrats and one Republican in the existing six districts in the three counties. Population gains in the southern part of the State led to the proposal for an additional congressional seat for Camden County.[54]

The remaining five Democrats on the Meyner Commission took an alternative view of the Essex-Hudson-Union area. First, they argued that Hudson County did not merit two districts, based on existing population figures.[55] Thus, the present 13th and most of the 14th district should form a new 13th district. Secondly, the city of Elizabeth should be kept in a Union County district, with the exception that three Union suburbs (Hillside, Springfield, and Union) be combined with west Essex suburbs to form the 11th district. Fourthly, the north ward of Newark together with a portion of Hudson County would become the 10th district. Finally, the rest of Newark and other Essex County suburbs was recommended for the 12th district.[56]

The minority plan had the same political effect as the majority plan, that is, a probable result of three Democrats and two Republicans from the five districts. The difference, of course, was that the minority plan favored

---

53 *Meyner Commission Report,* p. 22.
54 There was no internal disagreement on this issue.
55 *Meyner Commission Report,* p. 50.
56 *Meyner Commission Report,* pp. 50–51.

Democrats in Essex County, rather than in Hudson.[57]

Unable to decide on the proper realignment of the Essex-Hudson-Union congressional districts, the commission moved to its next recommendation. Again a partisan division took place. The Democrats attracted the vote of Bergen County's Harry L. Towe in proposing that congressional districts be designated as senate districts, with two senators elected at-large from each such district.[58] The other Republican members voted to subdivide each congressional district into two senate districts with one senator to be elected from each senate district.[59]

Finally, the commission divided over a plan for the assembly. Five Democrats and two Republicans voted for a 60 member assembly apportioned among 17 proposed assembly districts based on the Equal Proportions formula.[60] Thirteen counties would form separate districts for electing assemblymen, while four pairs of counties (Sussex-Warren; Hunterdon-Somerset; Gloucester-Salem; and Atlantic-Cape May) would be combined.[61] Again, the four Republicans dissented and argued for the integrity of a 1–2–4 plan. That is, the four dissenters wanted two assemblymen to be elected from each subdivided senate district.[62]

Thus, the Meyner Commission presented a rather disjointed set of recommendations to the legislature. None of the proposals were coordinated in an overall plan. The majority that prevailed on at-large senate elections and separate assembly districts was defeated on the realignment of congressional districts.

Following the release of the Meyner Commission Re-

---

57 Newark *Evening News,* January 28, 1965.

58 *Meyner Commission Report,* p. 2.

59 *Ibid.*

60 *Ibid.*

61 *Ibid.*

62 *Ibid.,* p. 32.

port, the apportionment conflict was dramatized by the actions of Governor Hughes and Senate Majority Leader Ozzard. Both leaders adopted alternative courses of action in attempting to resolve the issue of senate reapportionment.

Governor Hughes adopted a two-part course of action. First, he indicated that any 1–2–4 plans passed by the legislature would be vetoed.[63] While a threatened veto would not resolve the problem, the governor, in reality, wanted a solution that would forestall a court-imposed plan which might result in statewide at-large elections. Hughes did not phrase his veto threat in terms that placed him at an opposite pole from Republican legislative leaders. What the governor desired was a channel of communication with the Republican leaders through which negotiations could be arranged for a settlement. In seeking a bargaining situation, Hughes was asking for Democratic party participation in a plan that required Republican majorities in the legislature.[64]

Senator Majority Leader Ozzard was not willing to negotiate with Governor Hughes until the Republicans made an effort to pass a 1–2–4 plan. Ozzard's initial efforts were focused on getting the necessary Republican votes to pass a package plan. But the majority leader faced two difficulties which were evident in the Meyner Commission deliberations. First, Essex County was opposed to the congressional redistricting plan which gave Hudson County the advantage over Essex.[65] Second, Bergen County's leader opposed the division of congressional districts into senate districts and favored at-large senate elections within the newly aligned congressional districts.[66]

---

[63] Interviews with Governor Richard J. Hughes and Mr. Joseph W. Katz, special assistant to the governor, June 2, 1965.
[64] *Ibid.*
[65] Interview with Senator William F. Ozzard, May 20, 1965.
[66] *Ibid.*

The majority leader appeared to find the solution to the Essex County problem by permitting two votes to be taken on alternative 1–2–4 plans in the senate. Ozzard offered two bills which incorporated the 1–2–4 plan debated in the Meyner Commission. In addition, Senator C. Robert Sarcone (Republican—Essex) introduced two bills which supported the Essex County view on congressional districts in the Essex-Hudson-Union area.[67]

To pass the package plans Ozzard had to get the support of the rural Republicans who opposed any changes that disturbed the one-senator-per-county system. During the Senate debate, the majority leader argued that court guidelines required inevitable change:[68]

> I am going to tell you something. Whether you like this plan or whether you don't, whether this becomes law or whether it doesn't, not one man is going to run the same way he ever did before . . . So you just better make up your minds that you are going to be living in a different house from now on.

The Republicans then united on party lines to pass both package plans.[69] Ozzard's proposal was adopted by votes of 11–5 and 13–3, while Sarcone's variation passed by 11–4 and 11–5 votes.[70] All but the Morris and Ocean County senators accepted Ozzard's plea for change within rural Republican ranks, while Senator Sarcone of Essex abstained because

---

[67] Source: *NJSJ,* 121st February 17, 1965, pp. 333–334.

[68] *NJSJ,* 121st, February 17, 1965, p. 313. In recognizing the historic nature of imminent senate reapportionment, the senators agreed to record the floor debates in the official journal. This action represented the first time in the twentieth century that either chamber reported officially what was said during a reapportionment debate preceding a roll-call vote. In fact, this explains why newspaper sources are essential for discovering what occurred during debates on the floor of New Jersey Legislative chambers.

[69] *Ibid.,* pp. 308–309.

[70] *Ibid.,* pp. 308–310.

of his alternate view. Similarly, Senator Ozzard abstained on Sarcone's proposal. The Democrats were nearly solidly opposed to both packages, with the lone exception of Hudson County's William F. Kelly, Jr., who voted for Ozzard's congressional districting plan.[71]

TABLE 5.7. Senate Republicans united to pass Ozzard and Sarcone 1–2–4 plans

County Groups and Party	Ozzard Plan				Sarcone Plan			
	Yes	No	Not Voting	Cohesion	Yes	No	Not Voting	Cohesion
Rural Reps.	19	1	2	62.8	16	2	4	45.4
Urban Reps.	4	0	0	33.4	6	0	2	100
Minority Dems.	1	7	4	80.0	0	7	5	100
Totals	24	8	10		22	9	11	

While the senate Republicans had passed two 1–2–4 plans, the assembly Republicans were confronted by internal party rifts and the solid opposition of the Democrats. Republican Majority Leader Raymond H. Bateman (Somerset) had to get the support of Bergen County, which was split into two factions. The five Bergen Republicans, who supported county leader Walter H. Jones, solidly opposed the subdivision of congressional districts into senate districts. Jones faced an insurgency led by Bergen Senator Deamer. Senate districts might lead to the anti-Jones group gaining control of one of these new districts.[72] If the Jones faction bolted from party ranks, the Republicans would fall short of passing a 1–2–4 plan, assuming that all other Republicans and Democrats voted solidly on party lines.

While the Republican leadership was attempting to convince Bergen County to support the 1–2–4 plan, the

[71] This was consistent with the Hudson County vote on the Meyner Commission.

[72] Newark *Evening News,* February 18, 1965.

assembly Democrats tried to get support for two alternative proposals. These included a temporary senate plan based on 16 districts from which 40 senators were elected,[73] and a constitutional convention bill for a permanent reapportionment in 1966.[74]

But Majority Leader Bateman would not permit votes on either of these plans. The Republicans wanted to retain control over the situation. In the last caucus effort before the assembly roll-calls, Bateman was unsuccessful in changing the Bergen position.

Both the Ozzard and Sarcone package plans failed to gain sufficient votes and were defeated by 16–25 and 20–29.[75] The roll-calls showed that the Republicans could not pass an apportionment plan as long as the urban counties split. While overall Republican cohesion was weak (the 32 Republicans split 16–16 on the Ozzard plan and 20–12 on the Sarcone plan), the division among the urban Republicans was most significant. High urban cohesion was necessary in an assembly where the voting distribution included 18 urban Republicans, 14 rural Republicans, and 28 Democrats. While Majority Leader Bateman attributed the defeat of the 1–2–4 plan to Bergen County resistance,[76] the opposition of Essex and Union counties was equally important. The Essex Republicans refused to vote for the Ozzard plan on congressional districts, while the Union four-member delegation was almost solidly against both the Ozzard and Sarcone plans.

In contrast, the Democrats maintained a solid opposition bloc to both plans. The Hudson delegation did not support the Ozzard plan on congressional districts because a solid

---

[73] This plan had been introduced by Senate Minority Leader Robert H. Weber (Cumberland) on February 8.

[74] This proposal was introduced by five Democratic senators on February 15.

[75] *NJAM,* 189th, February 19, 1965, pp. 402–403.

[76] Interview with Assemblyman Raymond H. Bateman, May 6, 1965.

Democratic party position enhanced future bargaining power in forcing a senate reapportionment. The Democrats saw the defeat of the 1–2–4 plan as a turning point.[77] The Republicans, even with legislative majorities, were unable to pass a plan in response to court demands.

TABLE 5.8. Assembly Republicans failed to pass 1–2–4 plan due to urban county split

County Groups and Party	Ozzard Plan Yes	No	Not Voting	Cohesion	Sarcone Plan Yes	No	Not Voting	Cohesion
Urban Reps.	5	5	8	44.4	8	10	0	11.1
Rural Reps.	11	2	1	57.1	12	1	1	71.4
Democrats	0	18	10	100	0	18	10	100
Totals	16	25	19		20	29	11	
	Rep. Cohesion = 0				Rep. Cohesion = 25.0			

The next move by the Republicans was to attempt to heal the party rift in the assembly, while the senate Republicans tried to convince the state supreme court to delay senate reapportionment until after the November, 1965 elections.[78] Both efforts failed. Bergen County could not be moved by party loyalty appeals; and the state court was not convinced that the legislature was incapable of designing a temporary senate plan.[79] In fact, the supreme court felt that the Republicans should now try to carry out their "legislative responsibilities" by meeting directly with the governor.[80]

The bargaining position of Governor Hughes was in-

[77] Interview with Assemblyman J. Edward Crabiel (Democrat–Middlesex), June 2, 1965.

[78] Interview with Senator Ozzard, May 20, 1965.

[79] *Jackman v. Bodine,* 44 N.J. 312 (March 31, 1965).

[80] *Ibid.*

creased as a result of the court's views on developing a temporary plan for the senate. The Republicans were now forced to confine attention to a senate plan, which had been the major objective of the Democrats from the outset. On April 8, Governor Hughes and Senate Majority Leader Ozzard, after several negotiating sessions, agreed on the basic outlines of a plan: The plan must retain county lines and all Senators must be elected at-large. Political rather than population considerations were the key to an agreement. Ozzard and Hughes decided on a 28-member senate, consisting of 14 districts. The rural counties, which had 13 seats in the existing senate, would be reduced to eight seats in the new plan; and the urban counties were increased from eight to 20 seats.[81]

The estimated political effects of the 28-man plan were as follows: (1) The densely-populated urban northeastern counties would have a majority of 15 seats in the new senate as compared with five seats in the 21-member chamber. Bergen and Essex counties were each allocated four seats, even though Essex had more population;[82] (2) At least 14 incumbent senators, including 10 Republicans and four Democrats, were protected by the plan. As for the remaining seven seats, the Republicans from Cape May and Warren counties expressed interest in opposing Governor Hughes in the forthcoming elections; the Democrat from Salem County stated he would seek a congressional seat; the Republicans from Ocean and Sussex counties were retiring; and the Hunterdon County seat was vacant. This left only Gloucester County's John E. Hunt, a Republican,

---

[81] Newark *Evening News*, April 9, 1965; and *The New York Times*, April 12, 1965. Subsequently, the plan was modified to meet the objections of the Camden and Gloucester senators who wanted to remain in separate districts. Majority Leader Ozzard agreed to this change at the last minute. Thus, the senate passed both a 28 and a 29-member plan.

[82] According to the 1960 census, Essex County's population was 923,545, while Bergen's was 780,255.

TABLE 5.9. Political implications of Hughes-Ozzard agreement on a 28-member senate plan

Urban County Districts	Incumbent's Pol. Party	Estimated Future Pol. Party Composition
Bergen	Rep.	4 Reps.
Camden-	Rep.	2 Competitive
Gloucester (Rural)	Rep.	
Essex	Rep.	4 Competitive
Hudson	Dem.	3 Dems.
Mercer	Dem.	1 Dem.
Middlesex	Dem.	2 Dems.
Passaic	Dem.	2 Dems.
Union	Rep.	2 Competitive
Totals	4 Rep. 4 Dem.	4 Rep. 8 Dem. 8 Competitive
Rural County Districts		
Atlantic-	Rep.	Rep.
Cape May	Rep.	
Burlington	Rep.	Competitive
Cumberland-	Dem.	Dem.
Salem	Dem.	
Hunterdon-	Rep.	Rep.
Somerset	Rep.	
Monmouth-	Rep.	2 Reps.
Ocean	Rep.	
Morris-Sussex-	Rep.	2 Reps.
Warren	Rep.	
	Rep.	
Totals	10 Reps. 2 Dems.	6 Reps. 1 Dem. 1 Competitive

forced to run against Camden County's Frederick J. Scholz (Republican) in the newly-combined Camden-Gloucester district;[83] (3) The new senate lineup would

[83] This problem was subsequently modified under the 29-man plan.

probably consist of a slight Democratic party advantage in assuming that Governor Hughes was able to carry half of the districts in the competitive counties in his re-election.

Senator Ozzard then took the initiative to get a majority vote for the new senate plan. He was able to modify the 28-man plan to satisfy Senator Hunt of Gloucester. The Camden-Gloucester district was split, allowing Hunt to run in a separate district under a 29-man plan.[84] On the senate floor, Ozzard again confronted the rural Republicans with the necessity of passing the plan. He argued that there was no other alternative. Either the senate accepted the new districts or the supreme court would decide the issue:[85]

> I have been making speeches about reapportionment for at least six months and everywhere I go I run into lots of people who say, 'Leave it as it is. We like it this way.' And they mean it and they think you can do it, and you know you can't. So you have a bill today that is in part already approved by the New Jersey Supreme Court, and in the balance is something I think, at least, is the least inconvenient, the least unsettling of any of the plans that we have been able to devise that we think we can get through the front office.

The senate thereupon passed both the 28 and 29-member plans by votes of 14–1 and 14–0.[86] Seven rural Republicans joined two urban Republicans and five Democrats on the 28-man plan; while eight rural Republicans combined with one urban Republican and the same five Democrats on the 29-man plan.

Ozzard was successful in guiding the temporary senate plan through passage because he knew that the rural counties could no longer fight for their objectives of re-

---

84 Interview with Senator Ozzard, May 20, 1965.

85 *NJSJ,* 121st, April 12, 1965, p. 515.

86 *Ibid.,* pp. 511–513.

taining control. By holding together eight of the ten rural Republicans (on the 29-man plan), Ozzard was fully aware that the minority Democrats would add the remaining votes. The last-ditch opposition was from the northeast urban bloc and rural Monmouth and Morris counties. But even these senators realized the futility of trying to prevent adoption of a plan which had necessitated such careful bargaining by Ozzard with Governor Hughes. The only Republican to cast a negative vote was Senator Hunt (Gloucester) on the 28-man plan. Hunt then voted affirmatively for the 29-member plan. The other dissenting Republicans abstained from the voting. Thus, an "alliance" of rural Republicans and minority Democrats resulted in the senate agreeing to a new (but temporary) senate apportionment plan.

Legislative adoption was completed when the assembly approved both plans by votes of 43–16 and 46–13.[87] The senate voting pattern was duplicated in the assembly. The urban Republicans showed no cohesion as Bergen, Camden, Essex, and Union counties split their votes. Bergen and Union counties split internally on both roll-calls; Camden supported the 29-man plan and opposed the 28-man plan; and Essex County opposed both plans on the grounds that it merited more senate representation than Bergen County. Otherwise, most of the rural Republicans voted with a nearly solid bloc of minority Democrats to pass both plans.

Table 5.10 summarizes the voting position of the three county groupings in the two chambers. The most obvious conclusion is that the Republicans voted with weak cohesion, due to both scattered resistance to any change by a few rural Republicans and the lack of agreement among the urban Republicans. When the Republicans were so badly split, the minority Democrats, by maintaining a high

---

[87] *NJAM,* 189th, April 12, 1965, pp. 587–590.

degree of unity, were able to achieve their goal of gaining the first senate reapportionment in 189 years.

TABLE 5.10. Legislature adopts 29-member plan to reapportion senate

County Groups and Party	Senate Yes	Senate No	Senate Not Voting	Senate Cohesion	General Assembly Yes	General Assembly No	General Assembly Not Voting	General Assembly Cohesion
Rural Reps.	8	0	3	60	10	4	0	42.8
Urban Reps.	1	0	3	50	10	8	0	11.1
Democrats	5	0	1	100	26	1	1	92.6
Totals	14	0	7		46	13	1	
Rep. Cohesion = 28.6					Rep. Cohesion = 25.0			

Conclusions

The senate apportionment battle ended when Governor Hughes signed the 29-member plan into law. Throughout the struggle, the senate Republicans attempted to outmaneuver the governor in meeting state supreme court guidelines. Both weighted voting and the 1–2–4 plan represented rural Republican efforts to maintain control over senate reapportionment. But the senate Republicans were forced to work out a plan with Governor Hughes. This happened when the senate Republicans were unable to convince the assembly Republicans to support a party position in opposition to Governor Hughes and the Democrats. The assembly Republicans were not a united party due to the lack of agreement among the urban county delegations. Torn by internal rifts and inter-county rivalries, the urban Republicans were so badly split that they could not act effectively. The urban Republicans could not agree on the anti-court resolution, weighted voting, or a 1–2–4 plan.

The most effective voting bloc in the assembly was the minority Democrats. As long as this group voted with relatively solid agreement, they could force a solution most favorable to their interests. The Democrats were aided by the consistent position of Governor Hughes, who played the key role in negotiating a senate plan.

When all other efforts failed, Senate Majority Leader Ozzard, representing a rural county, accepted the inevitability of change. Ozzard was able to hold together most of the rural senators when he convinced them that no other alternative was available. Ozzard also tried to protect most rural county incumbents under the new plan.

Thus, the 1964–1965 case illustrated that senate reapportionment was achieved when there were strong external pressures forcing legislative action. The legislature in this case lost control over the problem when the highest state court imposed the "one man, one vote" standard. A Democratic governor was then able to enter the struggle directly and participate in a solution because the court made reapportionment a high priority legislative issue.[88]

[88] The "temporary" senate plan of 1965 served only through the November, 1965 elections. At that time, Governor Hughes was re-elected by an overwhelming majority and the Democrats captured two-house control with 41–19 assembly and 19–10 senate majorities. A constitutional convention, established by legislative enactment in 1965, met in 1966 to work out the details of a final apportionment solution. The 1966 legislature then adopted a permanent reapportionment plan based on the convention's recommendations. Due to time limitations this final phase of the 1964–1965 struggle has not been included within the scope of this study.

6

Major Strategies in New Jersey Reapportionment Politics

Introduction

ON EIGHT DIFFERENT OCCASIONS IN THE TWENTIETH CENTURY, the New Jersey Legislature faced various types of reapportionment problems. At the root of these problems was the clash between groups that wanted to retain power and control and other groups that desired a greater share of legislative representation. By preserving existing representation, particular legislative groups were able to maintain power at the expense of other groups. Group conflict was therefore a persistent feature of reapportionment controversies. Every reapportionment involved a "life cycle" of conflict and resolution. The "life cycle" is:[1]

> . . . conceived and born, it flourishes for a while, and then certain processes that are probably inherent in its own dynamic system eventually bring it to an end.

[1] Kenneth E. Boulding, *Conflict and Defense: A General Theory* (New York: Harper and Row Publishers, 1962), p. 307.

To analyze the process of conflict resolution, it is necessary to identify the major *strategies* employed by various legislative groups in state legislative apportionment. By identifying these strategies, it may be possible to discover how power is retained, altered, or redistributed in a legislature. Reapportionment politics in New Jersey provides the framework for identifying and analyzing various legislative strategies.

This chapter focuses attention on legislative strategies, although consideration has been given to two other approaches, both of which are important in understanding legislative behavior in reapportionment politics. The first approach would consider New Jersey's experiences as part of the series of comparative case studies of state legislative apportionment. In this regard, the study of New Jersey reapportionment politics would add to the findings of such representative authors as Baker,[2] Hanson,[3] Jewell,[4] and Steiner and Gove.[5] As a case study, various legislative responses in New Jersey would indicate what "rules" or "principles" have been followed in reapportionment politics. The purpose of the study would be to confirm or refute "principles" suggested elsewhere[6] by examining reapportionment problems in New Jersey. This chapter will consider the validity of "principles" in view of major strategies employed by legislative groups in reapportionment politics.

---

[2] Gordon E. Baker, *The Politics of Reapportionment in Washington State* (New York: Holt, Rinehard and Winston, 1960); and *Rural versus Urban Political Power* (New York: Random House, 1955).

[3] Royce Hanson, *The Political Thicket* (Englewood Cliffs, New Jersey: Prentice-Hall, 1966).

[4] Malcolm E. Jewell, Ed., *The Politics of Reapportionment* (New York: Atherton Press, 1962); and Jewell, *The State Legislature* (New York: Random House, 1962).

[5] Gilbert Y. Steiner and Samuel K. Gove, *Legislative Politics in Illinois* (Urbana: University of Illinois Press, 1960).

[6] See: Chapter I, *Supra*, pp. 35–36 for a discussion of these reapportionment "principles."

A second important approach to the study of reapportionment politics would consider New Jersey's legislative activities as part of the state's historical, legal, constitutional, and political development. The purpose of the study would be to place reapportionment politics into perspective. New Jersey's experiences with twentieth century reapportionment problems would then add to the state's inventory of political analysis, which is represented, in part, by Bebout's study of urbanization.[7] Lockard's examination of governors,[8] McKean's analyses of city politics and the legislature,[9] and Rich's text on state government and administration.[10] Hopefully, the study of reapportionment politics does add to the literature on New Jersey government and politics. In subsequent discussions, attention will be directed to the unique constitutional, executive, judicial, and legislative elements of New Jersey reapportionment politics as well as to recent constitutional changes that will change the strategic environment for future legislative responses to reapportionment problems.

To analyze legislative strategies, a particular theoretical model, the theory of games, will be used.[11] Before identi-

---

[7] John E. Bebout and Ronald J. Grele, *Where Cities Meet: The Urbanization of New Jersey* (Princeton: D. Van Nostrand Co., Inc., 1964).

[8] Duane Lockard, *The New Jersey Governor* (Princeton: D. Van Nostrand Co., Inc., 1964).

[9] Dayton David McKean, *The Boss: The Hague Machine in Action* (Boston: Houghton Mifflin Co., 1940); and *Pressures on the Legislature of New Jersey* (New York: Columbia University Press, 1938).

[10] Bennett M. Rich, *The Government and Administration of New Jersey* (New York: Thomas Y. Crowell Co., 1957).

[11] There is much difficulty in adapting game theory to the legislative process and caution must be exercised. To the author's knowledge, there are no other studies of legislative apportionment which have employed game theory. The closest approach is found in an analysis of game theory as applied to legislative elections in the state of Illinois. See: Jack Sawyer and Duncan MacRae, Jr., "Game Theory and Cumulative Voting in Illinois," *American Political Science Review,* Vol. 56, No. 4 (December, 1962), pp. 936–946.

fying the major components of this model, three preliminary qualifications must be noted.

First, all twentieth century New Jersey reapportionments cannot and will not be explained by game theory. All of the facts and particular events in New Jersey's reapportionment experiences cannot fit into this model.

Secondly, the identification of strategies represents only one way of understanding the exercise of power and control in a state legislature. In addition, the game theoretical model cannot be used to analyze all legislative strategies. A process of selection is necessary. Subsequent discussion of major strategies will represent only a sampling of the total range of strategies that may be used under particular conditions.

Thirdly, the theory of games has several inherent limitations when it is applied to practical political problems. These limitations naturally prevent the theory from offering a complete explanation of various political phenomena.

The basic limitation of game theory is that it assumes *rational behavior* by the participants in selecting strategies.[12] Under pure game theory conditions, strategy is defined as follows:[13]

> A strategy is a complete description of the choices a player will make under any possible set of circumstances. A strategy cannot be invalidated either by nature or by an act of an opponent, given the rules of the game, for the strategy is a complete specification of the action that will be taken for all states of nature and all moves of opponents.

Clearly, it is impossible to analyze legislative strategies under such strict limitations and no such effort is intended

---

[12] John McDonald, *Strategy in Poker, Business and War* (New York: W. W. Norton & Co., Inc., 1950), p. 52.

[13] Morton A. Kaplan, *System and Process in International Politics* (New York: John Wiley & Sons, Inc., Science Editions, 1964), p. 173.

here. Strategies will be identified for purposes of understanding how various actors behave under given conditions. Instead of considering strategies as "a complete specification of the action that will be taken," strategies in reapportionment politics will be assumed to be flexible and subject to change.

A second serious limitation of pure game theory is the assumption that the rules of the game are not under the control of the players.[14] The rules of the game determine the moves (or strategies) the player may make.[15] In reapportionment politics, however, the rules do change over time and many of these rules are subject to control by the players.[16] By not allowing for changes in the rules, game theory deals with static situations. In contrast, reapportionment politics is a dynamic process and changes are essential in order to displace entrenched legislative groups who will not yield power under existing rules of the game.[17] In subsequent discussion of legislative strategies, it will be assumed that the players have control over many of the rules of the game.

In addition to the static nature of game theory, a third limitation is the assumption that "values are defined from the outside, that they do not change, and that they are independent from the results of the game."[18] But legislative groups are concerned with more than the moves or strategies selected in reapportionment conflicts. There are no "single-purpose"[19] calculations in reapportionment poli-

---

[14] *Ibid.*, p. 171.

[15] *Ibid.*

[16] For example, legislators can amend or revise the state constitution, which will change the rules of the game.

[17] For example, if changes of the rules were not possible, there would have been no way of changing the one-senator-per-county system in the senate. See, Chapter V, *Supra.*

[18] Karl W. Deutsch, *The Nerves of Government* (New York: The Free Press, 1963), p. 59.

[19] *Ibid.*, p. 60.

tics. In fact, the difficulty of identifying strategies in a legislature is due to the multipurpose objectives of various legislative groups which select different courses of action for different and often conflicting reasons. Although no presumptions will be made subsequently to explain all legislative motivations, values, and reasons for selecting various strategies in the "reapportionment game," it will be assumed that the players will seek to obtain maximum gains or to avoid minimum losses, which can be measured in terms of legislative seats. This represents, perhaps, a serious limiting condition on analysis of legislative strategies.

A final limitation of game theory is the emphasis on one dominant principle, the principle of "minimax."[20] Minimax assumes that nothing more than a minimum gain is possible in any game. Minimax is defined as a strategy "that seeks to incur the least risk of loss, even at the price of accepting the smallest chance of gain."[21] The criticism of minimax is that it is clearly a conservative strategy.[22] Pure game theory does not allow for an alternative "maximin" strategy, where some players may seek to obtain maximum gains. Only minimax is chosen because it is assumed that competing players will know all the relevant information about the game, that such information is available to all players, and that the strategy of one player will always be known by the other players.[23] Thus, the minimax principle assumes that strategies in all games are predeterminate. This restriction is too limiting for analyzing reapportionment politics. In place of minimax, the following discussion will focus upon two competing objectives, both of which are essential for understanding the "life cycle" of conflict and resolution,[24] and both of which are known to

[20] McDonald, *op. cit.*, p. 81.
[21] Deutsch, *op. cit.*, p. 61.
[22] Kaplan, *op. cit.*, p. 188.
[23] Deutsch, *op. cit.*
[24] *Supra*, p. 217.

all the players in the game. Those players who want to alter the existing legislative pattern of power and control will seek a *maximizing* objective. These players will attempt to maximize their gains, and the gains will be measured in terms of winning additional legislative seats. In contrast, those players who want to retain the *status quo* will seek to avoid losses. Such players will attempt to preserve existing legislative representation by employing various types of *minimizing* strategies.

Having discussed the most important limitations of game theory, it is now possible to summarize the major components of the model which will be used in the study of legislative strategies in reapportionment politics:

1. *Payoffs:* The gains and losses in the "reapportionment game" are measurable in terms of legislative seats. Payoffs are obtained either by employing a maximizing strategy or a minimizing strategy. Those groups that desire change will seek maximizing objectives. In contrast, those groups that wish to preserve the *status quo* will seek to avoid losses and therefore will employ minimizing strategies.

2. *Rules of the game:* The rules of the game determine the moves the players may make. In the "reapportionment game," several of the rules are under control of the players. The rules consist of legal-formal, or constitutional rules; and the prerogatives of political parties when they control one or both legislative chambers and/or the governor.

3. *Players in the game and their resources:* The players in the "reapportionment game" will consist of various legislative groups, the governor, and the state supreme court. Each of the players will have various resources at his disposal. The resources of the players will determine what strategies will be selected in seeking the maximizing or minimizing objectives.

4. *Strategies:* Strategies will consist of three major elements: the resources of the players; the moves made by the players in the game; and bargaining to resolve differences among diverse groups. Six major strategies will then be identified for purposes of analysis. The strategies include: party unity; institutional loyalty; areal unity; blocking and obstructionism; reciprocity; and anticipated partisan gains.

Several elements of game theory will therefore be used in analyzing reapportionment problems in New Jersey. Again, it should be re-emphasized that what follows represents only a tentative and theoretical attempt to explain a few of the very complex considerations of reapportionment politics in New Jersey. Caution is required because a total explanation is not intended. The remaining part of this chapter attempts to discuss reapportionment politics in a new way and the limitations of the approach should be evident throughout the following discussion.

The New Jersey "Reapportionment Game"

Payoffs: The maximizing and minimizing objectives

New Jersey reapportionment politics deals directly with the distribution of power and control in the State Legislature. As various legislative groups compete for power, two conflicting objectives become clear in the reapportionment struggle: First, those groups that view change *favorably* will seek to *maximize their gains.* Achievement of this objective results in one group gaining power at the expense of another. The second major objective represents a direct reaction to the first objective. Those groups that view change *unfavorably* will attempt to *minimize their losses.* The goal is to preserve the *status quo,* which can be achieved through inaction, delay, or diversionary maneuvers.[25]

Success or failure in attaining and maximizing or minimizing objectives has an immediate and direct impact on various legislative groups. In every reapportionment of the New Jersey General Assembly, the gains of the winners were equal to the losses of the losers.[26] Every maximum gain and every minimum loss was therefore reciprocal for particular winning and losing county delegations; and, furthermore, all results were directly measurable in terms of gaining or losing representation in the assembly.[27] Maximizing strategies were employed by county delegations that sought seating gains in the assembly, while minimizing strategies were primarily evident in the senate, where the one-senator-per county-system of representation resulted in rural county control.[28]

The rules of the game

To achieve gains or avoid losses in reapportionment, diverse legislative groups are constrained and must act within certain specified limits or "rules of the game."[29] In New Jersey reapportionment politics, the "rules of the game" consisted of formal-legal or constitutional limita-

---

[25] Refusal to reapportion has been a key problem in state legislatures. See Jewell, *The State Legislature, op. cit.,* p. 18.

[26] Thus, assembly reapportionment in New Jersey fulfills the "zero-sum" condition of game theory. See: William H. Riker, *The Theory of Political Coalitions* (New Haven: Yale University Press, 1962), p. 28.

[27] It will be shown below that reciprocal gains and losses in assembly reapportionment were caused by state constitutional requirements, that is, a 60-member maximum limitation, and a guarantee of at least one seat for each of the state's 21 counties.

[28] This held true up to 1964, when the state supreme court declared the senate basis of representation unconstitutional in *Jackman v. Bodine,* 43 N.J. 491 (1964).

[29] See discussion, *Supra,* p. 221.

tions; and the prerogatives of political parties when they controlled one or both legislative chambers and/or the governor.

Formal-legal rules are found in the state constitution which established seven conditions for legislative action on reapportionment:[30] (1) The senate was composed of equal county representation; (2) The assembly must be reapportioned every ten years in accord with decennial census figures; (3) Assembly reapportionment must take place within a 60-member maximum limitation, and with a guarantee of at least one member for each county; (4) A majority vote is required to pass reapportionment bills at the roll-call stage; (5) Both chambers must agree to the same reapportionment plan; (6) The governor must approve the plan before it becomes law or he can exercise a veto in which case the legislature needs a two-thirds vote to put the plan into effect;[31] and (7) The state supreme court may exercise judicial review to determine if the legislature has followed the procedural and substantive requirements previously listed.

Political party considerations established a second set of constraints on reapportionment activity in New Jersey. In every case where one party, the Republicans, had a majority of members in both legislative chambers, the party caucus controlled the initial introduction of reapportionment proposals. Party caucus control was directly attributable to tight discipline in the majority party.[32] The party caucus selected the formal leaders in both chambers. Party

[30] *Constitution of 1947,* Articles IV, V, and VI.

[31] Prior to adoption of the 1947 constitution, the governor's veto power was not as strong. Under the constitution of 1844, only a majority vote in the legislature was required to override a governor's veto. See: *Constitution of 1844,* Article V, Paragraph 7.

[32] See: McKean, *Pressures on the Legislature of New Jersey, op. cit.,* pp. 30–40; Rich, *op. cit.,* pp. 52–56; and Belle Zeller, Ed., *American State Legislatures* (New York: Thomas Y. Crowell Co., 1954), p. 207.

leaders were bound by caucus agreements on reapportionment plans and generally presented bills for floor consideration. Prior consensus in the caucus indicated that the majority party sought to control reapportionment policy-making.[33] A corollary rule was that the legislative minority party, which was usually the Democrats, was excluded from offering initial reapportionment bills.

Majority party prerogatives were less certain when the Republicans controlled one chamber and the Democrats had a majority of members in the other. This occurred, for example, in the 1911 and 1961 reapportionments, when the Democrats controlled the assembly and the Republicans had a senate majority. In both cases the two parties competed for control over the sponsorship and resolution of the reapportionment problem. The principle of "to each his own,"[34] indicating that a legislative chamber will control its own reapportionment was not evident in either case.[35] In 1911 and 1961, the original plans proposed by senate Republicans were eventually adopted by the assembly Democrats.

A second modification of majority party prerogatives took place when the legislature was controlled by one party and the governor was a member of the opposite party. Divided legislative-executive control, which was evident

---

[33] This finding represents a modification of an original hypothesis in Chapter I, *Supra*, p. 35. There, it was stated that "the legislative interest is clearly predominant in reapportionment policy-making." The modification is that under conditions of one-party legislative control, the majority party caucus will control reapportionment policy-making.

[34] See: Hanson, *op. cit.*, pp. 35–36; and Chapter I, *Supra*, p. 35, which suggested that "each house should handle its own apportionment problem separately and the other house should accept the result."

[35] Thus, on at least two occasions, the senate proposed the plan finally adopted by the assembly. This disproves the hypothesis of "to each his own." In fact, New Jersey legislative practices in reapportionment appear to include regular inter-chamber participation in developing reapportionment proposals.

in the 1911, 1921–1922, 1941 and 1964–1965 cases, as well as in portions of the constitutional revision (1941–1943) and assembly deadlock (1954–1961) cases, did not alter the rule of initial sponsorship of reapportionment measures by the legislative majority party. Rather, the governor, who was a Democrat in all the aforementioned cases, retained certain constitutional and legislative leadership resources which he could employ to modify the impact of majority party caucus decisions. The governor's resources will be discussed in detail subsequently.

Players in the game and their resources

Constitutional restraints and political party prerogatives determine the "rules of the game" in New Jersey reapportionment politics. Within these two sets of constraints, various players in the game, including legislative groups, the governor, and the state supreme court, have a number of resources at their disposal in attaining the maximizing or minimizing objectives.

RESOURCES OF LEGISLATIVE GROUPS

Most prominent throughout all New Jersey reapportionments were four distinct legislative groups. These included the rural Republican senators, the urban and rural wings of the majority party in the assembly; and the assembly minority party.

The rural county senators, whose control of the upper chamber was maintained by equal county representation until 1965, had three resources in responding to reapportionment problems. First, the *constitutional rule* of one-senator-per-county afforded the rural Republicans with a strong bargaining position. For example, revision was impossible in the constitutional reform case (1941–1947) until retention of the restrictive constitutional provision was assured for the rural county senators.[36]

The second resource of the rural county senators was their *voting power*. In a twenty-one member senate, 11 senators constituted a majority. As long as 11 of the 13 rural senators had the same party affiliation, which was consistently Republican in all reapportionment cases, these 11 senators were assured of control. Control was exercised in the majority party caucus, in the selection of majority party leaders, and on the senate floor when roll-call votes were taken.[37]

High voting cohesion led to a third resource for the rural county senators. Not only did the rural senators have strong voting power, but they also voted frequently as a *bloc*. Regional differences did not inhibit a bloc vote between the northwestern, southern, and seashore representatives. The rural senators oftentimes voted together to promote action or to withstand assaults on their control. Bloc voting was particularly important when the rural senators remained *consistent* on one particular reapportionment plan. When the assembly was torn by urban-rural differences or controlled by the Democrats, a consistent rural bloc vote in the senate could effectively exploit assembly divisions. This was especially evident in the assembly deadlock case of the 1950's when the senate passed Equal Proportions Plans on ten separate occasions from 1953 to 1961. The assembly finally adopted an Equal Proportions Plan in 1961.

---

36 This finding confirms an original hypothesis in Chapter I, *Supra*, p. 36 that the maximum objective in reapportionment is to disturb the *status quo* as little as possible. This objective is achieved, in part, by securing constitutional provisions that restrict change. Also, see: Jewell, *The State Legislature, op. cit.*, p. 18; and Duane Lockard, *The Politics of State and Local Government* (New York: Macmillan Co., 1963), pp. 311–312.

37 *Supra*, p. 226.

The combination of resources held by the rural county senators, including retention of restrictive constitutional provisions, voting power, and consistent bloc cohesion, led to a situation where the rural bloc was able to exercise powerful influence in most reapportionment conflicts.[38]

Resources were dispersed rather than concentrated in the assembly. Majority party control did not always ensure agreement in reapportionment policy-making.[39] The assembly majority party, whether Republican or Democratic, was split into urban and rural wings.[40] Potentially, the urban wing had the greatest *voting* resources. But the urban wing did not vote cohesively because of the impact of reapportionment on particular counties.[41] Thus, the eight urban county delegations in the assembly could not effectively pool their voting resources to achieve control over reapportionment. This situation characterized the problems encountered by the assembly Democrats in 1911, the urban Republicans in 1921 and 1964–1965, and both parties in the assembly deadlock case of the 1950's.

The second resource of the urban county delegations was the ability to form *alliances* with the governor.[42] Reciprocity was an important consideration in the relationships between the urban county delegations and the governor. Urban assemblymen did not want the governor to intervene in reapportionment conflicts when they could

---

[38] This finding represents another refutation of the "to each his own" hypothesis. The senate was not constrained from regularly participating in assembly reapportionment problems. *Supra,* p. 227.

[39] Jewell, *The State Legislature, op. cit.,* pp. 59–61.

[40] *Ibid.,* p. 60; and V. O. Key, Jr., *American State Politics: An Introduction* (New York: Alfred A. Knopf, 1956), pp. 229–233.

[41] David R. Derge, "Metropolitan and Outstate Alignments in Illinois and Missouri Legislative Delegations," *American Political Science Review,* Vol. 52, No. 4 (December, 1958), p. 1065.

[42] Alliances between urban county legislative delegations and the governor were evident throughout most of the reapportionment cases. Alliances were due to the support that the urban counties provided to the governor in gaining electoral pluralities in the State. See: Baker, *Urban versus Rural Political Power, op. cit.,* p. 25.

handle the problem alone.[43] In return, the urban delegations would lend their support to the governor in other programs.[44] Reciprocity explained the refusal of Governor Edison to veto the 1941 reapportionment plan even when the Camden County Democrats had a strong case for an additional assembly seat. Edison, a Democrat, needed the support of the Essex County Republicans for his program of constitutional reform. On other occasions, the urban assemblymen expected the governor to enter the legislative arena directly and help to resolve reapportionment conflicts. Without Governor Meyner's insistence on legislative action in 1961, several urban county delegations would not have gained increased representation in a deadlock that persisted for nearly ten years.[45]

Finally, urban assemblymen of either the majority or minority party who sought direct benefits for their own counties could take advantage of the absence of precise constitutional guidelines relating to a mathematical formula for assembly reapportionment. The state constitution did not have any provision for a reapportionment formula.[46] By changing from the variation of the Vinton Method to the Vinton Method in 1941, the Essex Republicans avoided a seat loss. Similarly, the Union County legislators in both chambers focused attention in Equal Propor-

---

43 This confirms the hypothesis that the "legislature resents outside interference by the governor." See: Chapter I, *Supra,* p. 36.

44 Generally, the governor is not expected to play an active role in legislative reapportionment because of the fear that the rest of his legislative program might be endangered. See: Jewell, Ed., *The Politics of Reapportionment, op. cit.,* p. 31.

45 Thus, the originally stated hypothesis should be modified to state that under conditions of persistent deadlock, the legislature will not always resent outside interference by the governor. See: Chapter I, *Supra,* p. 36.

46 *Constitution of 1947,* Article IV, Section 3. The constitution only provided for a vague population standard in assembly reapportionment: "The members of the general assembly shall be apportioned among the several counties *as nearly as may be* according to the number of their inhabitants. . ." (Emphasis added.)

tions Plans in the 1950's to assure a maximum seating gain.

Although the rural wing of the assembly majority party lacked the voting power of the urban wing, the rural assemblymen could be effective in reapportionment conflicts when they employed the resource of *consistent bloc voting cohesion*.[47] By joining together, the members of the rural wing could demand changes in plans favored by the urban wing. The rural wing was most concerned with losing existing representation. The effort was to preserve minimal representation and prevent any increase in the size of the assembly that would favor the urban counties. Thus, the Atlantic County delegation was successful in preventing adoption of the Cavicchia Plan in 1952 and 1953 by mobilizing a rural bloc vote. Atlantic was not willing to yield one of its two assembly seats under any reapportionment plan. Also, in the assembly deadlock case, the rural wing was firmly opposed to the 67-member plan which increased urban county representation and discriminated against rural county power.

The urban and rural wings of the majority party in the assembly were not always opposed to each other in seeking reapportionment objectives. In fact, as it will be shown later, the strategy of party unity required urban-rural agreement within the majority party. When the political environment was characterized by divided legislative-executive control, the majority party in the legislature could sometimes use the *statewide electorate* as a resource. By appealing to the state's voters, the legislature could bypass programs sought by a governor who represented the opposite political party. In the constitutional revision case, for example, the *referendum* device was employed on three separate occasions. To bypass both the governor (who was a Democrat) and the legislature (which was controlled by the Republicans), the Hendrickson Study Commission

[47] Consistent bloc voting cohesion was thus an important resource for the rural legislators in both the assembly and the senate.

recommended that a new draft constitution be presented directly to the voters for approval. The Republican controlled legislature opposed this approach and agreed on the Feller Referendum proposal of 1943. The Feller Plan represented an effort to circumvent participation by Democratic Governor Edison. The 1943 plan was designed to seek voter approval in authorizing the legislature to draft a new constitution in 1944. After the draft was completed, another referendum was required for final adoption of a new basic State charter.

Diversity rather than unity was usually present within the ranks of the assembly majority party. Due to the urban-rural split in the majority party, the assembly minority party could be effective when it employed the resource of *consistent bloc voting cohesion*.[47a] This suggests that the minority party was not always suppressed in New Jersey reapportionments.[48] A cohesive minority party bloc vote was effective when the minority party was able to attract allies from the divided ranks of the majority party. When this was achieved, the assembly minority party could hold out for alternative reapportionment plans. Such alternatives might eventually be adopted when the assembly minority had a majority of members in the senate. This occurred in the 1911 and 1961 cases when the senate Republican plans were finally accepted by Democratic controlled assemblies. Also, the minority bloc could form alliances with the governor when both were members of the same party. By refusing to vote for Republican plans in 1965, the minority Democrats aided Governor Hughes in promoting a temporary senate reapportionment plan.

A second resource was available to particular county

[47a] Thus, consistent bloc voting cohesion was perhaps the most powerful resource that could be employed by any of the diverse groups within the legislature.

[48] This finding appears to modify the "principle" that the minority party will be unable to prevent seat losses. See: Chapter I, *Supra,* p. 36. Also, Hanson, *op. cit.,* p. 35.

delegations within assembly minority party ranks. A unified assembly majority party that appealed to the statewide electorate in referenda had to take into account the voting power of individual urban counties in minority party ranks. At the height of its influence, the Hudson County Democratic machine was able to generate huge voting pluralities due to the great power wielded by Boss Hague in Jersey City.[49] Hague's propaganda campaign against the 1944 referendum for a new constitution was not overcome by revision advocates and the proposed charter was overwhelmingly defeated at the polls.

RESOURCES OF THE GOVERNOR

The New Jersey governor was an active participant in reapportionment conflicts.[50] The governor had three *constitutional* resources that promoted his intervention in the legislative struggle. First, he had the power to veto reapportionment plans.[51] But the *threat* of a veto appeared more effective than its actual employment. The one time that a governor vetoed a reapportionment plan (1922), the legislature swiftly responded by overriding the veto and enacted its own plan. In contrast, the threatened use of a veto by Governor Hughes in 1964 and 1965 showed his intentions to remain an active participant in developing a temporary senate plan. Hughes insisted that he was opposed

---

49 Will Chasan, "The Decline of Boss Hague," *Nation,* Vol. 151, No. 24 (December 14, 1940), p. 606.

50 Other findings have suggested that the governor usually is passive in legislative apportionment struggles. See: Jewell, Ed., *The Politics of Reapportionment, op. cit.,* p. 31. Jewell observes that "the governor seldom perceives his role in legislative reapportionment to be a forceful one." The findings in New Jersey appear to refute this observation.

51 The governor's veto power was more effective under the 1947 constitution than under the 1844 constitution. Only a majority vote was required to override vetoes prior to the 1947 constitution, while a two-thirds legislative vote is required under the present constitution. *Supra,* p. 226.

to any legislative plans going beyond senate realignment. By threatening to negate alternative Republican plans, Hughes, due to a stronger veto power,[52] occupied a more powerful position in 1964 and 1965 than Governor Edwards in 1922.

Two other constitutional resources were available to governors. Governors had the right to outline courses of legislative action and offer recommendations in *speeches* and *special messages.*[53] For example, the major guidelines for constitutional revision were outlined in inaugural addresses delivered by Governors Edison, Edge, and Driscoll. Secondly, governors had the power to *convene special legislative sessions* to act on reapportionment problems.[54] Such action was taken by both Democratic and Republican governors in the constitutional revision, assembly deadlock, and senate reapportionment cases.

In addition to their constitutional resources, New Jersey governors could use the *statewide electorate* as a resource. When an incumbent governor was running for re-election, he would attempt to mobilize a solid legislative bloc vote from his own party in return for a *promise* of a *maximum party gain* at the next election.[55] Governor Hughes was particularly successful in holding together the legislative Democrats in 1964 and 1965. Both Hughes and the minority Democrats foresaw two-chamber legislative control and the governor's reelection following adoption of the temporary senate reapportionment plan. Therefore, both the governor and his legislative party opposed Republican plans to realign congressional districts and reapportion the assembly. Both of these Republican efforts represented a

---

[52] *Ibid.*

[53] *Constitution of 1947,* Article V, Section 1, Paragraph 12.

[54] *Ibid.*

[55] Sarah P. McCally, "The Governor and His Legislative Party," *American Political Science Review,* Vol. 60, No. 4 (December, 1966), p. 940.

counter-assault on existing Democratic party electoral strength.

Governors were most effective in resolving reapportionment disputes when they exercised *leadership* in mobilizing winning legislative coalitions.[56] Positive leadership came from the governor's success in influencing and bargaining with various legislative groups. The essence of the governor's leadership task has been particularly well-stated by Richard E. Neustadt.[57] In dealing with legislators, the governor must:

> induce them to believe that what he wants of them is what their own appraisal of their own responsibilities requires them to do in their own interest, not his.

Thus, Governor Edison was unable to achieve constitutional reform from 1941 to 1943 because he did not exercise effective legislative leadership. Edison failed to accommodate the competing claims of the rural county senators who opposed revision until their existing power position was guaranteed. On the other hand, the successes of Governors Driscoll, Meyner, and Hughes were evident in their skillful employment of persuasive and bargaining powers in dealing with diverse and conflicting legislative groups.

RESOURCES OF THE STATE SUPREME COURT

The state supreme court sought neither minimizing nor maximizing objectives in reapportionment politics. Instead, the basic role of the court was to exercise judicial review over legislative actions in view of the requirements of the state constitution.[58] The court did not participate in reapportionment politics until 1960. In exercising the

[56] The governor had to overcome the "natural" legislative inclination to preserve the *status quo*. See: Chapter I, *Supra,* p. 36.

[57] Richard E. Neustadt, *Presidential Power* (New York: John Wiley & Sons, Inc., Science Editions, 1960), p. 46.

[58] It should be emphasized in this section that the court always

power of judicial review under the state constitution, the court in the *Asbury Park* case[59] concluded that the "equal protection of the laws" was denied to New Jersey voters when the legislature refused to reapportion seats in the general assembly. The effect of the court ruling in *Asbury Park* was to change the strategic environment of New Jersey reapportionment politics. Prior to 1960, the court had refused to rule on the constitutionality of apportionment matters and had deferred final judgment to the legislature.[60] Following the *Asbury Park* ruling, the court employed three resources as part of its formal powers in interpreting the state constitution. In demanding legislative adherence to the population equality standard, the court could use *sanctions.* The court could threaten to impose a plan if the legislature refused to act. Such threats were never carried out. Rather, a court threat promoted legislative response, especially in 1961 and 1965, when there was much internal resistance and contention over developing a final plan in the legislature.[61] A second resource used by the court was to establish *deadlines* for legislative action in complying with court orders. Thirdly, the court reserved the right to *negate legislative efforts* to circumvent pervious court rulings. For example, the court refused to accept weighted voting as a solution to the senate reapportionment problem in 1965.

---

acts on the basis of legal interpretation of the state constitution. However, the court will be considered part of the "reapportionment game" only with regard to the effects of their actions and not with their intentions. Also, see: Walter F. Murphy, *Elements of Judicial Strategy* (Chicago: University of Chicago Press, 1964) for a discussion of bargaining on the United States Supreme Court.

59 *Asbury Park Press, Inc. v. Woolley,* 33 N.J. 1 (1960).

60 In 1922 the court had refused to overturn a reapportionment plan passed by the legislature. See: *Botti v. McGovern,* 97 N.J.L. 353 (1922).

61 Thus, the legislature could no longer resist outside interference by the courts in settling reapportionment problems. Court intervention modifies legislative efforts to preserve the *status quo*. See: Chapter I, *Supra,* p. 36.

Strategies in New Jersey reapportionment politics

When various groups seek the maximizing or minimizing objectives within the rules of the game, they will employ their resources and develop *strategies* in reapportionment politics. *Strategy* will be defined as follows:[62]

> Strategies will refer to the over-all plans under which maneuverings against specific obstacles are coordinated and for which scarce resources are allocated in order to further the accomplishment of the broad policy objective.

The *elements* of strategy will include the use of *resources* by diverse legislative groups, the governor, and the state supreme court; the *moves* made by these players in the game; and *bargaining* to resolve differences between them.

The *resources* that are available to the various groups in reapportionment politics have been discussed previously. To bring together previous findings, Table 6.1, below, offers a summary.

In developing their plans or courses of action, the players will attempt to employ their resources effectively by calculating the choices that are available to them under given conditions.[63] The second element of strategy will therefore consist of the *moves* made by the players in the game.

Third, every strategy will take into account the conflicting objectives sought by diverse groups. *Bargaining* is a necessary element of strategy when a number of groups are involved. Bargaining, according to Dahl and Lindblom, takes place when four conditions exist: non-hierarchic controls, mutual interdependence of the bargainers, initial disagreement of the bargainers, and the expectation of

---

[62] Murphy, *op. cit.,* pp. 9–10.
[63] Kaplan, *op. cit.,* p. 173.

TABLE 6.1. Resources available to players in New Jersey reapportionment game

Legislative Groups	Governor	State Supreme Court
Rural Senate Reps.: 1. Retain restrictive constitutional provisions 2. Voting power 3. Consistent bloc voting cohesion	Constitutional: 1. Veto power 2. Threatened veto 3. Speeches and special messages 4. Call special legislative sessions	Constitutional (After 1960 only): 1. Judicial review a. Sanctions b. Deadlines c. Negation of diversionary legislative maneuvers
Urban wing of assembly majority party: 1. Potential voting power 2. Alliances with governor 3. Manipulate reapportionment formula*		
Rural Wing of Assembly majority party: 1. Consistent bloc voting cohesion 2. Alliances with rural GOP in senate	Statewide electorate: 1. Promise a maximum partisan gain to his legislative party at next election	
Unified assembly majority party: 1. Voting power 2. Appeal to statewide electorate in referenda to by-pass governor of opposite party		
Assembly minority party: 1. Consistent bloc voting cohesion 2. Alliances with governor 3. Alliances with dissident elements in assembly majority party 4. Alliances with senate 5. Voting power of Hudson County in statewide referenda	Leadership: 1. Persuasion 2. Bargaining 3. Compromise 4. Reciprocity 5. Forming alliances	

* This resource was available to any legislative group that wanted to take advantage of vague constitutional language in the assembly apportionment provision.

mutual gains.[64] In reapportionment politics, any accommodation between competitive political parties in the legislature or *vis-a-vis* the governor will involve non-hierarchic controls. Tight party discipline is maintained only under conditions of one-party control.[65] Mutual interdependence of competing groups is obvious considering the resources each has at its disposal. Initial disagreement of the bargainers will occur when there are efforts to change the *status quo* in reapportionment.[66] The expectation of mutual gains occurs when initial disagreements are resolved and the bargaining parties can attain mutually satisfying objectives.

Plans of action, strategic moves, and bargaining occurred throughout New Jersey reapportionment politics. Six major strategies have been identified to explain the nature of conflict and accommodation between contending groups in the legislative process: party unity; institutional loyalty; areal unity; blocking and obstructionism; reciprocity; and anticipated partisan gains.

THE PARTY UNITY STRATEGY: WHEN THE MAJORITY PARTY IN BOTH LEGISLATIVE CHAMBERS IS IN AGREEMENT, THE REAPPORTIONMENT PROBLEM IS QUICKLY RESOLVED AT THE ROLL-CALL STAGE. OR, A UNIFIED MINORITY PARTY WILL SEEK TO BUILD ALLIANCES OR FORM BLOCKING COALITIONS TO ACHIEVE ITS GOALS.

Under conditions of one-party control of both legislative chambers, the strategy followed is to maximize party

[64] Robert A. Dahl and Charles E. Lindblom, *Politics, Economics, and Welfare* (New York: Harper & Row Publishers, Harper Torchbooks, 1963), pp. 326–333. Also, see: James M. Buchanan and Gordon Tullock, *The Calculus of Consent* (Ann Arbor: The University of Michigan Press, 1965), pp. 97–116; and Charles E. Lindblom, *The Intelligence of Democracy* (New York: The Free Press, 1965), pp. 87–101.

[65] This will be shown below.

[66] See: Chapter I, *Supra,* p. 36.

gains. Such strategy focuses on rewarding urban counties of the majority party at the expense of both urban and rural counties of the minority party. For example, urban county seating gains were evident in the 1901, 1922, and 1931 reapportionments proposed by the Republican majority party, which had overwhelming two-chamber legislative control on all three occasions. The minority Democrats were unable to prevent urban and rural county seat losses because their voting power was insufficient to offset party unity.

Majority party gains will also be achieved when urban-rural gains and losses are balanced within majority party ranks. For example, the 1922 plan gave two urban counties (Bergen and Union) seating gains, while one majority party rural county (Morris) was designated for a seat loss.

The key requirement for majority party unity is developing a consensus prior to the roll-call vote. Caucus decisions will ensure majority party unity at the roll-call stage.[67] Party caucus agreement will ensure that individual county gains and losses are acceptable to all groups in the majority party, or that dissatisfied delegations are unable to form blocking coalitions.

Finally, the strategy of majority party unity may be used to override vetoes of reapportionment plans by governors, when the constitution permits a simple majority vote for the legislature to supercede the governor.[68] In 1922, Democratic Governor Edwards opposed the reapportionment plan, but Republican party unity resulted in rejecting the veto. The legislative majority party achieved inter-chamber agreement by enacting its own plan over the governor's veto. This showed that the legislative majority party resented interference by the governor in reapportionment matters. The legislative majority

---

[67] *Supra,* p. 226.

[68] *Ibid.*

party sought to control reapportionment policy-making.[69]

The majority party unity strategy is rarely successful in New Jersey reapportionment politics for two reasons. First, two-party competition rather than predominant one-party control existed during the most controversial reapportionment cases.[70] Close party competition, especially in the assembly, could prevent inter-chamber agreement. A minority party bloc vote could exploit differences between various majority party groups. Also, the governor could intervene and present new programs or try to resolve differences between contending groups. Secondly, individual county delegations might oppose party unity in order to preserve existing representation. When these counties had sufficient votes to block formation of assembly majorities, caucus decisions were not automatically ratified. Thus, Essex County was able to alter the original apportionment plan of 1941 and retain all seats, while the Bergen delegation opposed the 1–2–4 plans in 1965 and blocked formation of a Republican majority in the assembly.

Although the assembly minority party lacked sufficient voting power to control the outcome of reapportionment problems, it could often be effective by adopting a party unity strategy. Minority status did not prevent the Democrats from playing an important role in reapportionment. Party unity enhanced the position of the assembly minority in two ways. First, the assembly minority could be effective when it voted as a unified bloc. A solid minority bloc forced the majority to join ranks to pass a partisan-oriented reapportionment plan. Secondly, the assembly minority could prevent action by joining ranks and forming a blocking coalition with dissident groups of the majority party.[71]

Three examples indicate the leverage of the legislative

---

[69] *Ibid.*

[70] See Chapter II, *Supra,* Figure 2.3, p. 78 and Chapter IV, *Supra,* Figure 4.1, p. 127.

[71] See: Riker, *op. cit.,* p. 40.

minority in exploiting internal disagreements within the majority party. First, in the constitutional revision case, the Hudson Democrats, by successfully holding together the minority, blocked constitutional revision under Governor Edison. In addition, the Hudson Democrats joined forces with the rural Republicans to prevent adoption of any convention proposals. Similarly, the minority Democrats and the Essex Republicans blocked assembly action on various proposals following the defeat of the Cavicchia Plan in 1953. Party unity was maintained by the Democrats particularly in 1955 when the Camden Democrats refused to be lured by a Republican offer of a seating gain. Camden did not accept the offer because a solid front of Democratic party opposition forced the Republicans to meet directly with the Democrats and develop a bipartisan plan. Thirdly, in 1964 and 1965, a cohesive position by the minority Democrats prevented the assembly Republicans from passing the 1–2–4 plan. The Hudson delegation did not break minority party ranks and vote for the favorable congressional redistricting proposal. A solid minority bloc forced the majority party to turn attention to senate reapportionment, where the minority could expect a maximum partisan gain at the next election.

THE INSTITUTIONAL LOYALTY STRATEGY: THE RURAL COUNTY BLOC IN THE SENATE SEEKS RETENTION OF RESTRICTIVE CONSTITUTIONAL PROVISIONS IN ORDER TO PRESERVE EXISTING CONTROL.

As long as equal county representation was the senate basis of apportionment, the rural Republican bloc focused on the institutional loyalty strategy which kept the one-senator-per-county system intact. The rural bloc could not hope to gain any more power under any reapportionment. The major objective therefore was to preserve the *status quo* by refusing to permit any changes in the constitutional basis of representation.[72] The resources of the rural bloc, including their voting power and consistent bloc voting cohesion, made resistance to change successful. In all confrontations with other legislative groups and the governor, the rural senators demanded assurances that their control over the upper chamber would remain intact.

The best example of the institutional loyalty strategy was found in the constitutional revision case. A definite conflict of objectives was evident in this case. Democratic Governor Edison sought comprehensive constitutional reform by means of a population-based convention from 1941 to 1943. His objective was to prevent the rural counties from having overweighted representation in the convention. Edison feared that the rural bloc would prevent effective reform of state government.[73] Alienated by Edison's "acres versus people" attack, the rural county senators refused to take any action on convention proposals throughout Edison's tenure. Senate inaction was due to partisan differences with Edison, but even more important was the reaction by the Republican bloc to the charge that rural county power should not be exercised effectively when the state constitution was revised. By keeping the *status quo,* the rural Republicans gave up nothing and stymied Edison in his crusade for constitutional reform.

If the institutional loyalty strategy focuses primarily on blocking reform proposals, how is the rural county bloc motivated to accept change? The answer is found in a *quid pro quo* arrangement. The key to constitutional reform was the "no apportionment" compromise developed by Governor Edge with the rural Republicans. The rural bloc in the senate permitted a referendum to authorize the 1944

---

[72] This confirms an originally stated hypothesis in Chapter I that "the maximum objective in reapportionment is to disturb the *status quo* as little as possible." See: Chapter I, *Supra,* p. 36.

[73] See: Baker, *Rural versus Urban Political Power, op. cit.,* p. 27; and Jewell, *The State Legislature, op. cit.,* p. 18.

legislature to draft a new constitution in return for an amendment which retained existing apportionment systems in both chambers. The "no apportionment" restriction was similarly evident when Governor Driscoll sought accommodation with the rural bloc in 1947. Driscoll attracted senate support when equal county representation was retained in the constitution and rural representation in the convention was the same as in the legislature.

The rural bloc strategy of institutional loyalty assumes that effective voting power will be exercised by a dominant group of senators who remain consistent in their demands. The "no-apportionment" demand in the constitutional revision case showed that rural county interests converged on one basic objective: The rural senators wanted to continue their predominant position in the upper chamber.[74]

The institutional loyalty strategy will not be effective when the state supreme court directly intervenes in the reapportionment thicket. When the highest state court adopted the "one man, one vote" rule in 1964, the rural senate bloc was forced to change equal county representation. The state court established a timetable for senate compliance and reserved the right to review plans in conformity with population reapportionment. In response, the rural senate bloc was compelled to discard the institutional loyalty strategy. With equal county representation no longer acceptable to the state supreme court, the rural senators tried first to retain control of the caucus through weighted voting. Weighted voting was to apply only at the roll-call stage of senate action. When the court nullified this diversionary maneuver, Majority Leader Ozzard had to convince the rural bloc that change was inevitable. Ozzard argued that the court might impose an at-large election, which would result in a Democratic party sweep of *all*

---

[74] Jewell, *The State Legislature, op. cit.*, p. 18; and Lockard, *op. cit.*, pp. 311–312.

senate seats. Under these conditions, the best that the rural Republicans could hope for was the retention of the maximum number of incumbents. The institutional loyalty strategy therefore gave way to the objective of individual senator self-preservation under the 29-man plan.[75]

THE AREAL UNITY STRATEGY: AREA INTERESTS PREVAILED IN REAPPORTIONMENT DISPUTES WHEN THE MAJORITY PARTY IN BOTH CHAMBERS COULD NOT EXPECT TO ACHIEVE MAXIMUM GAINS.

The areal unity strategy was employed when individual differences in the majority party could not be reconciled. Unless the majority party in both chambers expected to achieve a maximum gain in reapportionment, the tendency was for area interests to be asserted over party unity. As shown previously, the party unity strategy was adopted under conditions of one-party control and consensus in only three cases (1901, 1922, and 1931) when a maximum party gain was possible.[76]

Area interests were much more dominant than party interests in the most controversial reapportionment cases. When party affiliation is held constant, a major finding is that the urban Republicans in the assembly oftentimes clashed with the rural Republicans in the senate.[77] For example, area interest was evident in the strategy employed by Governor Edison throughout 1941 to 1943. Edison tried

[75] William J. Keefe and Morris S. Ogul, *The American Legislative Process* (Englewood Cliffs, New Jersey: Prentice-Hall, Inc., 1964), p. 89. Individual preservation is the desire of each legislator to be in a safe district. The strategy here is to design a plan which will retain the maximum number of incumbents.

[76] *Supra,* pp. 240–241.

[77] Recent studies have disputed the clash of urban-rural interests without considering party affiliation. See, for examples: Thomas A. Flinn, "The Outline of Ohio Politics," *Western Political Quarterly,* Vol. 13 (September, 1960), pp. 702–721; and Robert S. Friedman, "The Urban-Rural Conflict Revisited," *Western Political Quarterly,* Vol. 14 (June, 1961), pp. 481–495.

to get support from a bipartisan coalition of urban Republicans and independent Democrats (that is, Democratic assemblymen not under the influence of Hudson County) in the assembly for a constitutional convention over the opposition of the rural Republicans in the senate. Since the legislative Democrats were in the minority, Edison required the support of key urban county Republican delegations. But Edison was ineffective in gaining enough bipartisan urban county support over the blocking coalition formed by the Hudson Democrats and the rural Republicans. The problem was that the urban Republican delegations were *disunited*. While the Essex Republicans supported Edison in the goal of reforming state government, the other urban Republican delegations refused to lend support to a Democratic governor. The remaining urban delegations opposed Edison on partisan grounds and some favored an alternate route of reform by means of legislative rather than convention drafting of a new constitution.

Area interests were strongly evident at the outset of the assembly deadlock case. In 1952 and 1953, a major problem was the urban-rural split over the Cavicchia Plan. The Essex Republicans (urban) agreed to relinquish one of their seats, while the Atlantic Republicans (rural) were firmly opposed to losing any representation. The Atlantic County position prevailed when the plan did not pass in the assembly. The plan failed even when the Atlantic-led bloc lacked enough votes to form a blocking coalition. More importantly, the Essex Republicans were unable to mobilize an effective urban county bloc due to lack of a cohesive position among the urban delegations.[78] The urban Republicans did not effectively utilize their voting power and were prevented from adopting a plan that most urban delegations favored.

The areal unity strategy was especially ineffective

---

[78] Derge, *op. cit.*, p. 1065.

within the northeast group of urban county delegations of the majority party. These delegations generally had the lowest voting cohesion of any group in the assembly.[79] Area disunity characterized the interrelationships of the five northeast county delegations. Bergen, Essex, Hudson, Passaic, and Union counties were continually at odds with each other over various reapportionment proposals. The northeast group controlled the greatest proportion of assembly votes and a unified position among them would have ensured success in resolving any controvery. However, diversity rather than unity was the general pattern of response by these counties. Diversity was prompted by the desires for individual power. The obstructionist strategy, that is, the refusal to accept any seat losses, pursued by the Essex and Hudson delegations in the assembly deadlock case, ensured continued control over assembly leadership. At the same time, the Union County senators were promoting Equal Proportions Plans in order to gain increased assembly representation. Also, the Passaic delegation split away from Essex-Hudson leadership in the committee vote on the Equal Proportions Plan in a desire to be independent from Essex-Hudson influence.

THE BLOCKING AND OBSTRUCTIONIST STRATEGY: LEGISLATIVE GROUPS THAT CANNOT EXPECT TO GAIN UNDER A REAPPORTIONMENT WILL MAKE ALLIANCES TO PREVENT FORMATION OF ASSEMBLY MAJORITIES.

Blocking strategies are employed by county delegations that want to minimize their losses in reapportionment. Obstructionism focuses upon preventing legislative action.[80] This is achieved by refusing to vote for proposals at the roll-call stage, or by engaging in blocking maneuvers within the assembly majority party caucus. Two objectives are

---

[79] *Ibid.* Derge observes that "metropolitan legislators usually do not vote together with high cohesion."

[80] Jewell, *The State Legislature, op. cit.*, p. 18.

evident in blocking strategies: First, mutual bloc preservation, or the desire to retain existing personnel and strength,[81] is sought either by urban or rural county delegations of the majority party or by bipartisan urban county alliances that want to avoid seat losses. Secondly, individual urban county delegations may threaten to block action if alternative plans are not adopted.

Mutual bloc preservation was evident in 1921 and throughout most of the assembly deadlock case. By forming an alliance with Morris County and other rural Republicans, the Hudson Republican delegation temporarily prevented the loss of a seat in 1921. But the Hudson delegation lost a seat under the same plan in 1922 when it changed to Democratic party affiliation and the urban Republicans voted with high cohesion to pass the plan.

The most outstanding example of mutual bloc preservation was in the assembly deadlock case, where Essex and Hudson counties prevented assembly reapportionment for nearly ten years. Mutual cooperation operated both within the context of majority party control and as a bipartisan obstructionist force. When the Democrats gained control of the assembly, the Essex-Hudson bloc seized control of the leadership and overrode all efforts to pass a plan. The 1960 vote on the 67-member plan was in reality a diversionary maneuver since the senate was firmly opposed to increasing the size of the assembly. The final vote in 1961 represented a reaction to Essex-Hudson obstructionist tactics. In effect, the mutual bloc preservation sought by Essex and Hudson prompted a counterstrategy resulting in the formation of a bipartisan assembly coalition to pass the Equal Proportions Plan.

A potential blocking strategy led to an outright victory for the Essex Republicans in 1941. The Essex delegation was able to secure inter-chamber acceptance of an alterna-

---

[81] Keefe and Ogul, *op. cit.,* p. 89.

tive plan over the demands of the Camden County senator. The higher voting resources of Essex County accounted for the victory. The expectation of an overall party gain was the key consideration since the Camden delegation was Democratic in the assembly. Essex County's alternate plan eliminated its own seat loss and a Camden Democratic gain. Furthermore, a potential blocking vote by party leadership did not consider the stakes high enough to provoke a two-house deadlock.

THE RECIPROCITY STRATEGY: LEGISLATIVE GROUPS WILL ASSENT TO GOVERNOR'S DEMANDS ONLY WHEN A RECIPROCAL AGREEMENT IS NEGOTIATED.

New Jersey governors must bargain with diverse legislative groups and make reciprocal agreements. Otherwise, the legislative groups will reject the rewards promised by the governor and resort to the institutional loyalty, areal unity, or blocking strategies to promote their own interests. Legislators are most concerned with preserving their own representation before they will accommodate with governors.[82]

In bargaining with legislative groups, the governor's reciprocity strategy will include *compromise* and *direct intervention*. Compromise may be necessary in securing constitutional reform in order to give reassurances to entrenched legislative groups. Direct intervention may be required to end assembly deadlocks in order to supersede obstructionist majority maneuvers.

Maximizing objectives were sought by governors in both the constitutional revision and assembly deadlock cases. In both cases, governors used compromise, legislative leadership and direct intervention to promote a constitutional

---

[82] See: Chapter I, *Supra,* p. 36, which offers the hypothesis that "reapportionment should focus upon maintaining the maximum number of incumbents."

convention in 1947, where Governor Edison had failed from 1941 to 1943. After outlining his own program, Driscoll met directly with Republican legislative leaders and agreed to a compromise plan, whereby the convention would consist of 81 delegates apportioned on the same basis as the legislature. Driscoll also agreed to the "no apportionment" restriction, which had been demanded by the rural Republican senators since 1943.[83] While reforming state government was the maximum objective sought by Driscoll, the rural Republicans could have prevented adoption of a convention plan by a bloc vote in the senate.[84] When he agreed to maximum rural county representation, Driscoll gained approval for constitutional revision.

Governor Meyner directly intervened in the assembly deadlock case. His objective was to override entrenched assembly leadership of his own party, which had refused to permit a final vote on the Equal Proportions Plan passed by the Republican-controlled senate. Meyner reacted to state supreme court pressure. The court had threatened to impose its own plan by assuming responsibility for a legislative function which was not being carried out. Even though Essex and Hudson counties stood to lose three seats each, representing the greatest losses ever suffered by individual counties in twentieth century New Jersey reapportionment politics, Meyner felt that other urban counties of his own party deserved seating gains. Meyner's direct intervention promoted a "power play" in the assembly Democratic caucus. The strategy here was for the Democratic assemblymen to impose hierarchial controls on the Essex-Hudson leadership. The assembly Democrats put enormous pressure on the assembly speaker to permit a final vote before the court acted. The speaker acceded because the majority of Democrats threatened to replace him with someone who would permit a floor vote.

---

83 *Supra*, p. 245.
84 *Ibid.*

THE ANTICIPATED PARTISAN GAINS STRATEGY: THE GOVERNOR'S BARGAINING POSITION WITH HIS OWN LEGISLATIVE PARTY WILL BE STRENGTHENED WHEN MUTUAL PARTISAN GAINS CAN BE EXPECTED IN FORTHCOMING ELECTIONS. THE LEGISLATIVE PARTY WILL THEN ACCEPT THE GOVERNOR'S LEADERSHIP IN RESOLVING EXISTING REAPPORTIONMENT PROBLEMS.

In addition to compromise and direct intervention, the governor's bargaining position with his own legislative party will be increased when he can offer *promises of electoral success.* The anticipated partisan gains strategy may be successful under two conditions.

First, the prospective candidate for governor may support constitutional reform as a major issue leading toward an election victory. The governor will try to convince his legislative party that existing patterns of party control will not be disturbed if the entire party is united.[85] Governor Edge adopted this strategy in 1943. He argued that the Republicans would win in the forthcoming elections and gain both legislative and executive control. However, the rural Republicans would not lend their full support until they secured the "no-apportionment" amendment to the Feller Referendum plan. The promise of electoral success in 1943 by Edge tended to discriminate against the minority Democrats (who would continue to be a minority after Edge's election) and the urban Republicans of the majority party which could not hope to change rural county control of the senate under the "no apportionment" restriction. However, inter-chamber reciprocity was accepted by the urban Republicans as part of the arrangement for supporting Edge. Rural county control was continued in the senate, while the urban counties would maintain the dominant position in the assembly.

Secondly, a governor may be assisted in offering election promises to his legislative party when the state supreme

[85] McCally, *op. cit.,* p. 940.

court is forcing a legislative chamber to reapportion. Governor Hughes was able to hold out for a maximum partisan gain in 1964 and 1965 even when the Republicans controlled the legislature. By insisting that only a senate reapportionment plan be adopted, Hughes was successful in promoting a cohesive minority bloc vote in the assembly which forestalled passage of alternative Republican plans. Hughes convinced the minority Democrats that he would be reelected and that his legislative party would gain control of *both* chambers in the forthcoming elections. Having accepted Hughes' leadership, the minority Democrats witnessed the governor's direct participation in developing a temporary plan with the senate majority leader. The senate Republicans, having exhausted all other resources and strategies, then agreed to the temporary 29-man plan under which the maximum number of incumbents was retained. However, Hughes achieved a shift of rural to urban county control in the senate. This enabled the Democrats to move into a more competitive position in seeking control of the upper chamber, because the major areas of electoral strength for the Democrats were located in the urban counties of the state.

The New Jersey "Reapportionment Game" in perspective

Six major strategies have been identified to show the nature of conflict and accommodation in New Jersey reapportionment politics. One of the purposes of analyzing strategies is to test "rules" and "principles" which have been suggested by other studies of state legislative apportionment politics.[86] By way of a summary, Table 6.2, below, indicates the confirmation, modification, or refutation of these "rules" and "principles" when they are compared with New Jersey's experiences. It should be emphasized that the New Jersey findings represent only a tentative ex-

---

[86] See: Chapter I, *Supra,* pp. 35–36.

planation, since several of the conclusions will apply only under particular conditions in the legislative process.

TABLE 6.2. Comparison of legislative rules in reapportionment with New Jersey's experiences

Comparative Rules and Principles of State Legislation Apportionment	*New Jersey's Experiences*
1. The legislative interest is clearly predominant in reapportionment policy-making.	1. Under conditions of one-party legislative control, the majority party caucus will control reapportionment policy-making.
2. Each house should handle its own apportionment problem separately and the other house should accept the result.	2. New Jersey legislative practices include regular interchamber participation in developing reapportionment proposals.
3. The legislature resents outside interference by the governor.	3. Reciprocity will determine the degree of the governor's participation in reapportionment politics. When the legislature can handle the problem alone, it will resist the governor's participation, but may offer him support in other programs. But, under conditions of persistent deadlock, certain legislative groups will welcome the governor's legislative leadership.
4. The legislature resents outside intereference by the courts.	4. After the *Asbury Park* decision in 1960, the court entered the political thicket of legislative reapportionment and changed the strategic environment for legislative maneuvering.

Comparative Rules and Principles of State Legislative Apportionment	*New Jersey's Experiences*
5. Reapportionment should focus upon maintaining the maximum number of incumbents.	5. Reapportionment should focus upon retaining the maximum number of incumbents of the party that controls a legislative chamber.
6. The controlling political party will obtain maximum results by suppressing the minority party, especially when future legislative control is uncertain.	6. By forming alliances, the legislative minority party may be able to press for alternative reapportionment plans.
7. The maximum objective in reapportionment is to disturb the *status quo* as little as possible.	7. Legislative groups that favor change will seek maximum seating gains; legislative groups that have power and control will seek to preserve the *status quo* by avoiding seat losses.
8. The *status quo* can be achieved by refusing to reapportion.	8. The *status quo* can be achieved by consistent bloc voting cohesion in the Senate; or, by blocking and obstructionist strategies in the Assembly.
9. The *status quo* can be achieved by securing constitutional provisions that restrict change; or by passing bills that entrench prevailing political patterns.	9. The *status quo* can be maintained by the rural bloc in the senate which enters into a *quid pro quo* arrangement with a governor; Or, the *status quo* of restrictive constitutional provisions will not be maintained when the state supreme court adopts the "one man, one vote" principle.

One basic problem has not been solved in the preceding analysis. If contending groups in reapportionment politics employed their maximizing or minimizing strategies simultaneously at various stages of the "life cycle" of conflict and resolution, how are the demands of any single group satisfied? Ideally, only optimal strategies will be successful. Chapter 7 will examine the outcome of successful strategies by employing William H. Riker's model of a minimum winning coalition.[87]

[87] Riker, *op. cit.*, pp. 32–46.

7

Legislative Strategies and Minimum Winning Coalitions

Introduction

IF BOTH THE MAXIMIZING AND MINIMIZING OBJECTIVES WERE achieved by competing legislative groups in reapportionment politics, there could be no settlement of conflict. Each of the major strategies—party unity, institutional loyalty, areal unity, blocking and obstructionism, reciprocity, and anticipated partisan gains—would be mutually counterbalanced. The result would be an equilibrium or protracted deadlock.[1] Obviously, however, particular legislative groups do win in reapportionment politics. A theoretical framework is required to explain the outcome of successful strategies in building winning legislative coalitions.

Four theoretical models have been considered to explain the outcome of successful strategies. Each of the models has particular usefulness in understanding legislative behavior. However, for reasons outlined below, Riker's model

[1] Kenneth E. Boulding, *Conflict and Defense,* (New York: Harper and Row Publishers, Harper Torchbooks, 1962), p. 307.

of a minimum winning coalition[2] seems especially adaptable to an understanding of reapportionment politics. In the following discussion, justifications will be offered to explain why Riker's model has been selected over three other alternatives. The alternatives are Schelling's analysis of bargaining,[3] Buchanan and Tullock's economic study of "decision-making" costs,[4] and Downs' vote-maximizing principle.[5]

First, coalition-building could be considered in terms of applying Schelling's detailed analysis of bargaining to the legislative process.[6] Bargaining is a necessary requirement for resolving differences between competing groups seeking the same policy objectives. Rather than considering Schelling's approach in detail, it appears sufficient to observe that Schelling is basically concerned with games of cooperation rather than with games of conflict.[7] While analysis of strategies in reapportionment politics deals partially with coordination of efforts by diverse groups, the more dominant feature appears to be conflict between groups seeking either the maximizing or minimizing objectives. It is necessary to discover under what conditions maximizing or minimizing strategies will be successful in building winning legislative coalitions.

Secondly, Buchanan and Tullock have developed a model to explan how collective decisions are made. "Constitutional" and "operational" decisions are distinguished. Constitutional decisions are made when the state is first

---

[2] William H. Riker, *The Theory of Political Coalitions* (New Haven: Yale University Press, 1962), pp. 32–46.

[3] Thomas C. Schelling, *The Strategy of Conflict* (New York: Oxford University Press, Galaxy Books, 1963).

[4] James M. Buchanan and Gordon Tullock, *The Calculus of Consent* (Ann Arbor: The University of Michigan Press, 1965).

[5] Anthony Downs, *An Economic Theory of Democracy* (New York: Harper and Row Publishers, 1957).

[6] Schelling, *op. cit.*, pp. 21–52.

[7] Karl W. Deutsch, *The Nerves of Government* (New York: The Free Press, 1963), p. 67.

organized. These decisions will include the selection of rules for collective action. Operational decisions follow adoption of the constitution. At this stage, the authors discuss the "external" and "decision-making" costs for political organizations. In their chapter on the bicameral legislature,[8] Buchanan and Tullock consider decision-making costs associated with the type of voting procedure adopted (either unanimity or simple majority voting), the degree of voting intensity, bargaining, and log-rolling. All of these elements are essential to an understanding of building winning legislative coalitions. However, the *Calculus of Consent* is primarily an attempt to relate economic terminology to an understanding of democratic political theory. The practical application of the theoretical model requires comprehension of several highly abstract economic concepts. The usefulness of Buchanan and Tullock's model appears somewhat limited in analyzing successful strategies and building winning legislative coalitions.

A third theoretical model is available in Downs' discussion of the vote-maximizing principle in coalition-building.[9] Downs is concerned with political party competition and the objectives sought by parties in attracting voter support. Two major hypotheses are developed by Downs: (1) parties act to maximize votes; and (2) citizens behave rationally in politics.[10] However, Riker has indicated that these two hypotheses are contradictory.[11] In a two-party system, both parties will seek to attract as many voters as possible. This objective will be achieved when both parties present approximately the same programs to the voters. Rational behavior by the parties, that is, the effort to maximize voter support, will lead to campaigns in which personalities rather than issues are emphasized. Parties

[8] Buchanan and Tullock, *op. cit.*, pp. 233–248.
[9] Downs, *op. cit.*, p. 300.
[10] *Ibid.*
[11] Riker, *op. cit.*, p. 99.

therefore have a powerful incentive to achieve complete ambiguity.[12] Since both parties will have the same programs, Downs is forced to conclude that "rational behavior by political parties tends to discourage rational behavior by voters."[13] Riker suggests that the dilemma may be resolved by changing the vote-maximizing principle:[14]

> Instead of simply asserting that parties seek to maximize votes, one could assert instead the size principle: that parties seek to increase votes only up to the size of a minimum winning coalition.

Thus, Riker concludes that the outcome of successful strategies in building winning coalitions should focus on minimum winning coalitions rather than on maximum winning coalitions.

Riker is basically concerned with the "life cycle" of conflict and resolution.[15] A conflict will be resolved when strategies are directed toward building minimum winning coalitions. Riker's model of the minimum winning coalition therefore seems to be the best approach to an understanding of successful strategies in reapportionment politics. What is a minimum winning coalition? Riker defines it as follows:[16]

> In social situations similar to n-person, zero-sum games with side-payments, participants create coalitions just as large as they believe will ensure winning and no larger.

Coalition-building begins with a leader who tries to at-

[12] *Ibid.*

[13] Downs, *op. cit.,* p. 136.

[14] Riker, *op. cit.,* p. 100.

[15] Boulding, *op. cit.,* p. 307. Also, see Chapter VI, *Supra,* p. 217.

[16] Riker, *op. cit.,* pp. 32–33. "N-person" refers to games where there are more than two players. "Zero-sum" is a condition where the gains of the winners must equal the losses of the losers.

tract followers in making a decision on a particular issue.[17] The leader tries to build a winning coalition and is opposed by blocking coalitions. The leader tries to attract followers with "side-payments," that is, he offers rewards which followers are willing to accept.[18] In addition to side-payments, the leader employs strategies to overcome the countermoves made by potential blocking coalitions. If side-payments are accepted and optimal strategies chosen, the final result will be attainment of objectives in a minimum winning coalition.

The attempt to use Riker's model of a minimum winning coalition is frankly speculative and an effort to go to a high level of abstraction in analyzing the outcome of the "reapportionment game." The model is not intended to explain all of the empirical facts and no claim is made for any one model to explain the complexity of reapportionment politics, including judicial decisions, elections, and legislative action. The model represents but one way of explaining group behavior in the legislative process. It is useful as a means of understanding group behavior, but is not an attempt to probe motivations, intentions, or the sources of competing arguments. The model is therefore tentative and should not be viewed as a rigid deterministic scheme.

Minimum winning coalitions in the reapportionment game

The nature of side-payments

The first step in coalition-building takes place when a leader tries to attract followers with side-payments.[19] Side-payments are very closely related to the governor's optimal bargaining strategies of compromise, direct intervention, and promises of electoral success. In particular, three of the

---

17 *Ibid.,* p. 103.
18 *Ibid.,* p. 105.
19 *Ibid.*

possible side-payments described by Riker are relevant to an understanding of New Jersey reapportionment politics: (1) the threat of reprisal; (2) promises on policy; and (3) promises about subsequent decisions.[20]

THE THREAT OF REPRISAL: AT ONE EXTREME A LEADER MAY SO MANIPULATE EVENTS THAT HE IS ABLE TO THREATEN MEMBERS OF THE BODY WITH REPRISALS IF THEY DO NOT JOIN HIS COALITION. THE SIDE-PAYMENT THEN CONSISTS OF A PROMISE NOT TO CARRY OUT THE THREAT.

Under conditions of tight party discipline, either a governor or a dominant legislative coalition can threaten reprisals to recalcitrant legislative groups. The optimal strategy for the Republicans in 1922 was to punish Hudson County for returning a Democratic party assembly delegation. In return, Democratic party Governor Edwards threatened and carried out a reprisal by vetoing the Republican plan which took away an assembly seat from Hudson. However, the governor's veto power was a weak resource under the constitution.[21] The reprisal failed because the party unity strategy adopted by the Republicans focused on legislative control over reapportionment policy-making.

The threat of reprisal was also evident in 1961 when Governor Meyner directly intervened in the legislative struggle and sought to override the blocking strategy of Essex and Hudson counties. Assembly Democrats who wanted to gain seats sought to end the deadlock. Reprisal was therefore threatened by imposing hierarchical controls on the majority party leadership in the caucus. The opti-

---

[20] *Ibid.*, p. 109–113.

[21] The governor's veto powers was less effective under the 1844 constitution than under the 1947 constitution. Only a majority vote in the legislature was required to override vetoes prior to the 1947 constitution. Under the present constitution, a two-thirds legislative vote is required to override vetoes.

mal strategy for the anti-Essex-Hudson Democrats was to threaten a revolt in the caucus in order to replace the recalcitrant leadership. The final step was to form a bipartisan coalition of all but Essex-Hudson and pass the Equal Proportions Plan.

PROMISES ON POLICY: THE LEADER WILL MODIFY AND REINTERPRET HIS PROMISES ON POLICY TO ATTRACT ENOUGH FOLLOWERS TO FORM A WINNING COALITION.

A leader will usually be able to attract initial followers who support him because their side-payment is achievement of the policy itself. But if these initial followers do not form a winning coalition, the leader will have to modify his original proposal and compromise with other groups.

Governor Edison did not employ a successful strategy from 1941 to 1943 in contrast to Governor Edge's strategy in 1943. Edison indeed attracted initial followers in certain urban county assembly delegations. But he alienated others in his attack on rural county power and his assertion of independence from the Hudson County machine. These two groups then formed a blocking coalition which lured enough urban county votes to prevent constitutional revision during Edison's tenure. In contrast, Governor Edge did modify his side-payment to the rural county senators in 1943. The "no-apportionment" compromise ensured that Edge could campaign for constitutional reform while senate power was protected and legislative control over revision ensured.

PROMISES ABOUT SUBSEQUENT DECISIONS: THE LEADER MAY OFFER PAYMENTS CONCERNING PROMISES ON FUTURE DECISIONS.

When the leader can offer promises about the content of future decisions, his stock of political currency is greatly expanded.[22] Governor Edge's successful strategy in 1943 involved log-rolling. The compromise on "no-apportionment" permitted him to form a winning coalition based on the promise of electoral success in the next election. At the same time, Edge relinquished participation in future revision by agreeing to legislative control over the issue. The tradeoff or log-rolling agreement ensured a Republican party coalition controlling constitutional reform in the 1944 legislature.

Promises of electoral success were an inherent part of Governor Hughes' successful strategy in 1964 and 1965. Hughes prompted a minority bloc that foresaw future legislative control following senate reapportionment. The optimal strategy for the minority Democrats was to join forces and remain consistent in opposing Republican alternative plans. In this sense, the Democrats' blocking strategy focused on maximizing gains in future elections by forcing entrenched rural Republicans to give up existing control in the senate.

Building minimum winning coalitions

If the coalition leader is successful in offering rewards that followers are willing to accept, how are minimum winning coalitions formed? Minimum winning coalitions are necessary because a coalition of the whole (an overwhelming majority or a grand coalition) may contain too many interests to satisfy the demands of any one group.[23] A coalition of the whole cannot expect to gain any more power than it presently holds.[24] The coalition will be reduced in size as the leaders act to accommodate some groups and to deny the demands of others. In this way, the

[22] Riker, *op. cit.*, pp. 112–113.
[23] *Ibid.*, p. 65.
[24] *Ibid.*, p. 57.

maximum winning coalition will be reduced to a minimum winning coalition.[25] The maximizing objective may be somewhat modified when a coalition of the whole faces little pressure to settle internal conflicts. As long as there is no danger to retaining existing control, the coalition will remain intact.[26] However, when outside pressure is great, the coalition is forced to act. Two dangers then arise. First, the coalition of the whole may reduce itself too much so that two equally powerful blocking coalitions result.[27] Secondly, a losing coalition may become a minimum winning coalition by gaining enough adherents from one of the majority blocking coalitions.[28]

The following section will attempt to test the aforementioned hypotheses to coalition-building in New Jersey reapportionment politics.

GRAND COALITIONS WILL BE CREATED WHEN OUTSIDE PRESSURES CAN BE RESISTED AND EFFECTIVE LEGISLATIVE CONTROL CAN BE MAINTAINED.

Blocking coalitions will not form within overwhelming majorities as long as there is no outside pressure endangering existing one-party control. The conflict between legislative Republicans and Democratic Governor Edison from 1941 to 1943 can be explained in terms of an overwhelming legislative coalition refusing to take action when there was little reason to upset existing power positions. Edison's program of constitutional reform could not benefit the grand Republican coalition which already had overwhelming two-chamber control. While Edison did gain some support from the Essex Republicans, the stronger position was a blocking coalition formed by the rural Republicans

[25] *Ibid.*, p. 65.
[26] *Ibid.*
[27] *Ibid.*, p. 62.
[28] *Ibid.*, p. 65.

in response to Edison's attack on rural county power in the senate. Inaction was the more desirable response to the demands of a Democratic party governor.

The situation changed when the Republican candidate for governor wanted party unity for the next election. Edge recognized the blocking position of the rural senators. To get their support for his election, Edge agreed to the "no-apportionment" compromise and legislative control over future constitutional revision. The rural county bloc then agreed to support Edge in his bid for the governorship. The need for party unity thus overcame the blocking position of the rural senators. In this sense, it was necessary to restore a grand coalition to establish the basis of support for a Republican gubernatorial candidate.

A COALITION OF THE WHOLE (A GRAND COALITION OR AN OVERWHELMING MAJORITY) CANNOT WIN ANYTHING AND THEREFORE IS REDUCED TO A MINIMUM WINNING COALITION.

Two examples indicate how grand coalitions were reduced to minimum winning coalitions in New Jersey reapportionment politics. In 1921, the Republicans had overwhelming majorities in both chambers. The reapportionment plan gave seating gains to two urban counties (Bergen and Union) and took seats from one urban (Hudson) and one rural (Morris) county. All four counties were Republican. Since every reapportionment is zero-sum in New Jersey, that is, the gains of the winners must equal the losses of the losers, there is no reason for the losers in a grand coalition to accept a plan unless they want to. The losers in a grand coalition have the option of forming a blocking coalition to retain their existing representation.

In 1921, the losers in the grand coalition, Hudson and Morris counties, joined forces and formed a blocking coalition to preserve their existing representation. This prevented action by the grand coalition. Furthermore, the remaining urban Republicans saw no reason to adopt a plan in 1921, when the chief rival to Republican party power, Hudson, had a temporary Republican delegation. When Hudson returned a Democratic party delegation in 1922, the new strategy was to punish Hudson and override the claims of rural county power in Morris. A minimum winning coalition was formed when the urban Republicans voted with high cohesion to enact the same plan that was blocked in 1921, and, in effect, expelled Morris County from the coalition.

Secondly, the overwhelming Republican majority in 1941 was too large to accommodate the competing demands of both Essex County in the assembly and Camden County in the senate. Essex wanted to retain its existing representation, while the Camden senator argued for a seating gain. However, the Camden delegation in the assembly was Democratic. After both chambers had passed conflicting plans, the Republican coalition was faced with an impasse. Essex had enough votes to block adoption of the senate plan in the assembly, while the Camden senator, as majority leader, had sufficient influence to form an urban-rural area bloc to prevent adoption of the assembly plan in the senate. The grand coalition had become modified by two equally powerful blocking coalitions.

To pass the final plan, it was necessary to accommodate one of these blocking coalitions. The Republicans decided to accept the Essex County position on two grounds. First, there was no reason to reward the Camden Democrats in the assembly at the expense of the Essex Republicans. Secondly, the stakes were not considered high enough to accept the Camden demands. If Camden's claims had been accepted, a deadlock would have resulted. Thus, the potentially powerful blocking coalition of Essex County in the assembly was prevented and a minimum winning coalition established to override the competing demands of Camden in the senate.

A GRAND COALITION MAY REDUCE ITSELF TOO MUCH SO THAT TWO EQUALLY POWERFUL BLOCKING COALITIONS RESULT. ONE OF THE BLOCKING COALITIONS WILL THEN BE TRANSFERRED INTO A MINIMUM WINNING COALITION.

Inter-chamber disputes over reapportionment plans show the dangers of equally powerful blocking coalitions confronting each other. If the inter-chamber dispute is not resolved quickly, as in 1941, a protracted deadlock may result. In 1911, the Democratic coalition in the assembly could not agree on an alternative to the plan passed by the senate Republican coalition. The senate coalition was unified while the urban wing of the assembly Democratic coalition was seriously split. With both inter-chamber disagreement and several blocking coalitions within the Democratic majority, only one coalition could win. The minimum winning coalition in 1911 was formed by the assembly Republican minority, which gained enough adherents from the divided Democratic majority to pass the senate reapportionment plan. The several blocking coalitions of the Democrats became losing coalitions when the Republican minority was able to take advantage of the majority party split.

Similarly, the Democrats had two equally powerful blocking coalitions in 1961. The Essex-Hudson bloc had enough votes to prevent adoption of a plan within the Democratic assembly caucus. The other Democrats could pass a plan if they could form a bipartisan coalition with the minority Republicans on the assembly floor. Thirdly, the senate Republican coalition was consistent in passing Equal Proportions plans. The solution to the problem was twofold. First, the Democrats had to override their own blocking leadership in the caucus to permit a floor vote on the Equal Proportions Plan. Secondly, the Essex Republicans had to break away from their Democratic party counterparts to provide the necessary votes for a majority in a roll-call vote. When a bipartisan coalition was formed, the Essex-Hudson Democrats were isolated. A minimum winning coalition overrode the blocking and obstructionist efforts of the Essex-Hudson Democrats.

A LOSING COALITION MAY BE TRANSFORMED INTO A MINIMUM WINNING COALITION WHEN IT ATTRACTS ENOUGH VOTES FROM ONE OF THE MAJORITY PARTY BLOCKING COALITIONS.

When a minority party remains consistent in opposing majority party plans, it may be in a position to exploit one of the blocking coalitions of the majority party by attracting enough votes to form a minimum winning coalition. The solution to the senate reapportionment problem in 1965 showed that a minority party coalition can actually win when it remains consistently opposed to a majority party that is badly split. The senate Republicans attempted a series of diversionary maneuvers to prevent the full impact of population-based reapportionment ordered by the state supreme court. However, the assembly Republican coalition was badly divided over all senate Republican alternatives. Neither weighted voting nor the 1–2–4 plan was acceptable to the urban Republicans in the assembly. Weighted voting discriminated against the urban areas and the 1–2–4 plan threatened entrenched party leadership in Bergen County. In this dilemma, the Republican coalition could not act because of an inter-chamber impasse. The senate-assembly blocking coalitions were rendered helpless and could not adopt a mutually satisfactory solution for all groups. Therefore, the potentially losing coalition, the minority Democrats, took advantage of the situation. Led by Governor Hughes, the Democrats focused attention on senate reapportionment. The 29-man plan was adopted on bipartisan lines when the majority coalition of Republicans had no other alternatives left.

Relationship of minimum winning coalitions and legislative strategies in New Jersey reapportionment politics

The preceding analysis has suggested several applications of Riker's model of minimum winning coalitions in New Jersey reapportionment politics. By way of a summary, the following table indicates the degree to which Riker's model fits New Jersey's experiences. It should be emphasized, however, that the table represents only a tentative explanation and future testing of these findings will be necessary in order to verify the usefulness of Riker's model.

Conclusions: Speculations on strategies in the future

The findings in Table 7.1 apply only to past New Jersey legislative experiences with reapportionment problems. In order to test the validity of these findings, it will be necessary to consider three major elements in the future: (1) the impact of population apportionment on the senate; (2) the continued importance of negotiation to resolve competing reapportionment claims in the legislative process; and (3) the delegation of responsibility for reapportionment to a bipartisan commission.[29]

First, the successful strategy that maximized rural county power in the senate was retention of restrictive apportionment provisions in the constitution.[30] This was achieved

[29] This study has focused on legislative strategies within the context of the reapportionment issue. No efforts have been made to relate the impact of reapportionment on public policy. For examples of this approach, see: Thomas R. Dye, "Malapportionment and Public Policy in the States," *Journal of Politics,* Vol. 27, No. 3 (August, 1965), pp. 586–601; and Richard I. Hofferbert, "The Relation Between Public Policy and Some Structural and Environmental Variables in the American States," *American Political Science Review,* Vol. 60, No. 1 (March, 1966), pp. 73–82.

[30] This confirms an original hypothesis stated in Chapter I, *Supra,* p. 36.

through "no-apportionment" demands. The alternate strategy was delay, avoidance of change, or employment of diversionary maneuvers to prevent the full impact of population apportionment.[31] However, the maximum strategy of inaction is no longer available to *retain* rural county power in the senate. State supreme court demands on the "one man, one vote" principle have changed the basis of senate representation so that the urban counties have control. Under the new constitutional provision,[32] the senate is composed of forty members apportioned among districts. Population equality is now the rule for senate apportionment and this will be achieved by using the mathematical method of Equal Proportions.[33] In the future, the best strategy for the rural county senators will be to form blocking coalitions to exploit differences between urban counties.

Secondly, effective obstruction to assembly reapportionment can be maintained by urban county delegations that prevent formation of floor majorities at the roll-call stage. The obstructionist strategy consists of both refusal to vote for proposals at the roll-call stage and engaging in blocking maneuvers within the assembly majority caucus. The obstructionist strategy is successful in preventing legislative action.

To overcome resistance to change in the assembly, counterstrategies will be required. One future alternative is to form bipartisan coalitions to end assembly deadlocks when the majority party is rendered helpless by blocking coalitions within its own ranks. In such cases, negotiation will be an inherent feature of resolving reapportionment disputes. Negotiation is necessary unless preliminary agree-

---

[31] *Ibid.*

[32] In June, 1966, the New Jersey Constitutional convention met for the specific purpose of amending the state's constitutional provisions on reapportionment. See: New Jersey Constitutional Convention, *Report of Committee on Arrangement and Style,* June 14, 1966.

[33] *Ibid.,* p. 2.

TABLE 7.1. Relationship of minimum winning coalitions and strategies in New Jersey reapportionment politics

Riker's propositions concerning minimum winning coalitions	New Jersey's experiences in twentieth century reapportionments		
	Case Years	Strategies Employed	Outcome
1. Grand coalitions will be created when outside pressures can be resisted and effective legislative control can be maintained	1901 & 1931	Majority party unity	Plans adopted without any outside interference. Caucus control rendered cases non-controversial
	1941–1943	Blocking and institutional loyalty by rural GOP senators	No action on Governor Edison's constitutional reform proposal.
	1943	Reciprocity and anticipated partisan gains	"No apportionment" compromise between Edge and rural GOP senators permits legislative action on constitutional revision.
	1947	Reciprocity and majority party unity	"No apportionment" compromise between Driscoll and rural GOP senators results in adoption of 81-member convention proposal.
2. A coalition of the whole cannot win anything and therefore is reduced to a minimum winning coalition	1921	Blocking	Hudson and Morris counties join forces to prevent action.
	1922	Areal unity	Urban GOP in assembly votes with high cohesion to punish Hudson Dems. and expel Morris GOP.

TABLE 7.1. (continued) Relationship of minimum winning coalitions and strategies in New Jersey apportionment politics

Riker's propositions concerning minimum winning coalitions	New Jersey's experiences in twentieth century reapportionments		
	Case Years	Strategies Employed	Outcomes
3. A grand coalition may reduce itself too much so that two equally powerful blocking coalitions result. One of the blocking coalitions will then be transformed into a minimum winning coalition	1941	Potential Blocking	Essex demands in assembly accommodated over Camden demands in senate to prevent deadlock.
	1953–1961	Blocking	Essex-Hudson Dems. refuse to permit assembly action.
	1961	Hierarchical controls and bipartisanship	Anti-Essex-Hudson Dems. threaten to replace leadership; Dems. and GOP then join forces to pass Equal Proportions plan.
4. A losing coalition may be transformed into a minimum winning coalition when it attracts enough votes from one of the majority party blocking coalitions	1911	Minority party unity	GOP assembly minority gains acceptance of Senate plan by taking advantage of urban Dem. splits.
	1965	Minority party unity and anticipated partisan gains	Dem. assembly minority achieves adoption of Senate reapportionment by remaining consistently opposed to GOP alternatives.

ment is achieved in party caucuses under conditions of one-party control and inter-chamber agreement. Otherwise, a legislature characterized by two-party competition will have continued conflicts over reapportionment. If New Jersey continues to have two strong political parties, competing claims over reapportionment will have to be resolved by negotiation, compromise, or the formation of bipartisan coalitions to overcome resistance to change. In the future, the governor and the legislature will continue to resolve reapportionment disputes through mutual accommodation of competing claims.

Another counterstrategy for preventing assembly deadlocks is to delegate responsibility for reapportionment to an impartial body outside the legislature and automatically accept its recommendations. This has been partially achieved under the new apportionment provisions in the State Constitution.

The new constitutional provisions will create a whole new set of strategic problems, which will not be considered at this time. However, the legislature's future role in reapportionment will be changed by the new provisions, and it is important to note briefly the nature of these changes. In subsequent assembly reapportionments, the lower chamber will consist of 80 members. These members will represent districts rather than counties. Responsibility for drawing district lines and apportioning assemblymen among the districts after each decennial census will rest with a ten-member bipartisan commission chosen by the state committee of each of the two major political parties. Should deadlocks develop over reapportionment, the chief justice of the state supreme court will appoint an eleventh member to the commission to act as an impartial referee to end disputes. The apportionment commission will then certify its recommendations to the secretary of state.[34]

---

[34] *Ibid.*, pp. 2–4. It should be noted that these same provisions will also apply to senate districts and apportionment.

Bibliography

I. Theories and Methods

BOOKS

Anderson, Lee F., Watts, Meredith W., Jr., and Wilcox, Allen R. *Legislative Roll-Call Analysis.* Northwestern University Press, 1966.

Banfield, Edward C. *Political Influence.* New York: The Free Press, 1961.

Beyle, Herman C. *Identification and Analysis of Attribute-Cluster-Blocs.* Chicago: University of Chicago Press, 1931.

Black, Duncan. *The Theory of Committees and Elections.* London: Cambridge University Press, 1958.

Boulding, Kenneth E. *Conflict and Defense: A General Theory.* New York: Harper and Row, Publishers, 1962.

Buchanan, James M., and Tullock, Gordon. *The Calculus of Consent: Logical Foundations of Constitutional Democracy.* Ann Arbor: The University of Michigan Press, 1965.

Dahl, Robert A., and Lindblom, Charles E. *Politics, Economics, and Welfare.* New York: Harper and Row, Publishers, 1953.

Deutsch, Karl W. *The Nerves of Government.* New York: The Free Press, 1963.

Downs, Anthony. *An Economic Theory of Democracy.* New York: Harper and Row, Publishers, 1957.

Kaplan, Morton A. *System and Process in International Politics.* New York: John Wiley & Sons, Inc. Science Editions, 1964.

Lindblom, Charles. E. *The Intelligence of Democracy.* New York: The Free Press, 1965.

McDonald, John. *Strategy in Poker, Business and War.* New York: W. W. Norton, Inc., 1950.

Murphy, Walter F. *Elements of Judicial Strategy.* Chicago: University of Chicago Press, 1964.

Polsby, Nelson and Wildavsky, Aaron B. *Presidential Elections: Strategies of American Electoral Politics.* New York: Charles Scribner's Sons, 1964.

Rice, Stuart A. *Quantitative Methods in Politics.* New York: Alfred A. Knopf, 1928.

Riker, William H. *The Theory of Political Coalitions.* New Haven, Connecticut: Yale University Press, 1962.

Schelling, Thomas C. *The Strategy of Conflict.* New York: Oxford University Press, Galaxy Books, 1963.

Shubik, Martin, Ed. *Readings in Game Theory and Political Behavior.* Garden City, New York: Doubleday and Co., Inc., 1954.

Turner, Julius. *Party and Constituency: Pressures on Congress.* Baltimore: The Johns Hopkins Press, 1951.

Truman, David B. *The Congressional Party.* New York: John Wiley and Sons, 1959.

Williams, J. D. *The Compleat Strategyst.* New York: McGraw-Hill Book Co., 1954.

ARTICLES AND PERIODICALS

Dawson, Richard E. and Robinson, James A. "Interparty Competition, Economic Variables, and Welfare Policies in the American States," *Journal of Politics,* Vol. 25, No. 2 (May, 1963), pp. 265–289.

de Grazia, Alfred. "General Theory of Apportionment," *Law and Contemporary Problems,* Vol. 17 (Spring, 1952), pp. 256–267.

Deutsch, Karl W. "Game Theory and Politics: Some Problems of Application," *Canadian Journal of Economics and*

Political Science, Vol. 20, No. 1 (February, 1954), pp. 76–83.

Golembiewski, Robert. "A Taxonomic Approach to State Political Party Strengths," *Western Political Quarterly*, Vol. 11, No. 3 (September, 1958), pp. 494–513.

Rapoport, Anatol. "Critiques of Game Theory," *Behavioral Science*, Vol. 4, No. 1 (January, 1959), pp. 49–66.

Rice, Stuart A. "The Identification of Blocs in Small Political Bodies," *American Political Science Review*, Vol. 21, No. 3 (August, 1927), pp. 619–627.

Sawyer, Jack and MacRae, Duncan, Jr. "Game Theory and Cumulative Voting in Illinois," *American Political Science Review*, Vol. 56, No. 4 (December, 1962), pp. 936–946.

Schlesinger, Joseph. "A Two-Dimensional Scheme for Classifying States according to the Degree of Interparty Competition," *American Political Science Review*, Vol. 49, No. 4 (December, 1955), pp. 1120–1128.

Snyder, Richard C. "Game Theory and the Analysis of Political Behavior," *Politics and Social Life*, Ed. by Nelson W. Polsby, Robert A. Dentler, and Paul A. Smith. Boston: Houghton Mifflin Co., 1963, pp. 130–145.

II. State Legislative Apportionment

BOOKS

Baker, Gordon E. *The Politics of Reapportionment in Washington State*. New York: Holt, Rinehard and Winston, 1960.

Baker, Gordon E. *The Reapportionment Revolution*. New York: Random House, 1966.

Baker, Gordon E. *Rural versus Urban Political Power*. New York: Random House, 1955.

Congressional Quarterly Service. *Representation and Apportionment*. Washington, D.C., 1966.

David, Paul T. and Eisenberg, Ralph. *Devaluation of the Urban and Suburban Vote*. Charlottesville: University of Virginia, Bureau of Public Administration, 1961.

de Grazia, Alfred. *Apportionment and Representative Government.* New York: Frederick A. Praeger, Inc., 1962.

de Grazia, Alfred. *Public and Republic: Political Representation in America.* New York: Alfred A. Knopf, 1951.

Hacker, Andrew. *Congressional Redistricting: The Issue of Equal Representation.* Washington, D.C.: The Brookings Institution, 1964.

Hanson, Royce. *The Political Thicket: Reapportionment and Constitutional Democracy.* Englewood Cliffs, New Jersey: Prentice-Hall, Inc., 1966.

Jewell, Malcolm E., Ed. *The Politics of Reapportionment.* New York: Atherton Press, 1962.

Page, Thomas. *Legislative Apportionment in Kansas.* Lawrence: University of Kansas, Bureau of Government Research, 1952.

ARTICLES AND PERIODICALS

Abram, Morris R. "A New Civil Right," *National Civic Review,* Vol. 52, No. 4 (April, 1963), pp. 186–188, 211.

Baker, Gordon E. "Cities Resent Stepchild Lot," *National Municipal Review,* Vol. 42, No. 8 ((September, 1953) pp. 387–392.

Baker, Gordon E. "One Vote, One Value," *National Municipal Review,* Vol. 47, No. 1 (January, 1958), pp. 16–20, 50.

Barrett, Charles A. "Reapportionment and the Courts," *State Government,* Vol. 35, No. 3 (Summer, 1962), pp. 138–143.

"Battlefields of 1961," *National Civic Review,* Vol. 50, No. 1 (January, 1961), pp. 4–5.

Bendiner, Robert. "How the Farmer Rules Your City," *Collier's* Vol. 132, No. 13 (November 27, 1953), pp. 34–41.

Dauer, Manning J. and Kelsay, Robert G. "Unrepresentative States," *National Municipal Review,* Vol. 44, No. 11 (December, 1955), pp. 571–575, 587.

Dixon, Robert G. "Representative Goals," *National Civic Review,* Vol. 52, No. 10 (November, 1963), pp. 543–547.

"Downtrodden Majority," *New Republic,* Vol. 141, No. 19 (November 9, 1959), pp. 3–4.

Durfee, Elizabeth. "Apportionment of Representation in the

Legislature: A Study of State Constitutions," *Michigan Law Review,* Vol. 43, No. 6 (June, 1945), pp. 1091–1112.

Dye, Thomas R. "Malapportionment and Public Policy in the States," *Journal of Politics,* Vol. 27, No. 3 (August, 1965), pp. 586–601.

Eisenberg, Ralph. "Power of Rural Vote," *National Civic Review,* Vol. 51, No. 9 (October, 1962), pp. 489–492, 530.

Fleming, Roscoe. "America's Rotten Boroughs," *Nation,* Vol. 188, No. 2 (January 10, 1959), pp. 26–27.

Fordham, Jefferson B. "Challenge: Legislatures," *National Municipal Review,* Vol. 47, No. 11 (December, 1958), pp. 551–555, 571.

Friedman, Robert S. "Reapportionment Myth," *National Civic Review,* Vol. 49, No. 4 (April, 1960), pp. 184–188.

Gelman, Norman I. "Unequal Representation," *Editorial Research Reports,* Vol. 2 (October 29, 1958), pp. 815–832.

Harvey, Lashley G. "Some Problems of Representation in State Legislatures," *Western Political Quarterly,* Vol. 2 (June, 1949), pp. 265–271.

"How're They Going To Keep Them Down On The Farm After Reapportionment," *Senior Scholastic,* Vol. 79, No. 9 (November 8, 1961), pp. 8–9, 28–29.

Jewell, Malcolm E. "Constitutional Provisions for State Legislative Apportionment," *Western Political Quarterly,* Vol. 8 (June, 1955), pp. 271–279.

Kennedy, John F. "The Shame of the States," *The New York Times Magazine* (May 18, 1958), pp. 12, 37–40.

Key, V. O., Jr. "Procedures in State Legislative Apportionment," *American Political Science Review,* Vol. 26, No. 6 (December, 1932), pp. 1050–1056.

Kristol, Irving. "One Man, One Vote," *New Leader,* Vol. 46, No. 13 (June 24, 1963), pp. 12–14.

Larson, James E. "Awaiting the Other Shoe," *National Civic Review,* Vol. 52, No. 4 (April, 1963), pp. 189–193.

Lewis, Anthony. "Legislative Reapportionment and the Federal Courts," *Harvard Law Review,* Vol. 71, No. 6 (April, 1958), pp. 1057–1098.

Lewis, Anthony. "On the Trail of the Fierce Gerrymander,"

The New York Times Magazine, (February 19, 1961), pp. 17, 74–78, 90.

Lindsay, John J. "The Underprivileged Majority," *Nation,* Vol. 194, No. 10 (March 10, 1962), pp. 208–210.

MacNeil, Douglas H. "Big Cities and States' Rights," *Survey Graphic,* Vol. 33, No. 10 (October, 1944), pp. 405–407, 427–428.

Mathews, J. M. "Municipal Representation in State Legislatures," *National Municipal Review,* Vol. 12, No. 3 (March, 1923), pp. 135–141.

McClain, Robert H. "Compulsory Reapportionment," *National Municipal Review,* Vol. 40, No. 6 (June, 1951), pp. 305–307, 324.

McWilliams, Carey. "Rotten Boroughs in the United States," *Nation,* Vol. 167, No. 13 (September 25, 1948), pp. 346–347.

Moskin, J. Robert. "Where We Stand: The Revolt Against Rural Rule," *Look,* Vol. 27, No. 1 (January 15, 1963), pp. 58–61.

Neuberger, Richard L. "On Rotten-Borough Legislatures," *Survey,* Vol. 86, No. 2 (February, 1950), pp. 53–57.

O'Hallaren, William. "A Fair Share for the Cities," *Reporter,* Vol. 21, No. 8 (November 12, 1959), pp. 22–24.

Perrin, Noel. "In Defense of Country Votes," *Yale Review,* Vol. 52, No. 1 (October, 1962), pp. 16–24.

"Rural Overrepresentation Acute in State Legislatures," *Congressional Quarterly Weekly Report,* Vol. 20, Part I (February 2, 1962), pp. 170–178.

Shull, Charles W. "Reapportionment: A Chronic Problem," *National Municipal Review,* Vol. 30, No. 2 (February, 1941), pp. 73–79.

"Trouble for Cities, Suburbs—Power Stays in Rural Areas," *U.S. News and World Report,* Vol. 46, No. 23 (June 8, 1959), pp. 67–69.

Tyler, Gus, "Court versus Legislature; The Socio-Politics of Malapportionment," *Law and Contemporary Problems,* Vol. 27, No. 3 (Summer, 1962), pp. 390–407.

Walter, David O. "Reapportionment and Urban Representation," *State Government,* Vol. 11 (February, 1938), pp. 30–32.

Wheeler, John P. and Bebout, John E. "After Reapportionment," *National Civic Review,* Vol. 51, No. 5 (May, 1962), pp. 246–250, 262.

III. State Legislative Politics

BOOKS

Heard, Alexander, Ed. *State Legislatures in American Politics.* Englewood Cliffs, New Jersey: Prentice-Hall, Inc., 1966.

Herzberg, Donald G. and Pomper, Gerald M. *American Party Politics.* New York: Holt, Rinehart and Winston, Inc., 1966.

Jacob, Herbert and Vines, Kenneth N., Eds. *Politics In the American States: A Comparative Analysis.* Boston: Little, Brown and Company, 1965.

Jewell, Malcolm E. and Patterson, Samuel C. *The Legislative Process in the United States.* New York: Random House, 1966.

Jewell, Malcolm E. *The State Legislature: Politics and Practice.* New York: Random House, 1962.

Keefe, William J. and Ogul, Morris S. *The American Legislative Process.* Englewood Cliffs, New Jersey: Prentice-Hall, Inc., 1964.

Key, V. O., Jr. *American State Politics: An Introduction.* New York: Alfred A. Knopf, 1956.

Key, V. O., Jr. *Southern Politics.* New York: Alfred A. Knopf, Inc., 1949.

Levin, Murray B. *The Compleat Politician: Political Strategy in Massachusetts.* Indianapolis: Bobbs-Merrill Co., Inc., 1962.

Lockard, Duane. *New England State Politics.* Princeton: Princeton University Press, 1959.

Lockard, Duane. *The Politics of State and Local Government.* New York: The Macmillan Co., 1963.

Neustadt, Richard E. *Presidential Power.* New York: John Wiley & Sons, Inc. Science Editions, 1960.

Pomper, Gerald. *Nominating the President: The Politics of Convention Choice.* New York: W. W. Norton & Co., Inc., 1966.

Ransone, Coleman B., Jr. *The Office of Governor in the United States.* University, Alabama: University of Alabama Press, 1956.

Steiner, Gilbert Y. and Gove, Samuel K. *Legislative Politics In Illinois.* Urbana: University of Illinois Press, 1960.

Wahlke, John C. and Eulau, Heinz. *Legislative Behavior: A Reader in Theory and Research.* Glencoe, Illinois: The Free Press, 1959.

Wahlke, John C., Eulau, Heinz, Buchanan, William and Ferguson, LeRoy C. *The Legislative System.* New York: John Wiley and Sons, Inc., 1962.

Wood, Robert C. *Suburbia: Its People and Their Politics.* Boston: Houghton Mifflin Co., 1958.

Zeller, Belle, Ed. *American State Legislatures.* New York: Thomas Y. Crowell Co., 1954.

ARTICLES AND PERIODICALS

Derge, David R. "Metropolitan and Outstate Alignments in Illinois and Missouri Legislative Delegations," *American Political Science Review,* Vol. 52, No. 4 (December, 1958), pp. 1051–1065.

Derge, David R. "On the Use of Roll-Call Analyses: A Reply to R. T. Frost," *American Political Science Review,* Vol. 53, No. 4 (December, 1959), pp. 1097–1099.

Flinn, Thomas A. "Party Responsibility in the States: Some Causal Factors," *American Political Science Review,* Vol. 58, No. 1 (March, 1964), pp. 60–71.

Flinn, Thomas A. "The Outline of Ohio Politics," *Western Political Quarterly,* Vol. 13, No. 3 (September, 1960), pp. 702–721.

Friedman, Robert S. "The Urban-Rural Conflict Revisited," *Western Political Quarterly,* Vol. 14 (June, 1961), pp. 481–495.

Frost, Richard T. "On Derge's Metropolitan and Outstate

Legislative Delegations," *American Political Science Review,* Vol. 53, No. 3 (September, 1959), pp. 792–795.

Hofferbert, Richard I. "The Relation Between Public Policy and Some Structural and Environmental Variables in the American States," *American Political Science Review,* Vol. 60, No. 1 (March, 1966), pp. 73–82.

Jewell, Malcolm E. "Party Voting in American State Legislatures," *American Political Science Review,* Vol. 49, No. 3 (September, 1955), pp. 773–791.

Keefe, William J. "Parties, Partisanship, and Public Policy in the Pennsylvania Legislature," *American Political Science Review,* Vol. 48, No. 2 (June, 1954), pp. 450–464.

Lockard, W. Duane. "Legislative Politics in Connecticut," *American Political Science Review,* Vol. 48, No. 1 (March, 1954), pp. 166–173.

MacRae, Duncan, Jr. "The Relation Between Roll-Call Votes and Constituencies in the Massachusetts House of Representatives," *American Poltiical Science Review,* Vol. 46, No. 4 (December, 1952), pp. 1046–1055.

McCally, Sarah P. "The Governor and His Legislative Party," *American Political Science Review,* Vol. 60, No. 4 (December, 1966), pp. 923–942.

Ranney, Austin and Kendall, Willmoore. "The American Party Systems," *American Political Science Review,* Vol. 48, No. 2 (June, 1954), pp. 477–485.

Sindler, Allan P. "Bifactional Rivalry as an Alternative to Two-Party Competition in Louisiana," *American Political Science Review,* Vol. 49, No. 3 (September, 1955), pp. 641–662.

IV. U. S. Government Documents

Advisory Commission on Intergovernmental Relations. *Apportionment of State Legislatures,* Washington, D.C., December, 1962.

U.S. Bureau of the Census. *U.S. Census of Population.* Population of the State of New Jersey in the Twelfth to Eighteenth Censuses, 1900–1960.

V. U. S. Supreme Court Cases

Baker v. Carr, 369 U.S. 186 (1962).
Colegrove v. Green, 328 U.S. 549 (1946).
Reynolds v. Sims, 377 U.S. 533 (1964).

New Jersey References

I. State Documents

Constitutions of the State of New Jersey, 1776, 1844, and 1947.

Assembly Committee on Highways, Transportation and Public Utilities. *Public Hearings on Assembly Concurrent Resolution No. 41,* April 25, 1960.

Assembly Judiciary Committee. *Public Hearings on Assembly Concurrent Resolution No. 34,* May 12, 1960.

Journals of the Senate of the State of New Jersey. 1901; 1911; 1921–1922; 1931; 1941–1947; 1952–1961; 1964–1965.

Manuals of the Legislature of New Jersey. Trenton: Fitzgerald Publishers, 1900–1966.

Minutes and Proceedings of the General Assembly of the State of New Jersey. 1901; 1911; 1921–1922; 1931; 1941–1947; 1952–1961; 1964–1965.

New Jersey Constitutional Convention. *Report of Committee on Arrangement and Style,* June 14, 1966.

Proposed Revised Constitution (1944). Pending before the Joint Legislative Committee to formulate a draft for the State of New Jersey constituted under Senate Concurrent Resolution No. 1, adopted January 11, 1944. Published by Order of the Legislature. Distributed through the State Library, State House Annex, Trenton, New Jersey.

Senate Committee on Revision and Amendment of Laws. *Public Hearing on Senate Concurrent Resolutions Nos. 9 and 13,* March 19, 1958.

Senate Committee on Revision and Amendment of Laws. *Public Hearing on Senate Concurrent Resolution No. 4,* April 4, 1960.

Seate Committee on State, County and Municipal Government. *Public Hearing on Senate Concurrent Resolution No. 1,* April 2, 1959.

Senate Committee on State, County, and Municipal Government. *Public Hearings on Senate Concurrent Resolution No. 1,* February 1, 1961.

Senate Judiciary Committee. *Public Hearings on Senate Concurrent Resolutions Nos. 22 and 23,* May 22, 1957.

II. Court Cases

Asbury Park Press, Inc. v. Woolley, 33 N.J. 1 (1960).
Botti v. McGovern, 97 N.J.L. 353 (1922).
Jackman v. Bodine, 43 N.J. 453 (1964).
Smith v. Baker, 74 N.J.L. 592 (1906).
State v. Wrightson, 56 N.J.L. 126 (1893).

III. Reports

Bureau of Government Research. *Apportionment of the New Jersey Legislature: Alternative Paths of Action.* New Brunswick: Rutgers — The State University, June 22, 1964.

Legislative Apportionment in New Jersey: A Survey of Modern Methods Available. New Brunswick: Bureau of Government Research, Rutgers — The State University, January, 1952.

Mason, Alpheus T. and Harrison, Joseph. *The New Jersey Committee For Fair Representation: Reapportionment in New Jersey—Recommendations and Supporting Statements,* January, 1965.

New Jersey Legislative Reapportionment: A summary of legislative proposals to reapportion the seats of the General Assembly of New Jersey, 1951 to 1957. Trenton: Law and Legislative Reference Bureau, Division of the State Library, Archives and History, New Jersey State Department of Education, November, 1957.

Proceedings of the New Jersey State Constitutional Convention of 1844. Compiled and Edited by the New Jersey Writers' Project of the Works Progress Administration with an Introduction by John Bebout. Sponsored by the New Jersey State House Commission, 1942.

Proceedings of Rutgers Policy Forum. *Legislative Reapportionment Alternatives and Their Impact on New Jersey Citizens*. New Brunswick: Extension Service, College of Agriculture, Rutgers University, January 12, 1955.

Ralston, Anthony. *A Fresh Look at Legislative Apportionment in New Jersey*. A Report to the General Assembly of the State of New Jersey, June, 1960.

Reock, Ernest C., Jr. and Friedelbaum, Stanley H. *Congressional Districting in New Jersey*. New Brunswick: Bureau of Government Research, Rutgers–The State University, May, 1956.

Reock, Ernest C., Jr. *Population Inequality Among Counties in the New Jersey Legislature, 1791–1962*. New Brunswick: Bureau of Government Research, Rutgers – The State University, 1963.

Report of the Commission on Revision of the New Jersey Constitution. Submitted to the Governor, the Legislature, and the people of New Jersey, May, 1942.

Report of the New Jersey Legislative Reapportionment and Congressional Redistricting Planning Commission. Established pursuant to Senate Concurrent Resolution No. 21, 1964; reconstituted by Senate Concurrent Resolution No. 3, 1965. February 5, 1965.

Shank, Alan and Reock, Ernest C., Jr. *New Jersey's Experience With General Assembly Districts, 1852–1893*. Preliminary Draft. New Brunswick: Bureau of Government Research, Rutgers – The State University, May, 1966.

IV. State Legislative Apportionment

BOOKS

Baisden, Richard N. *Charter For New Jersey: The New Jersey Constitutional Convention of 1947*. Trenton: Division of

State Library, Archives and History, New Jersey Department of Education, 1952.

Bebout, John E. and Grele, Ronald J. *Where Cities Meet: The Urbanization of New Jersey*. Princeton: D. Van Nostrand Co., Inc., 1964.

Brush, John E. *The Population of New Jersey*. New Brunswick: Rutgers University Press, 1956.

Edison, Charles. *A New Constitution For New Jersey*. Addresses by the former Governor of New Jersey, 1941–1944. Trenton: Division of State Library, New Jersey Department of Education, Undated.

Edge, Walter E. *A Jerseyman's Journal*. Princeton: Princeton University Press, 1948.

Erdman, Charles R., Jr. *The New Jersey Constitution—A Barrier to Governmental Efficiency*. Princeton: Princeton University Press, 1934.

Lockard, Duane. *The New Jersey Governor: A Study in Political Power*. Princeton: D. Van Nostrand Co., Inc., 1964.

McKean, Dayton David. *The Boss: The Hague Machine in Action*. Boston: Houghton Mufflin Co., 1940.

McKean, Dayton David. *Pressures on the Legislature of New Jersey*. New York: Columbia University Press, 1938.

Rich, Bennett M. *The Government and Administration of New Jersey*. New York: Thomas Y. Crowell Co., 1957.

ARTICLES AND PERIODICALS

Alexander, Jack. "Ungovernable Governor," *Saturday Evening Post,* Vol. 215, No. 30 (January 23, 1943), pp. 9–10; 51–54.

Alexander, Jack. "King Hanky-Panky of Jersey," *Saturday Evening Post,* Vol. 213, No. 17 (October 26, 1940), pp. 9–11; 119–124.

Anton, Thomas. "The Legislature, Politics, and Public Policy: 1959," *Rutgers Law Review,* Vol. 14, No. 2 (Winter, 1960), pp. 269–289.

Bebout, John and Kass Julius. "How Can New Jersey Get a New Constitution?" *University of Newark Law Review,* Vol. 6, No. 1 (March, 1941), pp. 1–69.

Bebout, John E. "New Task For A Legislature," *National Municipal Review,* Vol. 30, No. 1 (January, 1944), pp. 17–21.

Bilder, Walter. "Useful Reflections on the Constitutional Election," *New Jersey Law Journal,* Vol. 67, No. 48 (November, 1944) , pp. 397–401.

Burritt, Richard D. "Another Edison Makes Some Sense," *The New York Times Magazine* (October 12, 1941) , pp. 16, 27.

Chasan, Will. "The Decline of Boss Hague," *Nation,* Vol. 151, No. 24 (December 14, 1940) , pp. 605–606.

Daily Home News (New Brunswick) . 1964–1965.

Edison, Charles "How To Wake Up an Old State," *National Municipal Review,* Vol. 40, No. 11 (December, 1951) , pp. 574–578.

Effross, Harris I. "Origins of Post-Colonial Colonies in New Jersey," *Proceedings of the New Jersey Historical Society,* Vol. 81, No. 2 (April, 1963) , pp. 103–122.

Friedelbaum, Stanley H. "Apportionment Legislation in New Jersey," *Proceedings of the New Jersey Historical Society,* Vol. 70, No. 4 (October, 1952), pp. 262–277.

Frost, Richard T. "Stability and Change in Local Party Politics," *Public Opinion Quarterly,* Vol. 25 (Summer, 1961) , pp. 221–235.

"Jersey Justice," *America,* Vol. 104, No. 20 (February 18, 1961) , p. 652.

Kerney, James, Jr. "Price of A New Constitution," *National Municipal Review,* Vol. 41, No. 1 (January, 1952) , pp. 14–17; 63–64.

Lockard, Duane. "Achieving Fair Representation in New Jersey," *New Jersey Law Journal,* Vol. 88, No. 1 (January 7, 1965) , p. 1.

McKaye, Milton "The Glamorous Governor of New Jersey," *Saturday Evening Post,* Vol. 229, No. 41 (April 13, 1957) , pp. 23–25; 124–129.

Morris, Joe Alex. "His Heart Belongs To Jersey," *Saturday Evening Post,* Vol. 225, No. 1 (July 5, 1952), pp. 36–37; 54–57.

Newark *Evening News*. 1921–1922; 1941–1947; 1950–1961; 1964–1965.

"New Jersey Assembly Must Be Reapportioned," *National Civic Review*, Vol. 49, No. 7 (July, 1960), pp. 366–367.

The New York Times. 1921–1922; 1941–1947; 1950–1961; 1964–1965.

Note. "Legislative Apportionment: A Judicial Dilemma?" *Rutgers Law Review*, Vol. 15 (Fall, 1960), pp. 82–97.

Pomper, Gerald. "New Jersey County Chairmen," *Western Political Quarterly*, Vol. 18, No. 1 (January, 1965), pp. 186–197.

Wilson, Edmund, Jr. "New Jersey: The Slave of Two Cities," *Nation*, Vol. 114, No. 2971 (June 14, 1922), pp. 712–714.

UNPUBLISHED MATERIAL

Bebout, John E. *Party Alignment in New Jersey, Especially Since 1925*. Master's Thesis. New Brunswick: Rutgers University, May, 1938.

Connors, Richard J. *The Movement for Constitutional Revision in New Jersey: 1941–1947*. Master's Thesis. New York: Columbia University, Undated.

PERSONAL INTERVIEWS

Clinton. Interview with Wesley L. Lance, former assemblyman and senator, Republican, Hunterdon County. May 6, 1965.

Milltown. Interview with Assemblyman J. Edward Carbiel, Democrat, Middlesex County. June 2, 1965.

Morris Plains. Interview with Governor Alfred E. Driscoll. May 18, 1965.

Newark. Interview with Dominic A. Cavicchia, former assemblyman, Republican, Essex County, and deputy attorney general. May 11, 1965.

Newark. Interview with Governor Robert B. Meyner. May 12, 1965.

New Brunswick. Interview with Senator John A. Lynch, Democrat, Middlesex County. May 5, 1965.

New Brunswick. Interview with Dr. Ernest C. Reock, Jr., Director, Bureau of Government Research, Rutgers – The State University, July 19, 1965.

Somerville. Interview with Assemblyman Raymond H. Bateman, Republican, Somerset County. May 6, 1965.

Somerville. Interview with Senator William E. Ozzard, Republican, Somerset County. May 20, 1965.

Trenton. Interview with Assemblywoman Marion West Higgins, Republican, Bergen County. May 24, 1965.

Trenton. Interview with Governor Richard J. Hughes. June 2, 1965.

Tranton. Interview with Joseph W. Katz, special assistant to Governor Hughes. June 2, 1965.

Trenton. Interview with Attorney General Arthur J. Sills. May 10, 1965.

Union City. Interview with Assemblyman William V. Musto, Democrat, Hudson County. May 21, 1965.

Index